A
PATH
WELL TRAVELED

DEDICATED

TO

RITA

PREFACE

All life journeys encounter forks in the road. Choices, path one or path two, are influenced by history. Choices made shape life journeys.

Twentieth century history shaped hills, valleys, plains, and scenery along my life's path. I watched my parents endure and overcome hardships during the Great Depression as they lived by standards worthy of emulation: a strong work ethic, self-discipline, love for and commitment to family. I observed and learned by their example.

World War II shaped my early adult journey. As an Army Aviation Cadet, I learned that a young man from southeastern North Carolina could successfully compete with other young men drawn from metropolitan and rural communities nationwide. The experience expanded my early, narrow view of the world to a worldwide horizon. As a combat fighter pilot in the Pacific, I found the limits of my ability and learned that successful campaigns depend on responsible men from all ranks performing, with little to no recognition, administrative, maintenance, housekeeping, security, and other mundane, unrewarding tasks needed to maintain their unit's well being in a threatening environment. That experience made me aware of the need to recognize and express my thanks to those who gave me a lift as I continued my journey.

The Cold War shaped my midyears. The new Air Force offered growth and promotion opportunities for young Army officers willing to transfer to the Air Force. During the 50s and 60s, research and development of advanced AF weapon systems, motivated by a Soviet missile threat, offered great educational and duty assignment opportunities in advanced aircraft, missile, satellite, and electronic weapon technology. I took advantage of those opportunities. Professional skills developed during my military career served me well later in civilian life as a satellite communications consultant.

After retirement from civilian employment, I have enjoyed a good life. In the late 90s, Alzheimer visited my Rita and she became a charming four-year old. I am blessed that she remained happy and easy to manage. As her primary caregiver, remembering examples set by my parents, I learned to cope with her infirmities and to enjoy those moments when she briefly appeared from within a dense fog, giving me occasional glimpses of my young Rita.

Index

Chapter 1
BOYHOOD

My earliest memories return me to a home in Godwin, North Carolina, with the Atlantic Coastline Railroad in front and the

Godwin Baptist Church in the rear. This photograph pictures a neighbor, George Sanford Honeycutt, my father, Garthae Williams, my sister, Jewel, and me, standing on the railroad tracks. A note on the photograph's back side lists Jewel (born 1920) as five years old and  me as three years old, so the photograph dates from 1925.

As contractors paved Highway 301, a major north-south road, while only streets of some towns were paved – some with cobblestone, the idea of a paved road stretching from Maine to Florida seemed miraculous. A cement  plant, located between my home and the Atlantic Coast Line Railroad, off loaded cement from railroad cars and mixed concrete for transmit by trucks to prepared highway sites. The cement plant shows behind this picture of me, my mother, Sudie Honeycutt Williams, my sister Jewel, my brother Rodney, and dog Ben. My brother Rodney, the smallest, born in 1925, appears about two years old. So, the highway-paving project remained underway until after 1927.

At the time railroads, the prime movers of freight and passengers inspired both culture and folklore. Fast and powerful steam locomotives powered clean, colorfully painted freight and passenger trains up and down the Atlantic Coast Line's well maintained tracks at high speed. A mystique surrounded railroads. The steam engine's whistle, heard in the distant, sang a song from miles away. Stations and crossings received different sequences of whistle notes, and a practiced ear could recognize each Engineer's signature in his mournful song as he approached distant landmarks. My father and friends, socializing on a front porch during early evenings after supper, debated the engineer's identity and the location of an approaching train as it passed distant stations and railroad crossings

No one failed to stop a task to watch a passing passenger train roar through town. As it approached on a dark night, the engine's furnace, opened for the fireman to add more coal, painted low hanging clouds with a fiery glow. As it passed in a shower of sparks, smoke, and sound, bright dining cars revealed well-dressed passengers dining in elegant splendor. The clickey-de-clack of a slow freight's iron wheels on steel tracks late at night could lullaby to sleep a restless child or comfort a worried parent.

Measured by norms of today, the Roaring Twenties' economy gave the good life. Fast, polished passenger trains roared north and south carrying passengers in evening clothes, dining in plush dining cars. Godwin enjoyed a thriving commerce based on access to railroad depots, separated by a day's journey in a mule-drawn wagon, the primary local transporter, Wholesale goods, purchased from distant markets, arrived at these depots for local retailer shelves. Farmers, living within a too-from wagon day's travel, shipped their harvest from the Godwin railhead and bought supplies from Godwin retailers. Mr. Jimmy Daniel Pope, a blacksmith gifted in wood and metal, enjoyed a good livelihood repairing, or making, wagons, buggies, and other farm implements.

With no electricity available in Godwin, norms of living knew nothing of electrical conveniences such as electric lights, washing machines, dryers, and air conditioning. Oil lamps provided light. Big cast iron wood-burning stoves cooked meals and warmed kitchens. On washdays, mothers boiled water in large black outdoor pots and scrubbed clothes by hand on scrubbing boards. An open fireplace heated the "sitting" room, the only heated room other than kitchen. Going to bed in an unheated bedroom on a cold winter night offered a chilling experience. Mothers often placed bricks, warmed by the open fire, under bed covers to keep feet warm. I do not recall my mother, though without connivances of today, being busier than housewives of today. The old adage is true: *"Work expands to demand all available time."*

My father's radio, with its headset, became the first radio in Godwin. The only reliable radio signal came from KDKA, a Pittsburgh station. The receiver required a 50-yard antenna stretched between two tall juniper poles planted in the back yard. A set of earphones provided audio. Each night saw visitors in the Williams' home take turns wearing the earphones and relaying what they heard to others in the room. A great advance occurred when my father purchased a "loud speaker" to sit atop the radio. Now all could hear at the same time. Often my mother and father went to bed leaving "Boll Weevil" Pope and others in our living room listening to the radio.

Primitive automobiles, mostly Model-T Fords, increased as the transporter of choice. My father owned a Model-T which could attain, perhaps, 35 miles-per-hour. With no starter, it had to be hand cranked, and canvas curtains with isinglass panes served to protect occupants from weather. They were ineffective, and each automobile carried a large, heavy blanket, called a horse blanket, as standard equipment but no heater. Travelers in cold and rain expected a wet, cold, uncomfortable ride. My father owned an automobile garage and parts store and made a comfortable living repairing automobiles and selling automobile parts.

One day, my mother drove the 17 miles to Fayetteville not knowing that Jewel and I had smuggled Dog Ben into the back seat of the family Model-T. Faced with options to return Ben home or to leave Ben in the automobile and complete her shopping, she chose the latter. Returning to the parked automobile, we found Ben missing. He had squeezed between curtains in order to pay Fayetteville a dog's visit. Mother returned home heartbroken with two heartbroken children. Late in the afternoon, my father returned to Fayetteville hoping to find Ben, only to return to weeping children in early evening, with no Ben.

Bedtime came and as we prepared for bed, we heard Ben's signature scratch on the door – wanting in. A muddy, wet, happy dog entered with wagging tail. Unable to see outside of the Model-T, Ben had traveled in a southern direction 17 miles east of the Cape Fear River, crossed the river approaching Fayetteville, and stopped in Fayetteville located west of the Cape Fear. Mankind's wisdom, scientific or otherwise, cannot explain how Ben could know to swim the river, travel north, and find home.

Our community, a friendly, close–connected community including all families within the Godwin school district, supported its churches and school. Some, native to the community, served for years as schoolteachers. Other teachers, not native, typically served for long periods, gained a wide circle of friends, and became true members of the community. Each Friday Miss Clevy Godwin, a Godwin native school principal, read to or told a story to a class selected on the basis of its week's academic performance. A great reader and storyteller, all students hoped she would select their class. Her readings and stories created student interest in a broad range of literature including poetry, fiction, and history. To this day, I read and enjoy good books. I remember Miss Maggie, my first grade teacher, Mrs. Margaret Williams, a Godwin native and wife of Marshall "Carbine" Williams, as a gracious and kind lady. Frequent contact and friendship between teachers and parents insured that if a child misbehaved in school parents soon learned, and the child received punishment at school and at home. School discipline posed no problem.

My mother enjoyed the Godwin Garden Club, a strong, active club with a large membership housed in a large brick-stone building on a lot adjacent to the schoolyard. Its several projects included a commitment to give each schoolchild a hot lunch each school day. Club members planned menus and scheduled members to serve as cooks. Notes, carried home by school children to their mothers, published menus and specified groceries needed from each home. Children brought farm vegetables, fruits and meats to school, and designated mothers cooked meals in the school kitchen on a large iron, coal-burning stove. Older school children delivered meals to the desk of each child. This community driven school lunch program fed children many years before the idea converted into a government responsibility.

My mother and father, members of the Godwin Baptist Church, gave me no choice but to attend church on Sundays and during any weekday activity. They also monitored my school performance, and I had no choice but to finish all assigned work. My church and school teachers often assigned me speaking, singing, or dancing roles in various stage performances – offers my parents would not let me refuse. Often, Nell Starling, a classmate and neighbor, partnered with me on stage – so much so that classmates unmercifully teased us.

One Mother's Day's church program called for me to recite the poem, Somebody's Mother. A family that had recently buried their mother sat in the second row before me. As I recited, the family began to weep. Their grief greatly unsettled me, but with difficulty, I completed the recitation.

Children enjoyed an unrestricted, carefree life. Free to roam the town, neighboring fields, and nearby woodland, they sometimes engaged in dangerous play. One summer, I found a long, small steel cable beside the railroad tracks and dragged it to nearby woods. Strips of wood nailed to a tall pine tree trunk formed steps so that I and my friends could climb. We attached one end of the cable, at a great height, to this tree. We threaded the other end of the cable through a piece of pipe and attached it to a distant pine at a low level. With the inside of the pipe greased, a

5

mighty heave sent it up the cable to a waiting child. Holding the pipe, the child could, and many did, ride to the ground. When their feet reached ground level, they began running sidewise to avoid the lower pine. I remain amazed that so few hurt themselves. Rodney suffered the most grievous hurt. At the top, with his head too close to the cable, the upcoming pipe struck him above his right eye. He still wears the scar from his courageous ride.

Most boys adeptly made effective bows from small sweet gum tree limbs and arrows from reeds. Playing Indian warfare one day, an arrow struck my chin, penetrated the skin, grazed around the chin bone and came out through skin below my chin, and remained struck in a near horizontal position.

I could turn my head and the arrow turned with the head. Running home, I gave my mother a fearful sight. Doctor McLean, our local doctor, unable to fully contain his laughter, gave my mother much annoyance. I still wear the arrow's scar.

At age 10, perhaps 9 or 11, I built and set rabbit boxes. A rabbit box, about six inches square and about three feet long closed at the rear, includes a front trap door held open by a bar pivoting on a forked stick held in place by a trigger extending through a small hole located near the rear of the box. In the Fall, I sat boxes along edges of nearby fields. Sweet potato, placed at box rear, enticed rabbits to enter, trip the trigger, and close the trap door. Opening a tripped trap door required care. Timid rabbits could be lifted out of the box by their ears. Possums walked out to freedom grinning, happily. Angry cats and raccoons came out fighting. Depending upon demand, I released caught rabbits, prepared them for my mother's table or for sale to neighbors.

As roads and automobiles improved, more members of the community moved their trade to more distant markets, and the Godwin railhead became less and less an economic engine. In the early 1930s, the depot closed and Godwin served no longer as a train stop. The 1929 stock market crash and subsequent depression decimated the national economy. Dry winds changed western lands into dustbowls. In the east, dust in the atmosphere darkened the sun making it a gloomy red. On worst days, dust clouds caused near blackouts.

Hungry men, called hobos, rode southbound freight cars looking for work. Hungry men rode northbound freight cars looking for work. These men, not reprobates, still lived as men of somber dignity. Some came to our home asking for food. My mother gave them a plate and let them eat outside sitting on kitchen steps. One cold winter day, I came upon one squatting in a ditch alongside the railroad. He had broken ice covering a puddle and was shaving in cold water. Cattle cars carrying skinny cattle from western state dust bowls traveled north and south looking for markets.

Unable to afford maintenance and operating costs, families converted automobile rear wheels into mule drawn "Hoover Carts," and demand for automobile repair diminished. Hoping to gain customers from Highway 301 traffic, my father moved his garage to the southwest corner of the Godwin Main Street-Highway 301 Intersection. The move offered little business improvement.

Godwin life became difficult. My mother planted, cultivated and harvested a vegetable garden in a vacant lot behind our home. The garden provided ample vegetables during summers and an ample supply of canned vegetables for winter. Children worked summers in nearby fields planting, hoeing, and picking cotton. My sister, Jewel, far more competent than me, with little effort picked twice the cotton than I picked.

In the fall, children worked in barns preparing cured tobacco for market. Jewel and I worked for Coot Smith, a black tenant farmer, in his tobacco barn "grading" tobacco. I cherish that memory. It gave me a deeper insight into the black culture existing at the time. Mr. Coot Smith, a good farmer, a good employer, a lay preacher, and a good man, enjoyed great respect within the community. Real superstition and real Witch doctors existed in the black community. A given pattern of chicken bones found in a mailbox caused real sickness. At the time, a witch doctor's influence on a young man became newsworthy. Sick for no discernable cause, he received treatment at the Duke Hospital. Unable to convince him otherwise, he died believing his hex deadly.

My father closed his business and purchased a new International truck and an old White truck. He and blacksmith, Jimmy Daniel Pope, removed the cab, engine, and front wheels from the White truck, and built a flatbed with removable sides over its frame resulting in a tractor-trailer rig. Such rigs, novel at the time, are well known today. He began hauling cotton, produce, and other goods up and down well paved Highway 301 from New York to Florida. Hauling fees available did not sufficiently cover gasoline, tires, and vehicle maintenance costs. Gasoline, in particular at 20 cents per gallon, was relatively as expensive as today. Those twenty cents, in today's dollars, would be about 4.00 dollars. This enterprise failed. He then began work, as a mechanic, for a Fayetteville automobile dealership. Later, seeking any means to earn a livelihood, he operated a battery and magna-flux shop in Fayetteville. At the time, automobile batteries were repairable. Dead cells could be replaced with new cells to prolong battery life. The magna-flux machine could identify cracks, not visible to the eye, in automobile parts, allowing their continued use with confidence.

To supplement income, my father began a paper and movie delivery route. Leaving home around 3:00 in the morning, he drove to Fayetteville, loaded bundles of newspapers and cassettes containing movie reels into his automobile and drove a 150-mile delivery route. The route took him through Hope Mills, St. Paul, Lumberton, Elizabethtown, White Lake, Garland, Clinton, Roseboro, Autryville, Stedman, and back to Fayetteville in time to do a day's work. In each sleeping town, he dropped bundles of newspapers in front of drug stores and movie reels in front of movie theaters. Weekend mornings, I often came along to help with drops.

By self-confidence, discipline, and hard work, my mother and father provided for their family during difficult years following the 1929 crash and subsequent depression. Their painful struggle, at times, likewise proved painful for me, for my sister Jewel, and for my brother Rodney. Each Christmas, I remember a Christmas when no Christmas presents appeared. Disappointed, Jewel and I cried. Seeing the depth of our disappointment brought tears to my mother and to my father. Their grief pained me more than the disappointment, and disciplined me to better accept disappointments in order to spare others pain. I am persuaded that a life of self-confidence, discipline, and commitment to family lived by my mother and father during those difficult years made me a better man - better able to overcome obstacles encountered during my life's journey. Finally, in 1937, my mother and father decided to build a new house on a Sampson County farm, inherited from my father's parents, and to become farmers.

THE BAREFOOT BOY

Blessings on thee, little man,
Barefoot boy with cheek of tan!
With thy turned up pantaloons,
And thy merry whistled tunes;
With thy red lip redder still
Kissed by strawberries on the hill;
With the sunshine on thy face,
Through thy torn brim's jaunty grace
From my heart I give thee joy,–
I was once a barefoot boy

Oh for boyhoods painless play
Sleep that wakes in laughing day
Health that mocks the doctor's rules
Knowledge never learned of schools
Of the wild bee's morning chase,
Of the wild flower's time and place,
Outward sunshine, inward joy.
Blessings on you barefoot boy
Ah! That thou couldst know thy joy,
Ere it passes, barefoot boy.

John Greenleaf Whittier 1855

Chapter 2
Young Adult

In 1937, my father inherited a farm in Mingo Township in Sampson County located near Spivey's Corner, about half way between Dunn and Clinton. He and my mother decided to move their family to Sampson, to build a house, and to become farmers. At the end of the 36-37 school year, our family moved to Sampson.

Some years earlier, fire destroyed my Grandmother Daisy's home. She converted a large garage, located in her yard, into living space and lived in the garage while building a new house.

Likewise my father, mother, sister, brother and I lived in the garage while building our new home. Trees cut from the forest went to a saw mill owned by my Grandmother and there sawed into lumber needed to build the house. Methods had little changed since the 19th Century, and I had an opportunity to observe and to participate in a vanishing technology. Manual crosscut saws cut trees, and logs moved to the saw mill by a log cart with very large rear wheels which pivoted a half-circle axel to lift a log. Mules pulled logs slung underneath the axel between the wheels to the mill. A single cylinder, 9 horse power diesel engine with two enormous fly wheels powered the saw.

Before use, freshly cut (green) lumber contains much water, and must lie stacked in open air for weeks until thoroughly dry, and to avoid warping, it requires weekly restacking. When dry, it must go to and from a commercial planning mill to plane away rough face splinters, and then stored. My father, Rodney, and I moved each board used during house construction dozens of times.

Bricks needed for foundation and chimneys came from a school site in Eastover, a small town near Fayetteville. In earlier years, fire destroyed the school building, and used bricks were free for the taking. Rodney and I spent days after day cleaning bricks and

chipping away clinging mortar. Brick masonry is a little chang-
ing building trade. Except for the presence of a powered mixer,
today's building site is that of years ago. Then, as now, the brick
layer lay each brick onto a layer of mortar, positioned it carefully, removed excess mortar, checked level, and placed a dab of
mortar on top.

Rodney and I mixed sand, cement, and water in a large, flat box
with mixing hoes. A single brick layer's demand for "more mud"
kept us constantly busy mixing mortar throughout days of foundation and chimney building.

For one of my many assigned tasks, fetch sand, needed for mixing mortar, from a distant site where white sand could be found, I
used my Grandmother's Model-T truck to haul the sand. The

truck offered a new, once in a
lifetime, experience. A Model-
T's throttle is mounted below the
steering wheel on the right side of
the steering pedestal similar, to
the gear shift on more modern
automobiles. On the left side of
the pedestal, a lever, similar to

today's turn signal, controlled (engine spark) ignition timing.
This photograph pictures a neighbor, Harvest Smith, standing on
Grandmother's truck.

The driver controlled three foot pedals. The right pedal applied
brake. The left pedal had three positions. Full down, moved the
transmission to low gear. Half way up moved the transmission to
neutral. Full up moved the transmission to high gear. A hand
lever to the left of the driver's seat, when in the up position, held
the left pedal in its mid-way, neutral position. The middle pedal
gave reverse. A typical procedure: lift the lever on the left side
of the driver's seat to its full up position, start the engine, usually
by hand crank, enter the cockpit, drop the left lever while holding the left pedal in its midway position, add throttle, and press
the left pedal to its down position. As speed increases, advance
the spark, release the left pedal, and the truck is on its journey.

Typical for the time in southeastern North Carolina rural communities, no architect influenced house design. A picture, probably from a magazine, provided initial guidance for the new house. My mother and father sketched a floor plan; and Mr. Edmund Smith, a local carpenter, began building foundations, floors, and walls. The result was a well-built house that looked like the guiding picture. Its design had but two flaws: closets were two small, and in later years, when electric power became available; it had no adequate space for a bathroom.

Under Mr. Edmund's supervision, my father, my brother Rodney, and I did much of the building. We learned skills that have served us well during our life's journey. In later years, Rodney built a nice beach house largely by his own hand.
Again, we used 19th Century building tools and methods. Tools consisted of hammers, hand saws, hand planes, and spirit levels. Again, I remain grateful to have observed and participated in a vanishing technology. Before winter, our family moved into a home largely competed.

During the 1930s and 1940s, farming required intensive labor. Most farms supported two or more families, the landowner and one or more tenants. Tenants, knowledgeable and skilled independent farmers, by unwritten agreements, sealed by handshakes, planted, cultivated, and harvested crops on a portion of a farm. The tenant provided needed labor and shared one-half of monies received in the fall from the crop sale. The landowner provided land, a tenant house, mules, and fertilizer and received one-half of monies received from the crop sale. Both were motivated throughout the year; bountiful harvests promised bountiful incomes. The tenant, a self-respecting man with quiet dignity of self-employment, well respected in the community, considered himself a cut above a hired hand. The term share-cropper is an invention of journalists and fiction writers wishing to paint an oppressed, less admirable character.

Farm tools included hand tools such as hoes, rakes, and pitch forks and mule drawn implements such as plows, harrows, mowers, and hay rakes. My father owned two mules, one young, one old. During plow days, I plowed the older, a mule of wisdom gained over many years. Upon reaching the end of a current row, without prompting, he turned  into the beginning of the next row and continued his work. He knew time. At noontime, when completing a row heading toward the barn, he stopped expecting to be unhitched. If not unhitched after, in his mind, a reasonable period of time, he continued to the barn pulling the plow, not to be stopped.

Tobacco and cotton, cash crops, provided income. Corn and hay provided sustenance for mules, and other farm animals. Cows, pigs, vegetables, and fruits provided sustenance for families. Though profitable, tobacco required much work. Early winter tasks cut and stacked firewood beside tobacco barns and prepared tobacco beds for seeding. A between Christmases (the twelve days of Christmas) task seeded beds and covered them with protective thin cloth to prevent frost damage. An early spring task transplanted seedlings from bed to field. Summer tasks cultivated and pulled, by hand, and stomped, by foot, large tobacco worms from growing plants. Late summer tasks collected leaves, strung them onto sticks, and hung them in a tobacco barn for curing.

With the week's harvest in the barn, the owner lit the furnace, and maintained fire for about seven days to gradually increase barn temperature. Wood stacked beside the barn during the previous winter provided fuel. Heat and gases flowing from the furnace's rear end, through two-foot diameter flues extending around barn perimeter, then up to exhaust through the barn's roof, heated the interior. A necessary high heat, at the end of the heating period, properly cured tobacco. Barn temperatures below a proper level damaged tobacco. Constant temperature required twenty-four hour attention to the furnace. A draw string, passing through the barn's front wall, drew a thermometer from barn interior to be observed through a small window. More or less wood went into the furnace as the temperature fell or rose.

My father, Rodney, and I took turns tending the furnace. A hot, long, lonely night shift sometimes became scary. From nearby woodland came strange sounds, some real and some imagined. Dawn brought a welcomed relief and a short walk to the watermelon patch for an early breakfast on melons still cool from night air.

I cherish my early years in a small town and early years on a small farm in a culture, a way of life, and a workplace that, in the words of Margret Mitchell, are *"Gone with the Wind."* A slow pace of life and a slow speech, unique to the area, made for peaceful, pleasant living. Neighbors shared work, joy, resources, tools, and sadness.

Not all time counted as work time. Often, Army airplanes from Fort Bragg flew over our fields giving us air shows. Some, in formation practicing formation maneuvers, some as singles doing acrobatics. One day a flight ran out of gas and landed in nearby fields. My father, Rodney and I arrived at one of the crash sites to see the airplane righted from a nose over position. A crowd gathered around the airplane. Some climbed on wings and peered into the cockpit. Intentionally, or otherwise, someone pulled a lever, and an inflatable life-raft fell from beneath each wing to the ground, in a cloud of powder, and began self-inflating. Thinking "bomb" the crowd, including myself, ran for the woods.

On another day, an Army P-40 made a forced landing in a nearby field. In that field, I first saw a P-40, an airplane that in the fullness of time I would fly. The P-40, with six exhaust stacks on each side of the engine nacelle, and its shark-like nose captured the public's imagination. Portals, alongside Buick hoods, mim-

15

icked the P-40's exhaust stacks. Remnants of that portal design remain on today's Buick.

The new DC-3 airliner's entry into commercial flight made front page news for several months. The News and Observer published its first scheduled Raleigh arrival. My father, Rodney and I drove to Raleigh to see the airplane on Raleigh's airport, at the time on the west side of highway 70, south of the city. That day in Raleigh, the DC-3 appeared as a huge airplane. By today's standard, the DC-3 is a tiny airplane.

Boys of my generation followed exploits of pilots flying national and international races. Charles Lindbergh, Howard Hughes, Roscoe Turner, Jimmy Doolittle, Ale Williams, Wiley Post, and Amelia Earhart filled our imaginations and captured our hearts. In later years, I would have an opportunity to spend an afternoon in a bar with Roscoe Turner.

I graduated with the twenty-six member Mingo High School Class of 1939 as valedictorian. With lack of foresight, I neglected to save my valedictorian address. I only remember its Latin title, Quo Vadis, meaning "where do we go from here." Only in later years did I realize that little community schools, such as Mingo and Godwin, well prepared their graduates to successfully compete in groups drawn from large and small urban and rural communities nationwide.

Unable to finance college, I remained at home during the 1939-1940 school year helping my father farm, surveying cropland for Sampson County Government, and spotting fires for the Forest Service from a tower located across a lake in front of my father's home.

A Federal crop insurance program seeking to boost farm income via price increases (Agriculture Adjustment Act of 1936) limited acreage planted to many crops including cotton, tobacco, and corn. Each farm received allotments specifying the maximum acreage allowed for each crop in the program. Program administration and control, vested in county governments, offered in mid-summer four to five weeks employment for those willing to visit farms, measure tobacco, cotton, and corn fields and prepare reports confirming no over-planting. I took advantage of this opportunity, purchased a very used Model-A Ford Roadster and measured cropland during the summers of 1939 and 1940. If a farmer over planted, the program required him to destroy the excess and a later measurement confirmed compliance. On one occasion, while making this confirmation visit, I found that the earlier measurement in error and that the farmer had needlessly destroyed a portion of his tobacco crop. It seemed prudent not to tell the farmer, and I do not know that he ever learned.

Our home, sited beside what is now the Dunn Road, offered a pleasant view of Williams Lake, about one hundred yards away. On the opposite side of the lake, a dance pavilion, a swimming area, and a picnic area offered popular recreation for surrounding towns and rural communities. Beyond the lake, a Forest Service fire tower stood well above the tallest pines. A company of the Civilian Conservation Corps (CCC), a part of President Roosevelt's New Deal, built the tower during the winter of 1937. The CCC Company of twenty to thirty young men, commanded by an Army Reserve Major, bivouacked on the site during construction. A semi-military entity, it remained active from 1933 to 1942.

During portions of 1939 and 1940 summers, I worked as an observer in the tower cab, watching for fires. At the time, our community enjoyed no telephone service. When spotting a fire, I drove about five miles to the home of Mr. Dewey Jackson who had the authority to gather a crew of fire fighters, drive to, and extinguish the fire with rakes and backpacked fire extinguishers. Best of all, Mr. Dewey submitted vouchers and within a few days crew members, including me, received a check that nicely augmented a spotter's salary.

In late August of 1940, at the urging of Jack Faircloth, my friend and High School classmate, I hitch-hiked to the campus of Appalachian State Teachers College in Boone, North Carolina, and made an appointment with the school's business manager, Bernard Daugherty, to say that I was on campus to commence classes with no money. Mr. Daugherty made arrangements for me to register and gave me a job bussing tables in the school cafeteria at breakfast, lunch, and dinner. Bussing tables earned my tuition, room rent, and meals. Each school day, filled with work, class time, and late evening study, left little leisure time. Surprisingly, my grade point average remained high throughout the school year.

During Christmas holidays, Jack and I hitched-hiked to and from home. En route home, in slow traffic, we ended up in Pittsboro, NC, very late on a very cold night with no money for room rent. Finally, around midnight, Pittsboro's police chief stopped and made us an offer we could not refuse. The remainder of the night, we spent in his city jail.

During the school year, Professor Joseph Williams, an elderly gentleman, came to regard me as one of his special students. During the winter, Mrs. Williams fell and broke a leg. In early spring, she began to walk with crutches. Professor Williams asked me serve as her chauffer during short afternoon trips in the countryside. My schedule made a trip possible once each week. I would go to their home, help her into the family automobile, and drive where she wished to go. Most trips visited homes along small remote mountain roads seeking antique mountain artifacts. Those trips gave me an opportunity to see Western North Carolina, unchanged since the middle of the 19th Century. The mountain people still spoke a nearly Elizabethan dialect.

The school year ended, and I left the campus fully intending to return in the fall. In the hallway ceiling outside my dorm room, a trap door allowed me to store, in the attic, belongings accumulated during the school year. If the building still stands, my things may still be in that attic. My greatest regret is that I left a wool quilt made, and given to me by my Grandmother.

While away during my college school year, historic events drastically changed the national condition. The war in Europe, beginning with the 1939 German invasion of Poland and Sino-Japanese war beginning in 1937, prompted urgent, high priority programs to greatly enlarge the US Army and Navy. The 1941 Federal Budget added an additional Essex class carrier, two Iowa class battleships, two light cruisers, eight destroyers and eight submarines to an already robust ship building program. US industrial production output changed from domestic products to ships, tanks, aircraft, and other war material. Between 1939 and 1941, aircraft production increased from 2.1 thousand units to 19.4 thousand units. In 1940, Congress inaugurated the draft. Between 1939 and 1941 the US Military grew from 334.4 thousand to 1,801 thousand active duty personnel. Large construction projects increased Navy, Army, and Marine base facilities needed to accommodate larger force structures. Radio and news print repeatedly called for workers to fill needed military equipment production related jobs.

VICTORY WAITS ON YOUR FINGERS—

KEEP EM FLYING, MISS U.S.A.

Men and women from across the nation answered the call, uprooted their lives, moved to new locations, and began building military base infrastructure, airplanes, ships, tanks, guns, ammunition, and other items needed to sustain deployed military forces.

In late 1940, my father, a gifted mechanic, began work in the Norfolk Naval Air Station's Engine Overhaul Plant as a mechanic. In a short time he became an Inspector, accepting or rejecting aircraft engine repair jobs. In mid-1941, he, my mother, and Rodney shuttered the Sampson County home and moved to South Norfolk, Virginia.

Returning to Sampson from Appalachian, my life's journey encountered a second fork. One path offered easy travel through known territory. I chose an uphill, rocky path through unknown territory.

19

The need for, and the lack, of trained aircraft, ship, tank and other military equipment technicians prompted universities, including North Carolina State College, to offer short, non-degree programs, similar to those offered by today's community colleges. Considering the national condition, these programs seemed a more appropriate path than returning to Appalachian. I registered for an aircraft technician's class along with two Sampson County neighbors, Howard Hamilton and Wallace Honeycutt. Howard, Wallace, Clayton Lee from Newton Grove, North Carolina, and I shared the same boarding house in Raleigh. In later years, Clayton's sister would become Rodney's wife, my sister-in-law. After program completion, Howard used skills gained in this class working for Martin Aircraft factory in Baltimore followed by an Army tour as a B-24 airplane mechanic. Wallace and Clayton used their skills as sailors. As part of the curriculum, one of the instructors gave me my first airplane ride in a Piper Club.

I traveled (hitch-hiked) to Sampson Friday afternoon, 5 December 1941, to visit my Grandmother. On Sunday, her radio announced the Japanese attack on Pearl Harbor. Though many, including myself, hardly knew the location of Pearl Harbor, the attack unified the Nation to a degree not known before or since. On Monday, 8 December, Congress declared war on Japan with but one dissenting vote by Jeannette Rankin, a Republican from Montana. The following Thursday, Germany and Italy declared war on the United Sates – causing the United States to be at war with Axis partners; Japan, Italy, and Germany.

With popular support, the Nation rapidly transitioned from peacetime to a war time footing with priority given to production of military goods. The government halted automobile production and limited production of farm equipment. It froze prices of Consumer goods and issued rationing books to each family limiting the amount of gasoline, tires, sugar, meat, silk, shoes, nylon, and other items the family could buy.

People endured limitations with little complaint. Mothers learned to work around pantry shortages and still make good meals. Cookbooks appeared tailored to use items most available. Fathers learned to extend the life of automotive tires with "shoes" glued inside tires.

Early in 1942, perhaps at the end of 1941, I completed the North Carolina State College Program, and returned to my Grandmother's home in Sampson. Within a few days, my father and mother came for me, and I joined them in South Norfolk, Virginia. The Norfolk harbor was behind their home, and I saw the USS Alabama battleship's 16 February 1942 launch. Spectators lined the harbor's shoreline. For better viewing, I joined many others and walked from the shoreline some distance on a very large sewer or water pipe extending, above water, into the harbor. The launch caused a large wave that crossed the harbor. I could see the wave coming. Blocked from the shore by others on the pipe, I braced myself. Many were knocked off the pipe into the water. Others, including me, were wet on a cold blustery day.

A seldom seen next door neighbor avoided others in the community. Periodically, static blocked all radio programming. My father began to suspect that the neighbor monitored ship traffic in the harbor and transmitted information to some distant receiver. He relayed his suspicions to his sister, Olive, who lived in Raleigh. She, in turn, relayed the suspicion to the FBI. A few days later, men in dark business suits visited the neighbor. He left with the men to be seen no more. So long as he lived, my father believed that he played a role in catching a spy.

Jobs in the Norfolk Naval Air Station were available for the asking; and, after some on-the-job training, I began work in the propeller repair shop as an Inspector assigned to pass-fail propeller repair work. My strongest technical recollection is that propeller blades having bullet holes could be repaired to pass inspection criteria with holes still in place.

Airplanes, in and around the aircraft hangers, also impressed me. They included (I later learned) the Grumman TBF Avenger torpedo airplane. I was not a lone admirer. Naval pilots often visited the hanger looking with lustful eyes upon the planes. In later life, I learned that the carrier Hornet waited in the Norfolk harbor to

21

receive TBFs newly received from Grumman, being prepared for the Hornet, and that the pilots came from the Hornet's Torpedo Squadron Eight. The Hornet unexpectedly sailed before all the TBFs arrived. History tells that it sailed through the Panama Canal into the Pacific and on to Pearl Harbor. From Pearl it carried Jimmy Doolittle's B-25 airplanes to a launch point from which they completed the famous Tokyo raid. Later, during the battle of Midway, all Torpedo Squadron Eight crew members lost their lives except Ensign Gay, the lone survivor.

Rodney attended South Norfolk High School during the 1941 to 1942 school year. At the end of the school year, my father moved his family to 4907 Sewell's Point Road located near the Norfolk Naval Station. In the prime of their lives at ages 42 and 37, my parents Garthae and Sudie continued to set examples for living worth emulating.

Rodney and I both approached a fork in our journeys. I reached draft age as Rodney approached draft age. Rodney chose to begin working for the Norfolk Naval Air Station as a magna-flux operator. In the fullness of time he would be drafted, become an Aviation Cadet, complete pre-flight training at Furman University in Greenville, South Carolina, and see the Army close down pilot training before he could complete flight training. He would fly fifteen missions over Germany in the B-17's ball turret gun position for the 15th Air Force, 97th Bombardment Group, 342th Bombardment Squadron stationed in Foggia, Italy.

During the summer, in a barber shop reading a <u>Life</u> magazine while waiting my turn, I saw an Army recruiting page announcing that the Army no longer required a college degree for Aviation Cadet Applicants. On the way home from the barber shop, I stopped by an Army Recruiting Office, and on 16 June 1942 volunteered as an Aviation Cadet. A few days later, orders arrived; remain at home until further notice. Orders to report to the railroad station in Richmond, Virginia, came by mail in late November. The orders appointed me an Aviation Cadet effective 10 December 1942 and assigned me to the Aviation Cadet Center, San Antonio, Texas, by the USA Aviation Cadet Manning Board, Richmond, VA. On 10 December, my father drove me to Richmond. A heavy fog enshrouded a major portion of the route to Richmond, and we arrived hours late. Fortunately, a train also arrived late and I received a sleeping berth in one of its Pullman cars going to Pittsburgh, Pennsylvania where it joined a troop train bound for Texas.

Riding a troop train is an experience. Depending upon train length, one or more cars serve as kitchens, and other cars serve as mess (dining) cars. Assigned dining times, throughout the day, queues filled aisles with soldiers moving to and from the mess cars. Day or night, troop trains often stop to add or to disconnect cars with much bumping, grinding, and jerking. After a long, long time, I arrived in San Antonio a brand new cadet.

Two roads diverged in a yellow wood,
And sorry I could not travel both
And be one traveler, long I stood
And looked down one as far I could
To where it bent in the undergrowth.

Then took the other, just as far,
And having perhaps the better claim
Because it was grasser and wanted wear,
Though as for that the passing there
Had worn them really about the same.

And both that morning equally lay
In leaves no step had trodden black.
Oh, I marked the first for another day!
Yet knowing how way leads on to way
I doubted if I should ever come back.

I shall be telling this with a sigh
Somewhere ages and ages hence.
Two roads diverged in a wood and I,
I took the one less traveled by.
And that has made all the difference.

Robert Frost 1915

Chapter 3
CADET DAYS

As one of 32 Army Aviation Cadets, Class of 43-I traveling in a
Pullman car, I departed Richmond, Virginia, on 10 December
1942. In Pittsburgh, Pennsylvania, the car joined a troop train
having destination San Antonio, Texas. Between Pittsburgh and
San Antonio, the train made many stops to add additional cars or
to detach cars, much like a mail carrier delivers mail and picks
up mail as he walks down the street. After several days of bumping and grinding to add or detach cars, our Pullman came to a
stop on a railroad spur leading onto Kelly Army Air Base. In a
short time we experienced our first Army formation and lecture.

We stood in a group, structured somewhere between a mob and a
disciplined military formation; in front of a recently constructed
WWII barracks located on a portion of Kelly Field called San
Antonio Aviation Cadet Center. The long, frame, two story barracks building, typical of thousands built during the war, offered
an open bay on each floor. A row off fifteen bunks lay along
each side of the lower bay and along each side of the upper bay.
The entire Center, recently developed on a desert site, became
muddy when wet and dusty when dry. Renamed in later years, it
became Lackland Air Force Base.

The lecture's theme focused on the Center's mission and what
we should expect to endure during our three month Center tour
of duty. That mission included three training components, academic, physical conditioning, and military. The military component would be an abbreviated boot camp designed to convert ci-
vilians into soldiers. Upper Class, 43-H, cadets and permanent
party soldiers would be our mentors, drill masters, and immediate supervisors. We would be assigned to the lower floor of the
barracks before us. Upper Class cadets would be living on the
second floor, and we should consider them, and all other Upper
Class cadets, our seniors and we should obey their commands
and instructions.

The academic component would include accelerated studies in aerodynamics, aircraft structures, aircraft engines, aircraft recognition, weather, radio, and Morse code. Frequent pass-fail tests would monitor each cadet's performance. If less than satisfactory, the cadet would be eliminated, washed out, from the program. The physical conditioning component would include running and calisthenics, with each cadet required to achieve physical performance standards. The bar for these standards would rise as time wore on. Those unable to get over the bar would wash out of flight training and be transferred to Navigator, Bombardier, Gunner, or other training Centers. We should expect that only two out of three of our class members would complete the program, graduate, and move on to pilot training.

The barrack's lower floor offered only 30 bunks, two less than our party of 32. Bunk assignments, made alphabetically, assigned Joseph E. Williams and me to the second floor– subject to upper class supervision or harassment. Recognized as a farm boy, among other things; they required me to sit up on my bunk and crow like a rooster each morning when revelry sounded.

During the following few days, perhaps a week, all cadets underwent many vaccinations and extensive eye, ear, dental, and physical examinations. My left eye is good and my right eye is excellent, far stronger than the left eye. The result is that I have always had poor depth perception, and could not pass a depth perception test. The testing device, a lighted square box about four feet long with a window at its front end, enclosed two pegs, mounted inside the box, that ran on tracks. A successful testee entered the test room, sat across the room from the box, held a string in the right hand, held a string in the left hand, and aligned the two pegs. The right string pulled the right peg forward while the left peg and left string moved rearward. Likewise the left string pulled the left peg forward and the right peg rearward. With room light dowsed, the testee could see the two pegs through the box window and with good depth perception could align the pegs. I could not do so, and poor depth perception caused certain elimination. The doctor giving the test said, *"Son, some days one is unable to pass this test and on other days is able to do so. I will give you another appointment and you will have one more chance to pass.* " The next day, at the appointed time, I returned to his office. Busy, he said, *"Go into the room and wait. I will be with you in a few minutes.* " I entered the test room, closed the door, walked to the box, pulled the right peg to its rear stop, leveled my fingers on taunt strings, and pulled the left string until the pegs were side by side. My left fingers touched my elbow. Investigation complete, I sat down in the testee's chair and waited. In a few minutes the Doctor entered the room, turned out the lights, and said *"Try again Son."* I passed the test without difficulty. I have often wondered whether I fooled the Doctor, or did the Doctor knowingly give me a chance to fool the box.

The final physical examination featured me standing stark naked before a committee of doctors. Looking at a file that I took to be my examination & test results, they discussed my fitness to continue pilot training as though I were not present. One remarked, *"He is awfully skinny."* Another remarked, "But, his muscles are well developed." Finally, they all agreed, *"Let's let him go."*

Examination week over, our group began a daily, extensive, highly scheduled routine from sunup to sundown. When revelry sounded, all rushed to shave, shower, dress, and stand outside in rank within a specified short period of time. Then we marched to the Mess for breakfast. Time scheduled for eating allowed neither leisurely eating nor a second cup of coffee.

Scheduled events, such as classes, calisthenics, running, lunch, drilling, guard duty, and dinner, filled the remainder of the day. We marched in formation from one event to the next with very short preparation time allowed between events. For example, when dismissed in front of our barracks after calisthenics, cadets began undressing as they ran to their bunks, quickly showered, dressed, and ran to join a new formation forming outside. Tardy arrivals earned demerits, spoiling an otherwise good record. Though young, by the end of each day, the regimen exhausted all. Taps, a restful lullaby, quickly lulled all to sleep.

One black, rainy night, while on guard duty, wearing a heavy Army great coat, and carrying a heavy Army rifle with no bullets, I heard in the distance a terrible screaming. The screams came closer and closer. As the screams approached my post, I began to hear heavy breathing between screams and footsteps pounding the street. When a dark, frightful figure finally appeared, I hid behind a bush and let it pass. Minutes later, when back on my post, MPs drove by. I later learned that the MPs picked the up the poor fellow and took him to a hospital psychiatric ward.

In retrospect, I admire the Army's use of all available manpower. A small permanent party, augmented with upper class cadets, provided extensive training for lower class cadets. By serving as mentors, drill masters, and immediate supervisors, the upper class cadets enhanced and deepened their knowledge and skills gained as under classmen. In turn, my class learned from doing. Though, as under classmen we endured a lot of hazing, we gracefully accepted hazing as good humor. The letter appearing on the opposite page reveals an example I related to my parents.

Tuesday, 16 February 1943, San Antonio Aviation Cadet Center graduated 208 successful 43-I cadets and transferred them to various primary flight schools scattered throughout the Gulf Coast Training Command. At that rate the Center processed 832 cadets per year. Similar Commands existed on the East Coast and the West Coast. Assuming equal performance, the three commands collectively processed 2,496 cadets per year into Army primary pilot training schools.

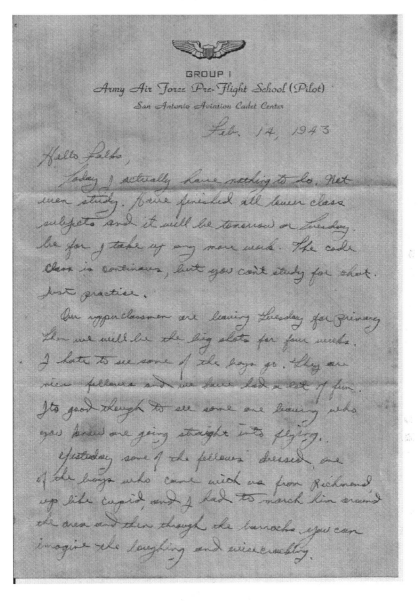

Orders transferred fifteen cadets, including me, to an Army Air Force Flight Training Detachment located near Bonham, Texas. Bonham, named for James Bonham who died at the Battle of the Alamo, remained House Speaker, Sam Rayburn's hometown. Jones Field, the Detachment's local name, served as a contract civilian flight school. In contrast to the San Antonio Aviation Cadet Center, Jones Field, well endowed with attractive buildings, offered a beautifully landscaped picture. Selected alphabetically, of the 32 who traveled with me from Richmond to San Antonio, only Joseph E. Williams and I transferred from San Antonio to Bonham. Conscious or not, alphabetic selection served to geographically mix cadets. Joseph came from Virginia. George W. Weston, a cowboy, came from Montana, and Russell A. Westberg came from Minnesota, still speaking with a Swedish accent. David K. Wolf and others hailed from homes scattered across the nation.

Flight line activities dominated Jones Field's schedule, a schedule more relaxed than that in San Antonio. Some academic studies of weather, aircraft recognition, and flight rules continued, and we continued to march from event to event. Our primary role, learn to fly the PT-19, a low wing, tandem two seat primary trainer built by the Ryan airplane company, dominated our schedule. The airplane, made of plywood wings, a canvas fuselage, with an inline engine and a fixed wooden propeller, made a good primary trainer. It had no air-ground radio and no intercom. From the back seat, the instructor could talk to the student through a gosport, a funnel-like horn inserted into a rubber hose extending forward to the front seat where it split into a pair of rubber hoses. These hoses, inserted into ear muffs on each side of the student's helmet, carried the instructor's voice, spoken into the horn, clearly to student ears.

My flight instructor, Joe Fraidy, proved to be a demanding, but great, instructor. The photograph on the following page pictures Joe standing beside the PT-19 with Joseph Williams standing on the wing. Note the hand crank used to spin an internal, heavy, inertial wheel up to a high speed, then removed; the spinner pulled a cable to engage a clutch, and kinetic energy, stored in the wheel, started the engine. Joe Fraidy also had Joseph Williams, George Weston, and Russell Westberg as students.

Joe Fraidy demanded that we fly a coordinated flight pattern. The pilot controls an airplane in three dimensions. An elevator controls pitch to raise or lower the nose; ailerons roll the airplane left or right, and a rudder causes the airplane  to yaw left or right. A unique application of pitch, roll, and yaw produces a coordinated maneuver. During coordinated maneuvers, a glass of water sitting on the dash before the pilot will not spill. More importantly, coordinated flight obtains maximum flight performance and maximum gun platform performance. What one learns from his first instructor stays with him throughout his flying career, and Joe Fraidy's demands served me well in later years.

I soloed the PT-19 within my allotted time and began a classical pilot training regimen including practice landings, simulated forced landings, stall entry and recovery, spin entry, and spin recovery. In addition, Joe Fraidy demonstrated classical coordinated maneuvers such as S-turns along a road, chandelles, lazy-eights, loops, and immelmanns, and demanded that we fly them with precision under his watchful and demanding eye. I gained 65 hours of daylight flight experience; twenty-seven hours duel with Joe Fraidy in the back seat, and 38 hours solo. Beginning in May, cadets flew evaluation flights with Army pilots in the back seat. All fifteen cadets assigned to Jones Field met standards and the evaluation declared all fit for Basic Flight training. Orders dated 17 May 1943 transferred all fifteen to Majors Army Air Field, Greenville, Texas, and we reported to Cadet Headquarters, Majors Army Air Field on 25 May.

In contrast to Jones Field, Majors Field featured tarpaper covered temporary buildings without landscaping. Its mission; provide cadets a higher level, more intense pilot experience in a larger, more powerful airplane. Though some academic studies continued and cadets continued to march from event to event, as pic-

tured right, flight line activities dominated the
schedule. The flight training
regimen experienced at
Jones Field continued with
additional instrument, formation and night flight
training.

Majors Field, an all Army installation organized by squadrons,
flights and sections, assigned one instructor and four cadets to
each section. Assignments placed me in a section within Squadron IV Flight B along with Joseph Williams, Cecil Roberts, and
John C. Roak. It seemed that, wherever we traveled, Joseph followed me or I followed Joseph.

At Majors, cadets flew the
Vultee BT-13 Valiant air-
plane. Significantly larger
and heavier than the Ryan
PT-19, the BT-13, powered
by a 450 HP radial engine,
with an adjustable pitch pro-

peller, offered greater performance. A wide fixed landing gear,
made the airplane easy to land. Canopied cockpits provided more
in flight comfort than did the open air PT-19 cockpit. The airplane, pilot friendly and easy to fly, is pictured at the right above.

Lt Richard E. Holzman
commanded Flight B. In all,
Flight B included eleven instructors. Four cadets assigned to each instructor
made a total of forty four cadets. All are pictured right.

Army Lieutenant flight instructors, recent graduates from pilot
training, had little more flight experience than that gained during
their cadet days. My instructor, Lt. Patterson, otherwise a good

instructor, seemed uncomfortable landing the airplane; a benefit for me because I made all landings. My first night landing, made at an auxiliary field, lighted with smudge pots along each side of the runway, proved terrible. After several hops, jumps, and skids, I finally regained control of the airplane. Lt Patterson asked me to stop at the field's traffic control station. He got out of the airplane, wished me well, and hitched hiked a ride back to Majors. I completed all landings, required by the mission, and flew back to Majors alone.

Daily schedules frequently included formation training flights in standard Air Corps four-ship formation flown by both Army fighter and bomber operational units. The formation is made up of two two-ship elements; a flight leader with one wingman and an element leader with one wingman. Initially, instructors flew flight leader and element leader positions and cadets flew wing. As time wore on, the four members of my flight, Joseph Williams, Cecil M. Roberts, John C. Roak, and I, flew the missions taking turns as flight leader, element leader, or wingmen. Performance standards remained high with cadets required to demonstrate high formation flight skill levels.

Instrument flight entered the flight training syllabus. A folding canvas mounted behind the front cockpit and pulled forward, much like a convertible automobile top, obstructed all front cockpit outside view. I flew all my instrument flights under this hood with Lt. Patterson in the back seat. The BT-13 airplane's cockpit, a typical Amy Air Corps cockpit, had instrumentation in  common with many cockpits of operational fighter and bomber airplanes. In 1943, thunderstorm turbulence posed a major instrument flight hazard. Without radar, airplanes often wandered into thunderstorms not included in weather forecast briefings. Heavy turbulence can, and often did, tumble gyros in gyro stabilized directional and roll instruments. Without these instruments, an airplane can be controlled, but without great precision. Major's instrument flight training syllabus, therefore, required that cadets cage gyro instruments and fly the airplane, under the hood, on needle, ball, and airspeed. Required maneuvers included recovery from unusual positions, including spin recovery. Instrument flight skills, learned in the BT-13 at Majors using these rudimentary instruments, transferable to the Army's advanced trainers and to operational fighter and bomber airplane cockpits, have served me well throughout my flying career.

This photograph pictures Joseph Williams standing left, David Wolf standing center, Russell Westberg standing right, George Weston squatting right, and me squatting center. The boardwalk kept feet out of mud while walking from our barracks to the street. We four became best friends. Joseph and I had trained together since the troop train ride from Richmond, Virginia, to San Antonio and had shared the rigors of San Antonio Aviation Cadet Center. Wolf, Weston, and Westberg joined us at Jones Field. We four survived primary flight training at Jones Field and basic flight training at Majors Army Air Field.

As Cadets approached the end of their Majors Field tour, they faced another fork in their journey, a fighter pilot path or a multi-engine pilot path, but the Army made the decision. Selection criterion included, among other things, cadet size. Small fighter cockpits of the day more fitted pilots of small statue.

Orders dated 28 July 1943 transferred me, Russell Westberg, and 186 other cadets to Aloe Army Air Field, Victoria, Texas, an advanced flight school for cadets destined to fly fighter aircraft. David Wolf, George Weston, and Joseph Williams transferred to advanced flying schools for multi-engine airplanes, and our paths diverged.

In time, Wolf and I met once more as we traveled on a Navy Seaplane Tender ship from San Diego to Hawaii, as Wolf journeyed to join a 5th Air Force B-25 bomb group in the South Pacific, and I to join a fighter squadron on Hawaii. Weston would die in a B-24, shot down over Germany. Joseph remained in the Service after the war. Our paths occasionally crossed, and he visited me in Washington, DC.

I reported to Cadet Headquarters, Aloe Army Air Field with 151 total flying hours, considered ready for advanced flight training. Aloe, another recently constructed Air Field consisting of tar paper covered buildings, sited in the desert, without landscaping, became muddy when wet, and dusty when dry.

Aloe's mission, to provide cadets a higher level pilot experience in a larger, more powerful airplane, used the AT-6, a low wing airplane with tandem cockpits and retractable landing gear. Its 550 HP Wasp engine powered a variable pitch propeller. Army developed the airplane during the 1930s as a  fighter. Japan purchased two in 1937, and the famous Japanese Zero fighter exhibited many AT-6 characteristics. Post WWII movies, such as Toro Toro Toro, filmed AT-6s, painted with Japanese colors, to represent the Zero. Main wheels, narrowly separated, gave the airplane a strong tendency to ground loop. An Army adage of the day stated that every pilot could expect one or more AT-6 ground loop.

Again, flight line activities dominated the schedule. The flight training regimen experienced at Majors Field continued with instrument, formation and night flight training with a more tactical flavor. Some academic studies continued, cadets continued to

march from event to
event and regular physi-
cal training continued.
Physical Training re-
mained a constant
throughout all cadet days,
consisting mostly of
marching to and from
daily events, with orga-
nized calisthenics a daily
torture. At Aloe, I proba-

bly enjoyed my best possible physical condition ever.

Aloe, another all Army installation organized by squadrons,
flights and sections, also assigned one instructor and four cadets
to each section. Recent cadet graduates, not seasoned and experienced pilots, served as instructors. A few days before my arrival,
my intended instructor spun on turn to final, crashed and died;
leaving no instructor available for his four intended cadets.

Each day I marched to the flight line with my fellow cadets. If
Doctors placed four cadets on sick-call one of the four free instructors flew with me. If less than four, I might get an instructor.
When administrative duties allowed, our Squadron Commander,
(a Major, his name is no longer in my files or memory, I shall
call him Major Aloe) served as our instructor. Major Aloe, older
and wiser, had more flying experience than the recently graduated cadets serving as 2nd Lt. Instructors. A tragic accident and
good fortune made him my part time instructor.

With no sick cadet and Major Aloe unavailable, Operations assigned an airplane to me and I flew solo. Having no instructor for
the day, I sat in the briefing room and listened to instructors brief
the day's mission to their cadets. I then flew alone and tried to
perform the mission as briefed. If the mission of the day required
instrument flight, I dropped my seat to its lowest position, accepted the risk of mid-air collision, and flew the briefed exercises on instruments.

At Aloe, instrument training included use of the Radio Range, a new navigational aid system being installed along the Nation's airways. A radio range station transmitted radio signals in each of four quadrants. Counting clockwise, the station transmitted the dash-dot signal for Morse code N (da-dit) in the first quadrant and the third quadrant, and transmitted the dot-dash code for A (dit-da) in the second and fourth quadrants. With broad beams on each side of the airway, a strong A or a strong N signal could be heard within a quadrant. Both signals overlapped a small portion of adjacent quadrants. Within this overlapped zone, signals merged (daditditda) to form a steady tone. These tones defined navigation airways. When on course, the pilot hears this steady tone.

A lost pilot must fly an orientation pattern before a Range signal is of value. For example, assume that a north-south airway intersected an east-west airway at station Aloe. A lost pilot hearing a solid N signal must determine whether he is in the station's north-east quadrant or the south-west quadrant. If south-west, by flying a north-eastern heading, the north bound airway or the east bound airway will intersect, but which airway intersected is still unknown. If flying a north or south heading and the tone continues, the pilot knows that he is on the north-south airway. If it slowly fades or increases, the pilot knows that he is north or south of the station. If the tone becomes a hard A, the pilot knows that he is leaving the east-west airway, can reverse course, intercept the airway and determine if East or West of station.

The Aloe syllabus continued formation flying employing tactical techniques. A two ship flight formed the Army's basic element. Combined elements formed four ship, eight ship, twelve ship, or larger formations. Typically in a four ship formation, an instructor

led with a cadet flying element, and cadets flying wing. The instructor flew the formation through acrobatic maneuvers, giving the cadets stressful workouts.

Some daylight solo navigational flights, called pilotage, required cross country flights using only compass, clock, and time. Some flights, along airways, used the Radio Range. Required solo night flights included pilotage cross country flights, and some along airways not equipped with a Radio Range. In 1943, beacons spaced ten miles apart still marked airways. Directly above a beacon, a red light flashed the Morse code for numbers ranging from one to ten. At night, in clear weather, a pilot flew from one beacon to the next. Halfway between the two, he began to see the third beacon ahead. So long as he kept track of the number of beacons passed, he could know, within ten miles, his location along the route. In weather, the beacons were of no value.

My first real Army mission required cadets to evacuate airplanes before a hurricane struck the Texas Coast. Orders assigned airplanes and destinations and told Cadets to go. Assigned an AT-6, I flew to Biggs Field, El Paso, Texas. After the storm, I returned to Aloe. Not a great successful mission, many airplanes ended up in a Texas cotton patch.

As the Aloe tour approached its end, the top 40% ranked cadets transitioned into the P-40N fighter. Initial check out proved a stressful experience. A single seat airplane with no pilot having P-40 experience able to ride along and help, the cadet flew alone. Cadets read the airplane's Tech Order, sat in the cockpit and memorize the location and function of all controls and instruments and, blindfolded, demonstrated to an instructor an ability to find the instruments and operate the controls. After completing blindfold tests, the instructor and the cadet crossed fingers and the cadet took-off.

Intentionally or not, this airplane challenged a young inexperienced pilot. It had extremely stiff controls. On takeoff, torque tended to force the airplane off the left side of the runway. Even with full right trim, it required right brake pressure until the airplane approached takeoff speed. In a slow climb with climb power, a small pilot could not roll the airplane to the right. In a high speed dive, he could not roll the airplane to the left. In the landing configuration at full power with hard right rudder, the airplane rolled over to the left. On landing approach, I rolled in as much right trim as I could hold with left rudder. If go-around became necessary, I could do so by holding hard right rudder and adding only cruise power while rolling more right trim. As speed increased and trim became more effective, I slowly added more power until climb power became possible.

A gunnery meet on Matagorda Island, a small island about sixty miles Southeast of Victoria, served as Aloe's grand finale. Each of the Gulf Coast Training Command's six advanced flight schools selected about 10%, of their cadets to represent their school. The event simulated a forward operating base, bivouacked in tents with typical field kitchens and other field support facilities.

The AT-6's standard configuration included a gun sight and gun mounts. On Matagorda a 30 cal. machine gun, mounted in the right wings of airplanes, let cadets make tactical firing passes at ground targets set up on a firing range, and at towed airborne targets. Ammunition tips painted red, green, blue, or other colors left color marks on targets. If a cadet hit a target, his color recorded the hit.

The AT-6's gun sight had no range finder. The pilot estimated target distance. Those with good depth perception, more often than not, wasted ammunition by firing beyond the gun's firing range. Having poor depth perception, I needed a crutch. Red concentric circles (bull eyes) marked both ground and towed targets. On my firing passes, I delayed firing until the red smudges became circles and approached airborne targets at target altitude. My hit rate remained consistently good.

I flew most of my Matagorda missions solo. However, Major Aloe used one mission to give me a required check ride. Too high on landing approach, I should have aborted the landing, gone around, and set up a proper approach. Instead, I raised the nose, reduced speed to near stall, and let the airplane drop like a rock. Approaching a proper landing glide slope, I lowered the nose, added a little power, regained approach speed, and made a good landing. After parking, as I sat in the cockpit filling out the airplane's log, Major Aloe stood on the wing, looked down at me and said *"Mr. Williams, if you were just half as good as you think you are you would still be a mediocre, inexperienced pilot."* Those well-deserved words, coming from a man I greatly respected, served me well.

For the Gulf Coast Training Command, the Matagorda Island Gunnery Meet served as its Super Bowl. Team members (about 15) from each of six flight schools competed for the highest school score, and cadets competed for the highest individual score. I won the highest individual score with a 63% hit rate. My win earned brownie points for Major Aloe and all other officers in the chain of command. Throughout my remaining cadet days, I received VIP treatment.

My last Aloe formation, a dress parade honoring cadet graduates, marched cadets, instructors, and permanent party personnel and formed a grand, memorable parade. In quick succession, Orders rated cadets as pilots, discharged them from enlisted status, commissioned them as 2nd Lieutenants, and granted them a ten day leave. Surprisingly, I did not receive a discharge certificate until 1947 when the Army Air Force became a new Department, the United States Air Force.

By bus to Galveston, Texas, and commercial air in a DC-3, I traveled to Raleigh – landing at a new airport that later became known as RDU. At the time, only one airport building existed. Too small for passenger services, the building provided only flight planning and weather briefing facilities for aircrews. However, some vending machines stood outside. My Mother and Father met me at the airport and I spent my ten day leave, less travel time, at home. At the same time, Rodney and our neighbor, Howard Hamilton, also enjoyed leave at home from the Army.

Returning from leave, the Personnel Officer summoned me to his office and showed me the location of assignments to be filled by the new 2nd Lieutenants. They included fighter squadrons in the Panama Canal, Alaska, the Continental US, and undisclosed locations. Given an opportunity to choose my next assignment, I encountered another fork on my life journey's path. I chose an undisclosed location. To my knowledge, personal gave no other cadet an opportunity to choose his next assignment.

Orders assigned 158 cadets to their next duty station with sixty-two (49%) P-40 qualified, and twelve (8%) fixed gunnery qualified. The orders assigned me to the undisclosed location and Russell Westburg to the 33rd Fighter Squadron, Dale Mabry Field, Tallahassee, Florida, both P-40 and fixed gunnery qualified. Our paths diverged, and within a year he would crash a P-39 in Alaska and die. The 40% loss rate of the five friends who survived primary and basic flight training is consistent with the wartime loss rate of USAAF aircrews, including both operational and combat losses.

MAJORS ARMY AIR FIELD
GREENVILLE, TEXAS

Here's a toast to the host
Of those who love the vastness of the sky
To a friend we send a message of his brother men who fly.
We drink to those who gave their all of old.
Then down we roar to score the rainbow's pot of gold.
A toast to the host of men we boast, the Army Air Corp!

Off we go into the wild sky yonder,
Keep the wings level and true.
If you'd live to be a grey-haired wonder,
Keep the nose out of the blue!
Flying men, guarding the nation's border,
We'll be there, followed by more!
In echelon we carry on. Hey!
Noting can stop the Army Air Corp!

The Army Air Corp song

Chapter 4
HAWAII

On or about 15 October 1943, a troop train, harvesting cadets recently graduated by the Gulf Coast Training Command, (renamed AAF Central Flying Command) arrived on Aloe's railroad spur. Except for a few remaining on Aloe as instructors, all Aloe's 43-I graduates boarded the train. Among the passengers, nine, all P-40 and gunnery qualified, shared Shipment AE 911 F orders to proceed to Camp Stoneman, Pittsburg, California. Though one of the nine, I knew neither the group size nor others in the group, with the exception of one 1st Lt, all newly commissioned 2nd Lts. After much bumping and grinding to add or detach individual cars, the train delivered me to Camp Stoneman.

A day or so after leaving Aloe, somewhere in West Texas or Arizona, the train stopped in a little desert town to take on water and coal. The conductor announced that a thirty to forty minute delay provided a good opportunity for passengers to get off the train and stretch legs. I did so. While in town, standing at an urinal, a 2nd Lt. standing to my immediate left turned to his friend, another 2nd Lt, standing to his immediate left, and said *"Yes I was in the Matagorda gunnery shoot-out and shot fifty six percent. Some son-of-a-*  *bitch beat me with a sixty three percent score."* I turned to my left and said, *"I am that son-of-a-bitch."* Most embarrassed and apologetic, he introduced himself as Tommy Riddle, the first among the group of nine that I came to know. Within a few hours he introduced me to his friend Lloyd Bosley. In time, I came to know all Aloe Nine members as fellow passengers.

After several travel days, the train stopped on Camp Stoneman's railway spur. Camp Stoneman, an Army installation about 100 miles north-east of San Francisco, located on the upper reaches of San Francisco Bay, served as a processing Center for Army personnel overseas bound. The Center issued to each pilot, among other things not remembered: a parachute, an A2 leather jacket, heavy wool lined jackets, trousers and boots designed for unheated cabins at high altitudes, a 45-calibre pistol with hip holster and belt, ammunition, and a large duffle carry bag. The pistol issued to me, a rare much desired true Colt, wore the Colt rearing horse logo. Most WWII 45-calibre pistols, manufactured by companies other than Colt, one being Singer Sewing Machine, did not carry the horse logo.

Camp Stoneman Orders 297, dated Monday, 25 October 1943 directed forty five officers to proceed, by rail, to San Diego. The group included two Majors, one Captain, one 1st Lt, one Flight Officer and forty newly commissioned 2nd Lts, including the Aloe Nine. While at Camp Stoneman and during the trip to San Diego, I came to know Max Bozarth and Robert Sadler, both Aloe graduates.

In route to San Diego, by ordinary passenger coach, civilian passengers gave the young, fuzzy chinned 2nd Lts wide berths as they walked down the railcar aisles wearing large 45 Caliber pistols on their hips. A stopover in Los Angeles, Riddle's home town, gave me an opportunity to meet his wife. The morning we departed Los Angeles for San Diego, she drove Tommy and me to the train station in a big red convertible.

The group reported to the US Navy Repair Base, San Diego, California and waited. During the wait, Sadler, Bozarth, and I visited the nationally known San Diego Zoo. For months thereafter, on cue, Sadler could and would, when asked, mimic a Seal's bark. I purchased two books of poems – one by Rudyard Kipling and one a collection of poems by various authors. Finally a call came, and some portion of Camp Stoneman's forty five boarded a Navy Seaplane Tender. A seaplane tender is a relatively small ship configured to refuel amphibious airplanes at sea. When well

44

out to sea, we learned that the ship traveled on a week's voyage bound for Hawaii. All new sailors, on their first voyage, formed the ship's crew. The small ship's wave induced pitching and rolling caused all sailors and many passengers to become sea sick. Those not sick had one thing in common, untested fighter pilots. Accustomed to pitching and rolling, they shared immunity to motion sickness; a distinction allowing me to know the entire Aloe Nine. In addition I came to know Class 43-I graduates from Flight Schools other than Aloe, including; David Wolf, my friend from Jones and Majors Field cadet days, and Harry Vaughan who became a lifelong friend. Days at sea are long and boring. To pass time, I read my poems. Out of character for the mythical fighter pilot, I endured a lot of teasing.

Visible from our ship, Monday morning, 1 November, an Island appeared on the western horizon. This same day, Marines, supported by the 13th Air Force, landed on Bougainville, the last Japanese stronghold south of Rabaul. Mid-day, our ship rounded Diamond Head, a world famous, extinct volcano on the south eastern point of Oahu.

Mid-afternoon, the ship docked at a Pearl Harbor berth, in Hawaii. Wreckage caused by the Japanese 7 December 1941 remained quite visible. Lt. Colonel Lew Sanders, Commander of the 318th Fighter Group, met the group on the dock and welcomed us to the Seventh Air Force, the Seventh Fighter Command, and to the 318th Fighter Group. A welcome by a Lt. Col. honored our group. Normal protocol would have a junior staff officer meet a group of new 2nd Lts. In time, I learned to hold Col Sanders  in high respect. I still do. A great commander, he gave first priority to care for his men and to the 318th mission. These two functions are so intertwined and mutually supporting that I combine them into a single priority.

Col. Sanders arrived in Hawaii in February of 1941 by an ocean voyage aboard the Navy's aircraft carrier Enterprise, a P-36 launch off the carrier's flight deck, and a landing on Wheeler Field. Flying P-36s, he led the first flight off Wheeler Field during the Japanese attack on December 7th, shot down two Japanese aircraft, and lost one wingman. The first Allied pilot to engage the Japanese agile Zero fighter, few believed his account of the Zero's performance.

Standing on the dock, Col. Sanders said that the 318th included three squadrons, the 19th flying the P-40, the 73rd flying the A-24, and the 333rd flying the P-39. Each squadron needed pilots, and we could each choose a squadron. Another fork in the road, I chose the 333rd because it offered me an opportunity to fly the P-39 rather than the P-40.

Choices made, a large Army truck transported six Aloe Nine members, Max K. Bozarth, Thomas P. Riddle, Lloyd L. Bosley, Elmer M. Harmes, Robert R. Sadler, and me, joined by Harry B. Vaughan along with their gear, to Bellows Army Air Field in its tarp covered bed.

On arrival, while gathering our gear from the truck bed, a four ship formation of P-39s flew low over Bellows runway at high speed. In order, after 3-second delays, the four pitched straight up in a high-G climb. When vertical, they rolled right, pulled the nose to the horizon, and rolled left onto their downwind leg beautifully spaced. In moist air, each airplane's two wingtip vortices drew contrail ribbons throughout the maneuver. The display matched the best of airshows.

Turning base leg and final, they made beautiful landings spaced about half a runway apart. Remembering Major Aloe's comment on Matagorda, *".....you are still a mediocre inexperienced pilot,"* I wondered if I could fly in the major leagues with such professionals.

Bellows, located on the south-east side of Oahu Island, shared the shores of beautiful Kaneohe Bay. Landward, behind Bellows, a mountain range provided insufficient space for landward directed takeoffs or forced go-a-round climb-outs. Right hand downwind landing patterns brushed the mountains before turning base and landing toward the sea. All takeoffs flew over the beautiful beach.

Pilots assigned to the 333rd are pictured right. Note the P-39. Bellows Field boosted only a few hardtop buildings, tarpaper covered constructions, reserved for func-

tions such as messing, pilot ready room, and storage of spare parts, tools, ammunition, and other critical items. Pyramidal tents, pitched on hills above the runways, served as living quarters. Tommy Riddle and I shared a tent with 1st Lt. Robert Rieser, and 1st Lt. Leonard Riggins, both combat veterans.

Major Joe Powell commanded the 333rd Squadron. The squadron served as a graduate school for fighter pilots. Young, inexperienced pilots, recent cadets, remained in the Squadron until judged fit for combat. Then orders transferred them to Gen. George Kenney's 5th Air Force in the South Pacific.

Training focused on formation, gunnery and tactics. Squadron aircraft allowed little Instrument training. An Army version of the Navy's SBD dive bomber with two tandem seats, made possible under the hood instrument flight with a safety observer, but with only one airplane in the inventory usually out of service, it gave few flight hours. Occasionally, a pilot spent a day at Hickam Field flying a Link trainer, a rudimentary forerunner of an instrument flight simulator. By the large, pilots remained poor instrument pilots.

My first flight in the P-39 served as a checkout and orientation flight in a two ship formation. As for the P-40, checkout required; read the Tech Order, sit in the cockpit and learn the

location and function of all instruments and controls; pass a blindfold test, cross fingers and fly. The flight leader flew around and above Oahu noting points of interest paying particular attention to all airfields. Returning to the Kaneohe Bay area, he flew several high-G chandelles, lazy eights, and loops, probably to evaluate and report my skill level.

The P-39, a small airplane with its engine mounted behind the pilot, a 20 mm gun or 37 mm gun firing through its propeller hub, and two 30-cal guns mounded in each wing, flew easily. It seemed to anticipate a pilot's intent; think turn and the airplane turned. The airplane, mid-1930s technology including its oxygen system, required pilots to wear 1930s era helmets. It had only a

single stage, engine driven supercharger. Below seven thousand feet, it gave good performance, but reduced engine power at higher altitudes made it a good airplane to fly for fun, but not an airplane in which to go to war.

Robert Rieser led my next flight, a four-ship formation. He intended, I later learned, to fly a required evaluation mission for all newly assigned pilots. He hoped to fly sufficiently high-G maneuvers that the two new wingmen lost position in the formation. He and the element leader would then quickly return to base and wait for the wingmen to return. When they arrived, he intended to chew them out unmercifully. I held my position throughout the flight and came home with Rieser

During the following days, new pilots flew two to three flights per day, all formation flights equally distributed between tactical training and gunnery training. Two-ship, four-ship, eight-ship and larger formation flights repeatedly performed accepted Army Air Force tactical maneuvers. The gunnery syllabus included shooting live ammunition at ground targets and at airborne targets. Riddle and I continued to compete for top-gun position. He remained a strong competitor.

On a regular schedule, new pilots practiced on a Bellows skeet range, and on a 45-cal pistol range. Range operators kept score, and Major Powell required all to reach and maintain acceptable score levels. We also practiced on a skeet range at Hickam Field designed much as a golf course. Pilots stood, buckled to a pedestal, on the flatbed of a truck. As the truck sped over the course, skeet disks flew from behind bushes. Hitting a disk as the truck bounced along challenged even Tommy Riddle. As a note of interest, I came to know a Sergeant from Fayetteville who managed this range.

Frequent missions, firing at ground targets on a gunnery range near Bellows and at large flag targets towed by a tow airplane over the ocean, tested and enhanced pilot skills. As a command responsibility, Major Powell often flew with pilots to evaluate the effectiveness of squadron training. A great aerial gunner, I flew his wing on several gunnery flights. Early in his attack run, he adjusted his bearing until satisfied, then closed on the target with wings lever, squeezed off a 37 mm round, and hit the target. In later years, while working with research programs developing automatic gun laying systems, I learned that he flew a collision-course, the path flown by Century Series fighters under computer control.

Rieser had a girlfriend, Charlotte. She worked in Fort Shafter's Command and Information Center (CIC) and often spent off duty time at Lanikah Officers Beach Club, located on a beach near Bellows. Behind the beach grew a row of tall evergreen trees. Returning from a two-ship mission with me on his wing, hoping to impress Charlotte, Rieser made a very low pass over Lanikah with a hard climb-out to avoid the trees. After landing, as I parked in my airplane's parking space, I noticed Col Sanders talking to an airplane's Crew Chief. As I filled out the airplane log, they walked over and began examining my airplane. Getting out of the airplane, I saw them picking small tree limbs out of the right wing's leading edge. I had not cleared the Lanikah trees.

As Col. Sanders began to give me the what-for, Rieser walked up and said, *"That is my fault. I buzzed Lanikah, with him on my wing flying a good formation, and flew him into the trees behind Lanikah."* Col. Sanders dismissed me with, *"Good work Lt."* and as I walked away he turned his attention to Rieser. In time Rieser would marry Charlotte and raise a son who would buy his Dad a P-39 of his own.

One day I learned another flying lesson on a mission to carry Bellows mail to Hickam Field in an L-5 observation airplane. An inexperienced pilot, able to fly an airplane, but without the wisdom of experience, I flew a short-cut route through the Pali.

From a high altitude, the Island of Oahu looks much like a ham floating peacefully on the blue waters of the Pacific with its shank pointing in a south-easterly direction. The eastern side of the island is separated from the western side by a mountain range. A valley, called the Pali, crosses the ham's shank exiting near Bellows Field on the eastern side of the island and near Honolulu, Pearl Harbor, and Hickam Field clustered on the western side of the range.

Since arriving on Bellows, I often flew P-39s through the Pali. Short on experience, without thinking, I flew the L-5 through the canyon. High bumpy, western winds raced through the canyon. As the L-5 progressed, the canyon narrowed, its venturi effect increased, and the winds approached maximum L-5 speed. With full throttle, my ground speed slowed to, at most, 5 knots, in a canyon too narrow to do a 180 turn. Turbulent winds tossed the airplane from a near miss on one side of the canyon to a near miss on the other. To my relief, after what seemed hours, the airplane finally reached the canyon's western exit. Later, Captain

50

Winston Park, a more experienced pilot remarked that I could have reduced throttle, let the wind drift the airplane reward out of the canyon, and flown around the southern tip of Oahu. A lesson well learned.

Sometime in early 1944 or before, a command decision stabilized the 318th Fighter Group and preparations began for a planned Marianas Campaign. In April of 1944, Major Paul Fojtik replaced Major Joe Powell as 333rd Squadron Commander. I later learned that Major Powell commanded the 47th Fighter Squadron as it flew B-29 escort missions and fighter sweep missions over Japan from Iwo Jima. In 1950, he endorsed my application for a regular commission and wrote a letter to an Air Force Selection Board recommending that I be given an Air Force Regular Commission as a 1st Lt. I was so commissioned by a Presidential appointment, dated 11 June 1952, signed by Secretary of the Air Force, Thomas K Finletter and General Laurence Kuter, Air Force Assistant Chief of Staff..

Major Fojtik, an experienced combat pilot flew with the 46th Fighter Squadron stationed on Makin, an island in the Gilberts, during the Mandates Campaign. Though wounded by a 7.7 mm round over Mili Atoll, he flew his P-39 back to Makin. Other officers, both administrative and flying, having operational experience, transferred into the 318th Group to replace an equal number of officers, having less rank and less experience, who then transferred to other units within the Command. Of the seven 333rd pilots welcomed to the 318th by Col. Sanders, on a Pearl Harbor dock in November, only Elmer Harms transferred out of the squadron.

April also saw the squadron transition from P-39 to P-47 aircraft. As P-47 airplanes arrived, our P-39s transferred to the 21st Fighter Group's 531st Squadron then transitioning from an A-24 dive bomb squadron to a P-39 fighter squadron. On 26 April, I flew my P-47 checkout flight. As the new airplanes arrived, Major Fojtik accelerated an already intensive formation and gunnery training program, and introduced two new training missions. Instrument missions entailed pilots dropping seats to their lowest position and flying the airplane on instruments with a wingman acting as safety. Major Fojtik asked Crew Chiefs to, inasmuch as possible; make pilots maintenance proficient and required pilots help maintain the airplanes.

Organizationally, the squadron formed and scheduled semi-permanent flights. My flight included: flight leader Captain Karl Mulligan flying lead with Riddle on his wing, and Arthur Bowen flying element leader with me flying his wing. Operations scheduled some, not all, pilots to fly a specific airplane; the idea being that the pilot would learn its unique flying qualities and be able to get maximum performance.

With the Group well equipped with P-47s and pilots reasonably comfortable in the airplane's cockpit, the time for three-day annual Army-Navy Maneuvers arrived. On the first day, expecting to earn an edge, Fojtik started engines early and positioned the squadron at the end of the runway ready for takeoff the moment scheduled maneuvers began. Before our first airplane cleared the runway, Navy F4U Corsairs began a mock strafing attack on Bellows. During the maneuvers, we flew simulated missions attacking designated ships at sea and in-bound Navy bombers designated as bogies.

Our attacks proved quite successful against targets defended by F4Us Corsairs and F6F Hellcats; both agile magnificent fighters. With an exhaust gas driven turbine supercharger, the P-47 had better altitude performance. Beginning attacks from altitudes above the Navy, we had the speed and energy needed to make successful attacks that Navy fighters could not defend. Later, our Intelligence Officer learned that, on the last maneuver day, Charles A. Lindberg flew one of the Corsairs.

In late April, airplane assignments gave me an airplane with 450 as it's the last three Serial number digits and gave Tommy Riddle an airplane with 449 as its last three serial number digits. He remarked *"Seems I can never beat you."* Robert Knox, left pictured right on opposite page, crewed my airplane and Elmer Rund, white shirt, crewed Riddle's airplane. Both survived attacks on Bellows during the 7 December Japanese raid. A stream of bullets, fired by a strafing Japanese Zero, straddled Rund as he lay on the tarmac. Knox considered the airplane his and me his pilot. His idea, a witch riding a broom across the moon, painted by Robert Rieser, a graduate from Stanford University's School of Art, became the airplane's nose art. Knox and Rund, both "Old Army," rightly expected me and Riddle to be Army worthy. When needed, Knox called me aside, beyond the hearing of others, to give me a good dressing-down  for failing to abide by Army rules and good discipline. I accepted his criticism because he deserved and held my highest regard. I suspect that Rund gave Riddle the same treatment.

A message from Amy Headquarters ordered the 318th to demonstrate its close air support capability with simulated dive bombing and strafing attacks on Wheeler Field while senior Navy and Army Officers, sitting on bleachers, watched. Given the mission, the 333rd launched a three flight formation led by Captain Winston Park.

I do not remember who led my flight. Thomas Benechasa flew his wing. I flew element and Harry Vaughan flew my wing. On climb-out, Vaughan reported engine malfunction, and Park ordered him to return to Bellows leaving me in a three-ship flight. As the formation approached the target, Park signaled right echelon as he started a diving left turn attack. The signal required me to move from the flight leader's left wing to Benechasa's right wing. As I started to move, Benechasa, contrary to flight procedures, moved right; a bad decision. Another bad decision; I began to move into number two position. Doing so, I necessarily had to look at the leader's airplane and could no longer see Benechasa. He then decided that he should return to his proper position. Our airplanes collided, and his propeller cut my tail section away.

All pitch and yaw control gone, my airplane began wild gyrations. Immediately, I unfastened my seat belt and manually opened the canopy. Another bad decision because the canopy slammed shut leaving me tumbling around in the cockpit as clothes tumble in clothes dryers. I began watching the canopy's yellow emergency release as it passed me by. On one of its passes, I grabbed it and held on. On my next pass toward the canopy, with canopy gone, a lurch threw me clear of the airplane. My senses recovered sufficiently for me to pull a ripcord and open the parachute, but I could not stop its wild swings. As I approached the ground, I realized that I would land in a large pineapple field; not a pleasant thought knowing that pineapple bushes have spurs. My guardian angel still rode with me. On a great upswing, the parachute set me, standing up, in the middle of the field on a small road used to truck pineapples to market.

Within minutes, medics arrived in an Army Ambulance. In less than an hour, I arrived in an Army hospital. Though doctors found only cuts and bruises, I remained in the hospital a few days. While there, I met Mary, a lovely brunette flight nurse. We became friends, but seldom saw one another. She spent much of her time on air evacuation flights, moving wounded from West Pacific battle fields to Hawaii and recuperating patients from Hawaii to the West Coast.

Returning to Bellows, Major Fojtik led my first flight, a strenuous two-ship formation. Not stated, but I knew his purpose – determine if I still had the nerve to fly fighters. After landing, he walked to the pilot's ready room without comment. Within a few days, a Witch replacement arrived for Knox to crew and for me to fly.

In order to better know and exploit the P-47's altitude capability, schedules routinely included high altitude missions. The airplane's exhaust-gas driven supercharging turbine became more efficient with altitude, and the airplane had better altitude performance than did its pilots. Above 25,000 feet, blood begins to boil, and nitrogen bubbles form in joints causing much pain. Above 30,000 feet, unpressurized cockpit atmospheric pressure is insufficient for lungs to absorb oxygen. Pressurized oxygen masks forced oxygen into lungs, but pilots had to forcefully exhale. After twenty minutes, or less, the pilot became exhausted. For longer periods he became near incapacitated.

With pilots beginning to show signs of fatigue, revised schedules gave them periodic two-day breaks. They spent those days visiting Honolulu or nearby Lanikah Officers Beach Club. The Beach Club, a favorite accessible by a long walk over a ridge, offered rooms for overnight with good beds, good dinning, a bar, and access to a beautiful beach. Flight Nurses and WARDS, <u>Women Air Raid Defense</u> girls from Fort Shafter's Command, Information and Control Center (CIC) employed to move friend-foe markers on its Situation Map, patronized the Beach Club. Occasionally, when not on an air evacuation flight, Mary met me here.

Waikiki Beach, another favorite destination for pilots free for a day or two, is pictured right. Note: that the beach is largely deserted, and the absence of vacationers on the beach. Shallow  water generated large long-running waves, great for surfing. Dark spots on the water are surfers waiting to catch a wave. Over a period of time, I learned to catch an occasional wave and ride a surf board to shore.

The large building to the left is the Royal Hawaiian Hotel. During WWII, the Navy used the Royal Hawaiian as a rest and recreation center for war weary sailors. The white building, right-center, is the Moana Hotel. Hawaii Calls, a radio program popular throughout the forty-eight states, originated under the banyan tree seen in the hotel's courtyard. The 318th patronized the Moana.

The photographs below picture 333rd pilots in front of the
Moana. The left one pictures from left to right: me, Tommy Riddle, and Max Bozarth. The right one pictures my then current
flight, again from left to right: Arthur Bowen element leader,
Captain Karl Mullian flight leader, me and Harry Vaughan
wingmen.

In May, the schedule became less demanding, and five-day passes became available. Tommy Riddle, Lloyd Bosley, Harry
Vaughan, and I flew to Hilo and spent five days on Hawaii, the
Big Island, in a hotel sitting on the lip of Mauna Loa, the island's
most active volcano. The hotel's large dining room window
overlooked Mauna Loa's glowing crater. We rented an automobile and toured the entire island, and experienced a surprise seeing native Hawaiians on the Kona (East) coast living the true
Hawaiian culture. The morning of our departure, the automobile's gas gage showed near empty, but, being on top of a mountain, we coasted downhill to the outskirts of Hilo, drove to the
airport and flew home. In Hilo I ate my first steak. Expecting it
to be dowsed in gravy, I ordered rice as its side dish – amusing
the party with my country boy taste.

Beginning in early May, with flight schedules minimized, all
Squadron Sections began packing equipment and belongings in
crates for shipment to an unknown destination. A few days later,
Sgt. Knox informed me that a beer can is the same length as that
of a 50 cal. machine gun round, and asked for my consent to

transport some beer to our next duty station. With my consent, he half-filled our airplane's ammunition bays with several cases of Black Label beer and topped off each bay with ammunition.

On 7 June the squadron, placed on a 24 hour alert, initiated the task of moving crates to a Pearl Harbor dock to be loaded onto the Seacat, an Army transport ship. On 13 June, the squadron ground echelon boarded the Seacat, and on 18 June, departed Pearl to join a sixteen ship convoy including two aircraft carriers, two destroyers, eleven transports, and one tanker. The Seacat, lacking gunners, depended upon 333rd Sgt. Victor Peterson's armament specialists to man the ship's 20 mm antiaircraft guns. On 27 June, the convoy anchored in Eniwetok's lagoon for a four day layover, and on 6 July the Seacat anchored in Saipan's harbor.

The squadron's thirty-seven P-47s and thirty-seven pilots, and a skeleton maintenance crew remained on Bellows. Pilots performed daily preflight inspections and any needed maintenance.
Minimized flight schedules reduced the need for maintenance. The photograph above illustrates the squadron's tarmac inactivity and near abandonment for three weeks following the ground echelon's departure. After an eight month, heavy, seven day per week, work load, pilots enjoyed twenty days of light duty.

On 3 July, thirty-seven pilots flew their airplanes to Luke Field on Ford Island in Pearl Harbor to be hoisted aboard the aircraft carrier, Sargent Bay

THE BRAVEST BATTLE

The Bravest battle that ever was fought!
Shall I tell you where and when?
On the maps of the world you will find it not;
'Twas fought by the mothers of men.

Nay, not with cannon or battle-shot,
With sword or noble pen;
Nay, not with eloquent words or thought
From the mouths of wonderful men!

But deep in a walled-up woman's heart–
Of a woman that would not yield,
But bravely, silently bore her part–
Lo, there is that battle-field!

No marshaling troops, no bivouac song,
No banner to gleam and wave;
But oh! These battles, they last so long–
From babyhood to the grave.

Joaquin Miller

Chapter 5
MARIANA'S CAMPAIGN

On the Fourth of July 1944, the Navy hoisted thirty-seven 333rd
Squadron P-47D airplanes onto the aircraft carrier, Sargent Bay.
Two days later, with thirty seven 333rd pilots, a 333rd maintenance crew, plus two spare pilots on board as passengers, the
ship, with one destroyer escort, sailed out of Pearl Harbor; beginning a twelve-day voyage with destination Saipan, an island
within the Mariana Archipelago.

The USS Sargent Bay, an
escort carrier with a normal
860 man crew, carried a
normal complement of 28
airplanes. Powered by twin
steam engines, it could attain
a 20 knot (23 MPH) top
speed.

Gracious ship crew members served delicious meals in an elegant dining environment. Passengers plus crew, however, over-
crowded sleeping quarters. Reduced vertical spacing between
hammocks like beds stacked from floor to ceiling accommodated
extra Army passengers. My hammock, at the top of a stack, gave
only about eighteen-inches of space below the ceiling. Climbing
into and out of bed offered a challenge and frequent head bumps.

The ship had excellent communications. Daily national broadcast
news told of American forces slogging through Normandy. But
for a choice made as a cadet, I might have been traveling to Europe rather than to the West-Central Pacific.

Briefings by the ship's Intelligence Officer gave pilots background information on the Mariana's Campaign. The Mariana
Islands, strategically located 1,500 miles southeast of Japan, offer secure basing from which B-29 airplanes can raid Japan. The
invasion of Saipan, now underway, is supported by the 318th

Headquarters Group and our three sister squadrons, the 19th the 73rd, and the 6th Night Fighter now operating off a captured Japanese airfield on Saipan providing air support for the operation.

Saipan is the most populated island in the Marianas Archipelago. Settled by Spain in the 16th Century, its people, the Chamorros, have a Spanish and Asiatic heritage. At the end of the Spanish American war, Spain ceded Guam to the US, and Guam became a US territory. Following WW I, the League of Nations awarded the islands north of Guam to Japan. The day following their 7 December 1941 raid on Pearl Harbor, the Japanese invaded Guam.

Squadron pilots, shown above on Sargent Bay's flight deck, include William Moreman in the airplane's engine nacelle and David Brunner on top between prop blades. I stand second from left on second row. The belts inflate as life savers.

Modified before leaving Bellows, our airplane's landing gear could accept Sargent Bay's catapult harness, and we expected to endure our first catapult launch and fly a last leg to Saipan. Launch procedures, briefed by the ship's Air Operations Officer, included an attention grabbing comment; *"If you go off the deck without flying speed, do not worry. Let the airplane settle. Just before it hits the water, it will begin to fly."* In time, that comment would ring in my ears making my survival possible.

Throughout the voyage, two airplanes remained on alert – ready to fly air defense. Pilots took turns on alert ready to launch if radar picked up targets not transmitting Friend-Foe (IFF) code. Before going on alert, pilot situation briefings described ship position, nearest friendly air fields, and nearest Japanese held territory. On one of my alert days, the distance to the nearest friendly air field equaled the P-47's maximum range. The Air Operations Officer advised that if launched, I should fly the mission and bail out and promised that the carrier's destroyer escort would pick me out of the water. During the afternoon, ship's radar detected an approaching unidentified airplane, the alert Caxton sounded, and I ran to the P-47 sitting on the catapult ready for launch. As I buckled parachute and shoulder harness, the crew chief started the engine. To my relief, ready for launch, radar identified the incoming airplane as friendly and canceled the alert.

Before reaching our destination, I became ill with a severe cold. Hoping to keep me fit to fly; the ship's doctor gave me a shot of penicillin, at the time a new medicine. The penicillin, dissolved in a large viol of warm wax and inserted into my buttocks with a very large, painful needle, worked. Fit to fly, I launched on launch day.

Airplanes launched as three twelve-ship formations. Major Fojtik launched the 37th airplane and joined the third formation. Led by Winston Park, the first formation launched three flights of four (12 airplanes) during the morning of eighteen July. I flew in the third flight led by Karl Mulligan with Harry Vaughan flying his wing, Charles Foster flying element, and me flying Foster's wing.

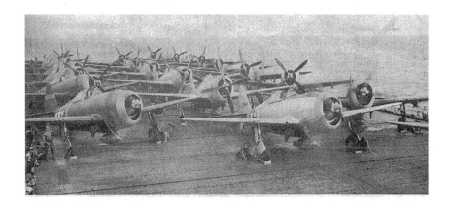

The photograph above captures the moment showing three airplanes with props turning and a wing tip of a fourth airplane on the catapult may be seen far right with crew members prepared to pull chocks so that taxi to the launch pad may commence. Twenty one airplanes may be counted, and four, not seen, are parked on the forward right side of the deck; therefore, airplanes with engines running belong to the second twelve ship formation. I have just launched, and the airplane on the launch pad is the first airplane to follow me off the pad.

After exposure to days of humid salty air, "grabby" brakes made taxing to the launch pad difficult and dangerous on a crowded, slowly pitching and rolling deck. A light touch on the brake pedal produced full brake and airplane lurch. Once on the launch pad, by hand signals, a Navy Launch Officer exercised control; hold full brakes while crew attaches the catapult harness to landing gear, release brakes, add power, let harness restrain airplane, add full power, lock throttle quadrant, right hand on control stick with elbow on hipbone. When ready  place left hand on right cockpit rail to signal "ready." On the next deck upswing – slam and away you go– beer and all. This photograph pictures a 333rd P-47 recovering from the catapult's kick.

We launched, with the carrier by perhaps fifty miles west of our destination, Aslito, a captured Japanese air field located on the southern end of Saipan , to join the 318th Group Headquarters, the 19th, the 73rd and the 6th Night Fighter Squadrons.

Navigating by clock and compass, Park drifted south of course. At the expected time, the formation approached a land mass with a large airfield straight ahead. Proud of his navigation and wishing to make a grand arrival, Park signaled for a close tight formation, and we made a low level pass over the airfield. When over the airfield, we realized that we were over Ushi Point, an airfield on Japanese held Tinian. See map below. No shots were fired. The Japanese took us to be their long hoped for air support and we could see them waving and cheering.

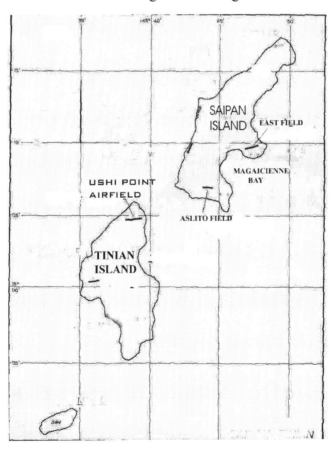

Recognizing his error, a chagrined Park led the formation on to Aslito. On my short final, perhaps at 500 feet, a battery of 105 artillery guns, located on the approach end of the runway, fired a salvo toward Tinian. Its shock wave lifted my airplane a few feet. I thought for a moment that someone considered me their target. In time Tinian would fall; Ushi Point airfield would become a B-29 airbase; and from Ushi Point Enola Gay would carry its atomic bomb to Hiroshima.

Landing, I received another shock caused by the racket of landing wheels on a runway of pierced, interlocked, steel planks. At first I thought I had landed wheels up.

After roll-out, following airplanes in the queue ahead of me, I taxied to a parking space where Sgt. Knox waited, pleased to reunite with his airplane and his pilot, and it pleased and comforted me to reunite with my friend, knowing that the airplane would again have the care and attention of a good crew chief. He promised to bring me a cache of beer during the evening. Noting that we had no refrigeration, he recommended I bury it in my tent's earthen floor for cooling.

While the Sargent Bay sailed the sea, the 333rd ground echelon established a squadron bivouac near the beach south of Aslito Airfield. Pyramidal tents pitched on sandy soil served as living quarters. Tommy Riddle, Max Bozarth, Harry Vaughan, and I shared one tent. Living in tents with sand for floors proved quite a large step down from Navy quarters with hammocks. A small piece of roofing tin, found nearby and placed beside a cot provided the luxury of something other than sand for bare feet when waking to begin a new day. Leaving the flight line, the pilots searched for and found their belongings shipped from Hawaii to Saipan by the Sea Cat, unpacked and stowed them in their tents. The following day, intelligence and operational briefings explained three 318th's missions. I recall those briefings as; "*Mission one required eight airplanes constantly fly combat air patrol during dawn and dusk periods and four airplanes constantly fly air patrol during bright daylight hours. A second mission required dive bombing and strafing flights to interdict Japanese*

64

airfields and other offensive facilities on Guam, Rota, Tinian, and Pagan to keep them inoperable. A third mission required close air support for Army and Marine infantry as they captured remaining portions of Saipan and during invasion and capture of Tininan and Guam."
A heavy flight schedule followed these briefings.

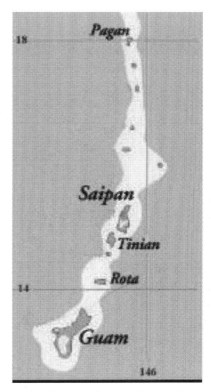

I flew my first sortie on the 21st of July on a mission to bomb and strafe targets within a Tinian town. The following day, the squadron launched a 36 ship mission, three 12 ship formations, to dive bomb and strafe a Japanese air field on Pagan Island, 200 miles north of Saipan. Captain Mulligan led my flight, the third flight in the third formation. As usual, Foster flew element and I flew his wing. That put me last over target after 35 airplanes had alerted the Japanese, had angered them, and had given all gunners adequate time to man their guns.

Foster's bombs failed to release. With me on his wing, Foster began a circling climb directly over the air field while every gunner on the island concentrated fire on us and filled the air with flack. Why we were not hit, I shall never know for certain – perhaps the hand of a guardian angel. Climbing to 5,000 feet, with me still on his wing, Foster rolled into a dive, dropped his bombs, and we strafed the air field, rejoined the squadron formation, and came home.

Two days later, another 333rd maximum effort supported two Marine Divisions as they established a beachhead on the northwest coast of Tinian. In formation, I arrived over the landing area at daybreak. To the west, flashes of gunfire lit the sky as big Navy capital ships bombarded landing sites. Below, I saw Marines climbing down rope ladders hanging over sides of troop ships and jumping into small landing craft.

When filled, landing crafts joined race track patterns aligned perpendicular to the coastline. At an appointed moment, the inbound leg of each race track continued its inbound heading; forming row after row of landing craft approaching shore. The ship bombardment ceased and the 333rd began strafing areas just behind the beaches. Before noontime, Marines secured the beachhead. Throughout July's remaining days, I flew daily close air support missions as Marines advanced across Tinian.

By the end of July, Army and Navy combat and air evacuation traffic exceeded safe traffic control on Aslito's single runway. (Note: Command renamed Aslito Field to honor Navy Commander Robert Isley who crashed while strafing the airfield.) Hereafter the name Isley will designate this field. A promise of relief came with the 318th reassignment to a new air field under constructed, soon to be operational, and the 318th began moving supplies and equipment across the island to East Field located on Kagam Point. See page 63. I made two, or more, trips driving a loaded jeep pulling a loaded trailer from Isley Field to East Field.

The twelve mile trip across the island offered a tourist's view of low land cane fields and jungle, and woodland at the higher elevations. Danger still lurked in these cane fields, jungles and woodlands. Although Japan's Army and Navy organized units had been defeated, and Japan's senior officers, Lt. General Saito and Admiral Nagumo (the Japanese hero who commanded Japan's First Air Fleet during the Sunday morning Japanese raid on Pearl Harbor two and one half years earlier) had committed suicide, and many Japanese families, both military and  civilian had committed suicide by jumping off the cliffs of Marpi Point, groups of Japanese, unwilling to surrender, still held out hiding in caves and jungle.

With a small group, organized by our Intelligence Officer, I visited Marpie Point and saw crumpled bodies still lying at the foot of the cliffs. Bodies, charred by Marine and Army flame throwers, filled a large concrete pillbox and gun emplacement, seen at the top left corner of the above picture. The crumpled bodies laying at water's edge, offered a truly gruesome sight. Another note of interest; Tom Clancy's book <u>Debt of Honor</u> begins at Marpi Point. The story begins with a man standing on Marpie Point looking eastward across the Pacific. The debt of honor is a debt owed by a son to a father who, among others, jumped over the cliffs in July of 1944. The son, a Japanese airline pilot, pays the debt in full by crashing an airliner into our Nation's Capital Building. Published in 1994, the book preceded and perhaps foretold the events of 9/11.

Learning of the field's completion and operational status, a quickly organized flight flew to, and became the first to land on East Field. Pictured in flying suits on the following page, from left to right, Lts. Wayne Duresmith and Marsden Dupuy, Major Paul Fojtik, and Lt Col Charles Taylor talk to four Army construction engineers. Col Taylor, 318th Deputy Group Commander, then held, and probably still holds, the record number of carrier take-offs for Army pilots. Major Fojtik, the 333rd Squadron Commander, stands at center. Lts. Duresmith and Dupuy provided strong leadership among junior officers.

After several hours in flight firmly strapped to its seat, the P-47 cockpit became a torture chamber and the life vest, seen hanging as bibs, became another instrument of torture. The parachute seat served as storage for a survival kit containing a small life raft, a first aid kit, a compass, maps, fish hooks, water and food. As flight time wore on, it became ever more bumpy. In time, it seemed as though one sat on rocks. Our Squadron Flight Surgeon, Captain John D. Van Valkenburg, gained a lot of medical experience treating sore butts.

My first trip to East Field crossed a recent woodland battle field. Japanese soldiers still lay where fallen. In the area, I noticed a nice stalk of ripe bananas beside the road and made a mental note to harvest the bananas on the return trip. Returning to Isley, I stopped beside the banana tree growing on the downside of the road's embankment. Standing beside the road, the stalk of bananas hung at my level just beyond my reach. Jumping, I grabbed the bananas. My weight pulled the bananas down, with me standing in some underbrush with the upper torso of a Japanese soldier looking up at me with both legs missing. Losing all banana interest, I returned to the jeep and continued on to Isley somewhat in shock. Hopefully, my report to our Intelligence Officer caused the body to be recovered and buried.

Assigned a bivouac area south of the runway and a maintenance area north of the runway, the 318th had to clear both areas, not covered with sugar cane, of damaged Japanese buildings and debris of war. The island's military government provided 40 Japanese prisoners to help clear the area and set up camp.

Bands of Japanese, hiding by day in the jungle, posed a threat. To remove cover for snipers, tracked vehicles smashed down all cane surrounding East Field, and Military Police posted guards around the clock. Nighttime often brought sounds of gunshots. Targets, most often, proved to be cows, or other animals that strayed into the area. Late one night a frightened hog, running through our sleeping area, awakened me. A hot night, all slept under mosquito nets with tent sides rolled up to allow some breeze to pass through the tents. The hog ran past my tent and through the adjacent tent's living space. Waking, Neal Obert first heard then saw an approaching squealing beast. The beast ran beneath his cot. Taller than the cot, the hog's back knocked Neil to the ground, helplessly entangled in the mosquito netting. He began shouting for help. Several hours passed before he regained his composure, but he never overcame his embarrassment, or constant reminders of his hollering ability.

Heavily loaded with rifles, hand grenades, and knives, disoriented Soldiers and Marines, clearly mentally disturbed, termed shell shocked in that day, wandering alone through our bivouac, posed another risk. Most carried battlefield artifacts such as Japanese swords, rifles, and pistols and wished to barter these items for delicacies such as candy, soft drinks, beer or whiskey. One came into my tent with a Golden Grain tobacco pouch filled with gold teeth gouged from Japanese dead. I gave them things they valued to get rid of them.

Beginning in July and continuing with less frequency through October, air-evac airplanes landed on Isley, loaded wounded soldiers, marines, and sailors from Army and Navy hospitals, and transported them to better medial facilities in Hawaii and in the States. Mary served as flight nurse on some of these flights, and I saw her occasionally. However, her airplane's short turnaround time made our visits brief. She usually brought me a tin of corned beef, a six-pack, a bottle of scotch, or other such item unavailable on Saipan. In October of 1944, McArthur's forces landed on Mindoro's Leyte Gulf, and the battle for the Philippines began, Philippine casualties became air-evac priority, and I saw Mary no more on Saipan. Battles for control of the Philippines continued through February of 1945. During that time, an air evacuation airplane crashed and burned on Eniwetok with Mary and patients aboard. Crash crews did not save all, and some of her patients died in the burning airplane.

One day Foster came to me and said *"There is a cow in the field out there. If you get me close, I will put a rope on it and we will eat it tonight."* Driving a jeep with him riding its hood as though it were a horse, Foster lassoed the cow with a single fling of a rope. Otis Bennett butchered the cow, and the squadron mess served small portions of fresh meat the following day. In later days, I came to regret my role that day. The cow belonged to some poor Chamorro family, and we had no right to eat it.

Again, Tommy Riddle, Max Bozarth, Harry Vaughan, and I shared a tent. With a scrounged tarp, we extended its living space, making it a squadron social center. A fox hole, augmented with sandbags, comforted all  when Japan's Nighttime Charlie came at night dropping strings of bombs. The sandbags also served as a soft stool for Tommy Riddle and Harry Vaughan.

Typically, Nighttime Charlie, a Japanese bomber, such as the Betty, flew from Truk, a Japanese held island 750 miles south of Saipan, dropped bombs on us, and continued on to Pagan or to Iwo Jima 500 miles north.

Most often the 6th Night Fighter Squadron's P-61 Black Widows failed to make an intercept. One night, however, one shot the intruder down. It broke into two burning parts and fell into the sea. As the two falling parts separated, an optical illusion persuaded all that the two lights, appearing as wing tip lights, showed the airplane fast approaching their positions. Many, including 1st Lt. Edmund Rogge, our Intelligence Officer, injured themselves jumping into foxholes.

August saw streets formed through the bivouac area, community latrines, showers and more foxholes built, and a motor-generator power station setup to provide light and electricity to all tents and squadron facilities. Flight operations supported the invasion of Guam, close air support for Marines firefights on Tinian, interdiction missions over Rota and islands north, and air defense over Tinian and Saipan.

One day, not on the flight schedule, I spent a miserable afternoon in and around my tent. In a clear blue sky, the large fireball sun steamed the weather to hot-hot. Sugar in the smashed sugar cane attracted swarms of flies, mosquitoes, and other unknown pests. My tent's OD colored canvas absorbed heat making the tent an oven. I could walk around, sit on an empty ammunition box in the sun, or sit inside the tent on a cot. Neither option offered comfort.

My tent stood on our bivouac's perimeter. Beyond the perimeter, about the length of a football field stood the remains of a farmhouse, with its roof gone, some walls down, and some walls standing. Miserable, bored, restless, but feeling reasonable secure, I walked over to the house. I could see in all directions

71

across a large field. I wore a big .45-caliber pistol in a shoulder holster, and I knew how to use it. As I walked around the corner of a standing wall, I came face-to-face with a Japanese soldier. Driven by hunger, he had come from out the nearby jungle to dig sweet potatoes in a garden hidden from our bivouac's view by the farmhouse. When seen, he squatted while looking at me over his left shoulder. Before him, lay a small bag of sweet potatoes. By his left side lay his rifle with its muzzle pointing away from me. He held his digging tool (bayonet) in his right hand. I experienced a mixed feeling; fear of a soldier and sorry for a hungry man.

While watching me and never breaking eye contact, he slowly picked up his rifle by the end of its barrel and arose in a non-threating manner. Though with a loaded and cocked 45 caliber pistol in my shoulder holster, I could not shoot him, but rather watched a hungry man walk away into the jungle with his bag of potatoes. I consider that my decision to do him no harm one of my life's finer moments. For months, I told this story to no one. Rules of engagement did not allow letting a healthy enemy walk away to fight another day. I could have been court marshaled for doing so.

The coastline of Magaicienne Bay offered a beautiful near-by beach, good fishing, and sheltered water. The fish augmented an otherwise unappetizing mess menu, and the beach offered an occasional refreshing swim. Having a fetish for battlefield artifacts, Lloyd Bosley searched nearby areas for guns, swords, grenades, and other such items. Among other things, he returned from a search with a small Japanese motorboat. Rigging a surf-like board towed by the boat, we enjoyed ski-like surfing across the Bay. However, with an underpowered boat, only those of small statue could surf successfully.

One day, while ski-like surfing on the Bay, a Navy Destroyer Escort, patrolling the Bay, stopped to watch. The ship's Captain signaled for us to come alongside his ship. He jumped into the water and joined us. Too heavy for our boat to get him out of the water, he signaling his ship to drop a tow rope, and we had all the power needed. For an hour or more we and the ship's captain surfed the bay behind a large Destroyer Escort.

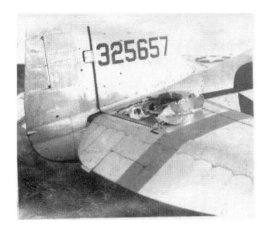

The P-47 could take a lot of punishment and still come home. The one pictured above took an anti-aircraft round and brought Wayne Bennett home seen siting on his jeep.

The airplane pictured right also came home.

The airplanes, however, could not withstand the forces of an exploding 500 lb. bomb, and a hanging bomb experienced by Foster over Pagan became a lingering hazard. During August, a total of 75 bombs failed to drop on target. Pilots jerked and shook some lose, but most came home with the airplane. Landing with a hung bomb is exceedingly dangerous. The landing jolt often shakes the bomb loose, and it follows bouncing, and hopping end over end alongside the airplane during rollout. Some exploded, destroying airplanes, killing one pilot and sending many to the boondocks running in fright. Major Fojtik landed with a hung bomb. Nothing concentrates the mind like a hung bomb while landing. All landings with bombs were great, smooth touchdowns.

In September, the Squadron continued to fly air defense and interdiction missions, 380 Combat Air Patrol (CAP) sorties over Saipan and Tinian and 172 sorties bombing and strafing Rota, Pagan and other islands north of Saipan. Seven Quonset Huts, in crates, arrived for the Squadron, including one setup as pilot living quarters, and I moved out of a tent into leisurely living space. Another served as an Officers Club. The officers themselves poured a concrete slab and erected the hut. The little experience mixing concrete for my father's house made me the squadron expert responsible for mixing the concrete. Willie Moorman, David K. Brunner, and Robert Rieser, all artists, decorated the interior, Lt. James C. Reed applied West Point engineering to design, sketch, and dimension furniture components. Others with some carpenter skills cut piece-parts from ammunition boxes and shipping creates and assembled needed furniture and a bar. In time, the hut began to look like a reasonable club with Willie Moorman's little elves peering from around each interior corner.

Major General Robert W. Douglass, Commander of the 7th Air Force, and Brig. General Ernest W. Moore, Commander 7th Fighter Command, visited East Field and decorated twenty three officers and enlisted men. All who traveled with me from San Diego to Hawaii received an Air Medal. This photograph pictures General Douglass presenting an Air Medal to Robert Sadler. To his left stands Richard
Peabody awaiting his turn to shake the General's hand. Fittingly, some enlisted men received equal recognition. Group enlistees, all magnificent soldiers, performed daily mundane, unrewarding tasks, with little recognition, and little hope of returning home in the near future. Thirteen pilots arrived from the States to replace veteran pilots suffering from recurring Dengue Fever, fatigue, and sore butts.

Daily routine saw little change through October. Generous applications of DDT greatly reduced mosquitos and other pests, but mosquito nets remained welcome and required. Interdiction missions encountered little opposition. The Mariana Trench, seven miles deep, lies just east of the Mariana Archipelago, and the area experiences much volcanic activity. En route to and from Pagan, pilots saw a small island form. Initially a small steaming spot of water became a small spot of smoking ground that grew into a small island. Eight more new pilots joined the Squadron and five more veteran pilots returned to the States.

Beginning in November, the arrival of B-29s on Saipan, Tinian, and Guam introduced a new and existential threat to the Japanese. A large airplane with pressurized cabins designed for high altitude, long range flight, it could easily fly bomb missions to mainland Japan and return home. Recognizing the threat, the Japanese increased air attacks on Saipan. Twin engine bombers, as many as nine on one occasion, attacked at

night. Zeke fighters strafed East Field on two occasions. On the 27th the Squadron launched all available P-47s while under attack by fifteen Zekes, Japan's Navy version of the formidable Zero.

William Fancher led my flight directly to Pagan to greet returning Japanese airplanes in their landing pattern. Harry Vaughan flew Fancier's wing. James de Yonker flew element, and I flew De Yonkers's wing. In the queue, waiting for takeoff clearance, I watched the flight ahead of our flight takeoff. Taking off in pairs, the flight leader and his wing man made a 270 degree left climbing turn as the element joined to make a perfect four ship formation. Crossing the field at about 5,000 feet, the flight leader, hit by friendly anti-aircraft fire, crashed and burned. Arriving over Pagan, we surprised two Zekes in the traffic pattern and some on the ground taxing. Fancher shot one down and De Yonker shot one as it was landing. We strafed those on the ground.

Following these raids, our Air Defense schedule changed. From dawn to dusk, the Squadron kept an element below 3,000 feet, an element at 5,000 feet, and a full 4-ship flight at 9,000 feet. In addition, from 0900 until 1600 an element loitered at 20,000 feet. In November, the Squadron flew 475 CAP sorties and 157 Interdiction sorties. In December, CAP missions demanded 1,005 sorties.

To clarify terms, one sortie is the flight of one airplane. The number of sorties flown within one month measures a squadron's productivity. A mission is a flight charged with the responsibility to achieve some objective. A four ship CAP flight counts as four sorties. A single ship reconnaissance flight over a target is both one mission and one sortie. A two ship reconnaissance flight counts as one mission and two sorties. A 36 interdiction flight counts as one mission and 36 sorties. A pilot's productivity is measured by flight hours, CAP sorties, and missions. By the end of November, I had flown 130 combat hours, 26 missions and 77 CAP sorties.

Frequent patrols over Saipan gave bird eye views of heavily loaded B-29s taking off from Isley and turning north en route to Japan. Underpowered, they used ever foot of runway to lift their load of bombs. Off times, needing more runway, one dropped from runway level to sea level to gain flying speed. As they neared water, "ground effect" most often provided the extra lift needed to fly. Sometimes they splashed. Watching, I remembered Sargent Bay's Air Operations Officer's words, *"If you go off the deck without flying speed, do not worry. Let the airplane settle. Just before it hits the water, it will begin to fly."*

Twelve P-38 fighters, ferried from Hawaii in late November, augmented the Squadron's P-47s fleet. Fighter command assigned eight of the P-38 pilots to the Squadron, and reassigned eight 333rd veterans to the 21st Fighter Group, stationed in Hawaii, including Tommy Riddle and Lloyd Bosley. Time and shipping space forced Bosley to leave his collection of battlefield artifacts on Saipan. In time, the 21st, flying P-51s, staged through Guam, Tinian, and Saipan en route to Iwo Jima. From Iwo, their

P-51s escorted B-29s over Japan, and on Iwo Bosley harvested another collection of artifacts. An early morning 300 man Japanese Banzai attack targeted the 21st pilot living area. Bosley gathered his collection of guns and hand grenades and formed a point of defense. Riddle lost an eye to grenade shrapnel and returned to civilian life. In years to come, when on the West Coast, I visited Tommy.

Its long legs put Truk and Iwo Jima within the P-38's range, and these two islands became interdiction targets. Over Iwo Jima, the 333rd shot down eleven Japanese airplanes. The eleven included two Japanese Betty bombers shot down by Captain Judge Wolfe, who in time became a 333rd Ace. Note him wearing the uniform of the day; a flying suit, a .45-Cal pistol in a shoulder holster, a knife, and a canteen of water. In January, Lt William Eustus, shot down over Truk, parachuted and picked up by the Japanese, spent the remainder of the war as a prisoner in Japan. He came home after the war, and lived a full life. Marines invaded Iwo in February and only Truk remained a P-38 target. I checked out in the P-38, but never flew a P-38 mission.

Before leaving Hawaii for Saipan, William Moreman and an Army Nurse became friends. Her hospital unit likewise moved to Saipan and operated a field hospital. They continued to see each other. One evening while on the beach of Magaicienne Bay, three Navy sailors attacked and killed both Moreman and the Nurse, but not before he shot one with his pistol. The following day a 333rd search team found their bodies on the beach in shallow graves.

The wounded sailor reported to the hospital bearing a .45 slug. When interrogated, he confessed, and implicated the other sailors. The Navy transferred them to Guam to stand Court Marshal for murder. The Squadron buried Moreman on Saipan. I served as a pall bearer, and saw my first <u>missing man formation</u> as a

77

333rd formation flew overhead during the burial ceremony. This photograph pictures William Moreman on the left and Arthur Bowen. Bowen survived the war and helped configure an airplane to represent a 333rd airplane, to be defined later, for display in the Cradle of Aviation Museum located in Garden City, Long Island, New York.

In early March, 1945 alert orders brought winds of change. The 318th would redeploy to operate under operational control of Tactical Air Force, Tenth Army. Preparations commenced for movement to an unannounced destination.

Sixteen 318th pilots and eight maintenance sergeants, ordered to Hawaii on detached duty, departed East Field 14 March on a mission to accept new P-47N aircraft from Hickam Depot and ferry them from Hawaii to Saipan. The group included twelve 333rd pilots including, Robert Sadler, Walter Peckham, Carlton Berry, and me. By Military Air Transport, we traveled to Guam, to Eniwetok, and on to Hawaii. In Hawaii, each pilot flight tested an assigned airplane and prepared for a flight back to Saipan.

The Squadron devoted activities during the first five days of April to last minute crating and packing equipment and personnel belongings. On 6 April, Group's ground echelon loaded crates and equipment on a freighter, the USS Hall Young, and boarded a troop ship, the USS Kenmore. The two ships joined a small convoy, traveled to Ulithi, joined a larger convoy, and waited. An air echelon composed of airplanes, pilots, and a skeleton staff of engineering, maintenance, communications, ordinance, and operations personnel moved to Kobler Field, the number two Isley landing runway and support area named for Lt. Wayne F. Kobler, a 318th pilot who crashed and died on Tinian.

On 7 April a four flight, sixteen ships, 318th formation, following a B-25 carrying a 318th maintenance crew and providing navigation, departed Hawaii flying new airplanes; destination Saipan.

The lead flight, an all 73rd flight led by Major Wilmer McCown, included Rodney Selfridge, Delmar Horner, and Thomas Martin. A second flight led by Donald Kane (73rd) included Robert Redfield (73rd), Otis Bennett (333rd) and Gordon Beecroft (333rd). I led a third flight, all 333rd. Walter Peckham flew my wing. Robert Sadler flew element, and Carlton Berry flew Sadler's wing. Edward Gray led a fourth flight with Howard Barrett, William Mathis, and Kenneth Elender, all from the 19th Squadron.

We flew the first leg, an eight hundred mile four and one half (4:30) hour flight to Johnson Island, in good weather. Well into the flight, my engine began to run rough. When over water, far from land, one often imagines a rough engine. This very real roughness caused much anxiety. However, the engine continued to give sufficient power for me to remain in formation. We remained on Johnson for three days waiting for a good weather forecast. During the stay, our maintenance crew checked, changed spark plugs, and retuned my airplane's engine – an airplane that would later be named "Cheek Baby." While on Johnson, I flew a test flight, and the engine performed well. Over time I flew that airplane many hours without another squawk.

The formation departed Johnson Island 11 April during early morning hours. We flew a second uneventful 1,400 mile leg to Majuro Island in seven (7:00) hours in good weather. Majuro is one of the southern islands in the Marshall Archipelago. Its culture, almost untouched by the outside world, claimed that, in the past, Robert Louis Stevenson lived on a nearby island that could be seen in the distance. Mili, an island fifty miles to the south, later in time, became the site of atomic and nuclear tests from 1948 through 1958.

This photograph, made somewhere during the trip, pictures one of our P-47Ns over the vast Pacific. Note the external fuel tanks.

While on Majuro, we learned of President Franklin Roosevelt's 12 April death. The formation departed Majuro early morning 14 April. The third leg, an eight hundred mile, three and one half (3:30) hour flight to Eniwetok, encountered a weather front with embedded thunderstorms.

Major McCown elected to penetrate the weather front beneath the weather at low altitude. With low visibility and high turbulence, the need to maintain eye contact with other airplanes demanded close formation incurring high collision risk. I chose to not take that risk and accept a possible reprimand.

Signaling Sadler, I suggested that we climb above the weather and proceed to Eniwetok above the clouds. He enthusiastically nodded agreement. By reducing my throttle a small amount, the main formation drifted ahead. When confident of sufficient separation, I added power and began to climb. After a few very turbulent minutes, my flight reached about fifteen thousand feet above all clouds. I knew; that a Radio Range station on Eniwetok beamed an east-west radio beam, that we flew west in its second quadrant, and that, in time, I should begin to hear its (dit-da) "A" signal. As time wore on, I began to hear the signal, faint, but increasing. Turing 5 degrees right of course, I soon intercepted the beam's steady tone. Now we needed to get below weather before landing without descending onto the main formation. Our preflight weather forecast promised clear weather over Eniwetok. If the forecast held, we could make a visual descent with no risk. If clouds covered Eniwetok, I planned to continue west beyond the weather front, descend, reverse course and fly the western range beam back to Eniwetok. My Guardian Angel provided; Eniwetok enjoyed clear weather. Descending, I called tower for landing clearance and set up a landing pattern. Major McCown heard my call and, by a return radio call, instructed me to hold until all airplanes in the main formation landed. The wait served as my reprimand.

The formation departed Eniwetok the following day. The fourth leg, an uneventful eleven hundred mile, five (5:00) hour, flight, delivered six new P-47N airplanes to the 333rd, six to the 73rd, and four to the 19th squadrons. Other ferry flights fully equipped each squadron with 37 new airplanes and retired the old D models. The P-47N; the final production model of the P-47; designed for very long range operations in the Pacific; fitted with a larger wing, larger internal fuel tanks, wing fittings for large external fuel tanks, and an improved engine; fully loaded, with 3,000 lbs. of ordinance and 710 gallons of fuel in external tanks; weighed 21,000 lbs. In its time, it weighed more than any other single engine fighter.

The USS Hall Young and the USS Kenmore, in convoy, reached Ulithi 9 April and anchored in its large lagoon. Ulithi is one of the Caroline Islands located 525 miles south-west of Saipan. At the time it served as a major Navy staging area. Within the Navy fleet anchorage, the ship's convoy merged into a larger convoy, and departed Ulithi for a 1,200 mile voyage to Okinawa. Late in the afternoon of 25 April, the convoy steamed past Okinawa. The USS Hall Young and Kenmore anchored off Ie Shima, a small island, about 5 miles north-west of Okinawa. During early morning hours of the 30th, a Kamikaze crashed into Hall Young's number five hold, and I lost my shipped-ahead belongings, including my clothing, uniforms, and books. Some Headquarters' lost files included some of my personnel records, most reconstructed by preparing extracts from files of other officers who shared a common order with me. My file today still contains tissue copies prepared on typewriters by squadron clerks. The afternoon following the morning raid, the Group's ground echelon disembarked and began preparing a Group bivouac on Ie Shima.

Returning from Hawaii to land on Kobler Field, we found the air echelon's mission to be largely training. Between 15 April and 4 May, I flew six check-out flights (7:40 hours) introducing pilots, unfamiliar with the airplane, to the P-47N.

On 6 May, the Squadron flew a 36 ship, 1,500 mile, 6:45 hour interdiction mission to Truk. The formation made one, line abreast, strafing pass. I led one flight. Over target, Gordon Beecroft in the flight to my left, hit by anti-aircraft fire, began to burn.

81

Signaling my flight to move into right echelon, I moved to a position below Beecroft to assess damage. Fuel leaking from his right wing fuel tank fed a flaming fire, but fire commenced below the wing. I believed, and still believe, that Beecroft had two to three minutes before the fuel tank emptied and exploded. I repeatedly radioed Beecroft to climb, slow down and bailout over Open Ocean. He and his flight leader, over excited, jammed the radio. He could not hear me and bailed out at high speed over Truk's lagoon. His parachute ripped, and he fell into the beautiful lagoon's turquoise water.

This photograph pictures Beecroft, wearing the cap, with Carlton Berry, his friend since cadet days. Berry survived the war. While at the University of Michigan in the early 50s, I had an opportunity to visit him and his family, at the time assigned to a fighter squadron stationed on Selfridge AFB in Michigan. A few weeks after my visit, Carlton died in an F-86 mid-air collision over Lake Michigan.

On a Wednesday, 9 May, we learned of people back in the States celebrating Germany's surrender in Europe on the opposite side of the globe.

Assigned primary pilot for the airplane ferried from Hawaii, I gave it a name. My mother's father, brothers, and sisters called my mother "Cheek." In their tender moments, my father called her "Cheek Baby." Hence, the airplane's name became "Cheek Baby."

This photograph pictures Crew Chief, Sgt. Nolan Fredericks, inspecting Cheek Baby's auxiliary section. The picture appears on the Cradle of Aviation Museum's WWII Web page. A P-47N display within the museum wears Cheek Baby's colors.

Following the Truk mission, we learned that the Ie Shima airfield had achieved operational status. On 13 May, the Squadron said goodby to Saipan and its fleet of airplanes departed on a 1,300 mile (6:45 hour) flight to Ie Shima, to commence another campaign on another island.

I flew Judge Wolfe's element. As I recall, Joseph Osner flew Wolf's wing and Walter Pechham flew my wing. En route the formation encountered a weather front with embedded thunderstorms. In rain and turbulance, one or more airplanes disappeared not to be heard from again. Fearing mid-air collisions, the mission commander instructed each flight to procede as individual flights.

Side Note: In the late 1980s, Robert Rieser, Arthur Bowen, and I provided the Cradle of Aviation Museum, Garden City, Long Island technical guidance as it configured a P-47N for exhibit in the museum. The airframe is the last P-47 to roll of Republic Aviation's production line. Its colors are those of the 333rd airplane Cheek Baby.

He often flew like a bird.
As a pilot in the 333rd
Often Courageous
Never Outrageous
We salute you for gathering this heard.

Barry Johnson

83

Who sees the wind?
Neither you nor I;
But when the wings are soaring high
The wind is flowing by.

Durwood B. Williams

Chapter 6
OKINAWA CAMPAIGN

The 7:00 hour flight from Saipan to Ie Shima introduced the 333rd to an unfamiliar weather environment. Frequent cold fronts, formed over north-east Asia, brought frontal weather to Okinawa and to its surrounding area. Instrument flight experience in Central Pacific's sub-tropical, air mass, cumulus cloud weather did not prepare the 333rd for cold, rain, low ceilings, and thunder storms associated with cold or warm fronts.

Well into the flight, the formation encountered a wide spread frontal formation extending from sea level upward. The squadron commander elected to penetrate the front at mid-altitude, about 5,000 feet. Within minutes, the formation began to experience heavy turbulence caused by embedded thunderstorms. Unwilling to accept the risk of mid-air collisions associated with poor visibility and turbulence, the mission commander directed the formation to separate into individual flights. Each four ship flight then bumped and bounced through the weather, and continued on as single flights.

In mid-afternoon, Judge Wolfe's flight first reached and landed on Ie Shima; introducing the first Army combat aircraft into the Okinawan Campaign. This photograph is from the National Archives, College  Park, Maryland. Its title is <u>P-47s arriving Ie Shima from Saipan</u>. A second photograph from the same source and same title shows the 333rd emblem on the side of the airplane. Typically, reporters and photographers record firsts. If indeed, these are the first Army fighters to arrive on Ie Shima, then Judge Wolfe pilots the first airplane, Alford Weeks the second airplane, me the third, and Walter Peckham the fourth. Note crew chiefs riding wing directing pilots to assigned parking hardstands on a taxiway paved with crushed coral, a substitute for cement. Crushed coral also paved parking revetments and runways. Though sufficiently firm to support aircraft, they produced dust when dry and a sticky surface when wet.

Once parked, crew chiefs helped their pilots out of the cockpit. After seven hours in a small cockpit, strapped to its seat, and sitting on bumpy survival kits, exhausted pilots welcomed help. They visited; first the squadron's equipment room (tent) to stow parachutes and other flying gear, then the ready room (big tent) for mission debriefing. The Intelligence Officer, in deference to pilot fatigue, canceled the debriefing. The Flight Surgeon's staff offered each pilot a shot of whiskey, and showed him to his tent quarters for rest.

Coming ashore on 30 April, the 318th ground echelon had been assigned a squadron bivouac area located southwest of a 3,700 foot runway, named Plum Field. Though adequate for Navy and Marine airplanes designed for short field takeoffs, it proved inadequate for a P-47 needing 5,800 feet of dry runway to lift 10 tons of airplane plus stores.

After a thirteen day effort since ground echelon arrival, the bivouac remained incomplete because the area had been heavily mined by the Japanese. Every square foot of the area required sweeping by Army Engineers before erecting tents and temporary buildings. The photograph on the opposite page shows the bivouac at the time of our air echelon's arrival. The peak in the background is the highest elevation on Ie Shima.

Nearby, a crude sign marked the spot where machine gun fire killed Ernie Pyle, a war correspondent who shared the infantryman's experience, and reported on the ugly face of war from an infantryman's viewpoint.

Buried, with his helmet on, in a long row of graves, he lay beside an infantry private on one side and a combat engineer on the other side. The sign correctly implies that the Army Infantryman and the Marine respected and revered him. Later in time, the Army reburied his remains in an Army cemetery on Okinawa, and later moved them to the National Memorial Cemetery located in the Diamond Head volcanic crater on the island of Oahu, Hawaii.

Given a few hours rest, pilots reassembled in the squadron ready room (big tent) for an intelligence briefing; given by our intelligence officer, Capt. Edmund Rogge. The briefing, as remembered, follows.

The 318th has been assigned to a new 301st Fighter Wing. The 301st is part of the Tactical Air Force, Tenth Army. The Tenth Army, Commanded by Lt. General Simon Buckner, includes the Army 24th Corp, and the Marine 3rd Amphibious Corp. A Marine, Major General Francis Patrick Mulcahy, commands the Tactical

Air Force and has operational control of all land based Navy, Marine, and Army fighters.

Japanese organized resistance has been defeated in the northern half of Okinawa, but fierce fighting continues in the southern half. More than a thousand Navy ships, including both capital fighting ships and supply ships, sitting near shore, are targeted daily by waves of Kamikaze pilots. US ground forces and ships are targeted nightly by Japanese bombers.

Though campaign plans project 318th long range offensive missions, today's ongoing ground fighting and wave after wave of Kamikaze attacks demand that first priority be given to air defense, and second priority be given to offensive missions.

The 333rd will augment the Navy's F4U Corsairs to maintain Okinawan air defense. A ring of fifteen radar equipped Navy destroyers, currently serving as picket stations, provide early warning of inbound hostiles. Stations are numbered from1 through 15 clockwise beginning with Station 1, located 51 miles north of Okinawa on a 007 degree radial, to Station 15, 35 miles north on a 343 degree radial. Pickets are concentrated in a sector from Station, 8 located 95 miles southwest of Okinawa on a 224 degree radial, to Station 3, located 65 Miles northeast of Okinawa on a 50 degree radial. The 333rd will maintain constant alerts, ready to scramble when called by a Central Fighter Control. While on patrol, usually over a picket, 333rd flights will be controlled by Central Fighter Control. Tactical intent is for Control to detect approaching inbound bogies at a distance, and to vector patrolling flights to

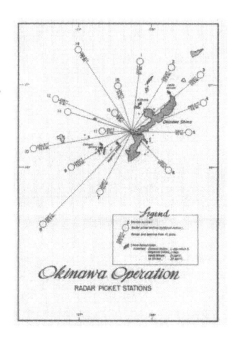

Okinawa Operation
RADAR PICKET STATIONS

intercept. Flight leaders will identify, and, if so directed, shoot down hostiles before they reach their intended targets – ground forces ashore and ships anchored in the Okinawan harbor.

Taking a longer view, 318th on Ie Shima puts most all Japanese military forces vulnerable to US air attack. From Ie Shima, the P-47N's long legs place all Japanese Islands, Korea, China's heartland, Formosa, and the Philippines within the Group's range of operation. In time, pilots should expect to fly fighter sweep and escort missions over any or all of these areas. If necessary, emergency procedures will allow pilots to seek a safe haven in China, Korea, Formosa, or the Philippine. See picture below.

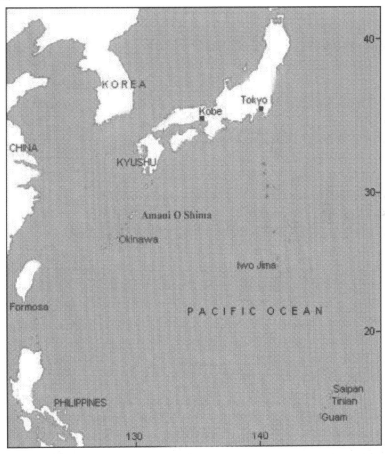

The 333rd flew its first Okinawan mission on May 14, the day following its arrival on Ie Shima. Two four ship flights, escorted a large, slow, Navy Martin PBM, amphibious airplane, named Mariner, as it searched for a pilot down in the ocean north of Okinawa. I flew element in one of the flights, but do not recall other members of the flight. After a four and one half hour orbit over the PBM during a fruitless search, the PBM returned to its harbor and our two flights returned to Ie Shima.

The 19th Squadron arrived on Ie Shima on the 16th May, and the 73rd arrived on the 17th May.

Okinawa did not offer a good life. Cold and constant rain made tent living miserable for people acclimatized to warm, comfortable weather of Hawaii and Saipan. With summer clothing and tents not suited to the cold and rain and an insufficient number of blankets available, we slept in flying suits or day clothing. Frequent bomb alerts sounded, kamikazes by day and bombers by night. Kamikazes came during the day knowing that pilots needed day light hours to visually select and attack targets. Bombers came at night to avoid a heavy concentration of ship and shore visually directed anti-aircraft weaponry. We endured seventy six alerts during the month of May. At the time, night fighter technology posed little risk for Japanese night bombers.

After a few days, recognizing that, rather than targeting us, the Japanese attacks targeted ships anchored in the harbor or US forces on Okinawa, we began to ignore night time alerts, remain on damp cots, in damp tents rather than jump into wet foxholes containing mud and water. During daylight hours, we had grandstand seats watching Kamikazes pilots fly overhead; select a target, dive, and crash. Some failed to survive heavy anti-aircraft fire from ship and shore. Some survived the dense cloud of flack, and crashed onto or near to their target.

Standing beside my tent, I watched a Zero fighter fly directly over my head at about 1,000 feet. South of our runway, just offshore, a large cargo ship sat at anchor off-loading equipment and supplies. As the Zero crossed the shoreline, it did a well-executed half-roll, a split-S, and hit the cargo ship amidships in a vertical dive. As a pilot, I could admire the pilot's skill and his dedication to what he judged to be his duty.

Other days, I watched Japanese aircraft fly over the harbor and attack Navy ships at anchor. One continued his dive to about 500 feet, lost his nerve, pulled up, and slowly climbed back to altitude while shore gunners and ship gunners filled the air with flak and tracers. After reaching about 7,000 feet, he started another dive. Again, he lost his nerve, pulled up, climbed back to altitude, and tried again. On the third try, he continued his dive, struck, and burned a large Navy warship. As a fellow pilot, I prayed that some gunner would end his terrible turmoil and conflict between duty, honor, and a wish to live.

Towering clouds, heavy rain, and poor visibilities, often encountered over the Ryukyus and Japan, required instrument flight beyond aircraft and pilot abilities. A low frequency radio range, located on Ie Shima, proved unreliable as a navigation aid due to weather and frequent Japanese jamming, In late May or early June a Ground Control Approach (GCA) System, installed on the island, offered radar assisted approach and landing voice guidance during approach and landing in weather, but our pilots, having little to no instrument flight experience since cadet days, had neither knowledge of GCA procedures nor instrument skills needed to make a GCA approach and landing.

As a last resort, if remaining fuel allowed, a pilot could chose to fly west and bail out over mainland China, but uncertainty that he would meet friendly people made this option unattractive. His survival gear included a message written on silk in French, Thai, Lao, Annamese, Chinese, Korean, and Japanese asking any would-be rescuer for help. In recent years, Rita's hairdresser, a Korean, interpreted the message as follows:

91

"I am an American aviator. My airplane is destroyed. I do not speak your language. I am an enemy of the Japanese. Please escort me to the Allied Military Bureau. My government will pay your expenses."

Mission tasking originated in TAC Headquarters – often by none other than the TAC Commander. Believing the Japanese pagan, that fire in the sky during dark nights would ignite their superstitions, and that superstition would contribute to Japan's defeat, General Mulcahy ordered the 318th to fly night-time fighter sweeps. Such missions came to be called "Heckler" missions.

Bordering on insubordination, our Group Commander, Lt. Col Sanders strenuously opposed these missions as a miss-allocation of resources that exposed aircraft and pilots to excessive risk. He limited them to single element (two-ship) missions. The WWII fighter airplane required visual target acquisition and visual ordinance delivery. During daylight hours, flown by an experienced pilot, it could, with precision, destroy airplanes in the air, locomotives and vehicles on the ground, ships at sea, or other high value targets. At night, the day fighter became ineffective. Experiencing the Japanese, both civilian and military on Saipan, all admired the tenacity of the Japanese. No one believed that fifty caliber guns and small rockets at night would panic Japan's population – particularly so after months of enduring heavy B-29 raids from Saipan, Tinian, and Guam.

The first Heckler mission, flown under clear skies the night of 17 May by Lt. Col Phillip Rasmussen, the 318th Group's Operations Officer, and 333rd 1st Lt. William T. Goff, could discern and strafe an airfield, and a small lighted town before it extinguished its lights, and find its way home.

The following night, Captain William Fancher led a mission with 1st Lt John Dooling flying wing. Clouds obscured the target area. While searching for a target, the two became separated. Fancher (pictured right) failed to return to base, and Dooling found Ie Shima only because, at his estimated arrival time, Okinawa, experiencing an air raid, lit the sky with gunfire. He turned toward the brilliant display of anti-aircraft fire and exploding bombs and found home base.

Three nights later, Rasmussen and Goff flew another Heckler mission. They encountered weather shortly after take-off. On instruments, they climbed above the clouds and continued, only to find a cloud cover over Kyushu. Turning south for home, they encountered rain, icing, and turbulence. Due to anoxia, vertigo, or otherwise, Goff, pictured right, disappeared, not to be seen again. Rasmussen reached home only by chance and good airmanship. Operations never scheduled me for a night mission.

During May, I led seven Combat Air Patrol (CAP) flights providing picket ship air cover, and learned the high risk of friendly fire from pickets. If, after hours of orbiting a friendly picket, alert klaxons indicated incoming hostiles sounded, every gun on the picket and its escorts opened fire on my flight. I quickly learned to extend my orbit beyond the picket's gun range during alerts.

On 28 May, the 318th Group first flew a large multi-ship mission over Japan; a fighter sweep over Kyushu, the southernmost Japanese Island. On takeoff one 333rd pilot, Lt. Melvin L. Byfield, pictured right, failed to become borne, crashed, and burned. The mission continued, engaged the Japanese Air Force and shot down sixteen airplanes. Each of four 333rd pilots, Capt. Judge Wolfe, Capt. Fred Stevenson, Lt. Dayton Rivas, and Lt .Dan Owen, destroyed one Zeke each. I did not fly this mission.

I flew my first mission over Japan Wednesday, 30 May, in a three flight (12 airplanes) fighter sweep over Kyushu, the southernmost island of Japan proper. Capt. Winston Park led the flight as mission commander. Lt. James De Yonker led the second flight, and I led the third flight. Lt. William Brooks flew my wing. I do not recall who flew my element

This mission gave me the most difficult flight during my entire sixty year flying career. An early takeoff, at first light on a wet Wednesday morning with a full internal load on a wet, sticky, 3,700 foot, coral runway, offered a marginal takeoff run. When tower cleared my flight, the third in the queue for takeoff, I taxied into takeoff position, locked brakes, let the engine stabilize at full power, and began a takeoff roll. At the end of the runway, the airplane broke ground without climb speed. Immediately ahead, a pile of dirt, dumped for runway extension use, lay on the overrun. I knew that my main wheels, not fully retracted, would hit the pile of dirt, and that the impact would reduce speed and cause the airplane to crash.

It is true that, when experiencing life threating events, the mind races and time slows. Seconds become minutes, allowing the brain adequate time to think and react. Just before striking the pile of dirt, I popped the airplane hard onto the overrun and pulled the stick back – elevator calling for nose high position. The airplane bounced into an extreme nose high attitude, the main wheels cleared the dirt, but the tail wheel struck, knocked the airplane back into a level position, and reduced airspeed to below stall speed. Beyond the overrun, the terrain sloped steeply down to the ocean fifty feet below. The words of Sargent Bay's Operations Officer rang loud and clear in my mind, *"If you go off the deck without flying speed, do not worry, let the airplane settle, just before it hits the water, it will begin to fly."* I did, and it did.

Outbound, Park's element leader reported engine trouble and Park instructed him to return to base. Later my element leader's wing man reported engine trouble and Park instructed the element leader to take him back to base. This reduced the mission to a nine ship formation, Park's three ship flight, De Yonker's full four ship flight, and my two ship flight.

Rain and low ceilings over Japan blocked our route. Unable to reach the primary target, Park turned south heading toward Amani O Shima, the largest Japanese island located about halfway between Kyushu and Okinawa. (See page 89)

On waters of a large Amani O Shima bay, we saw a number of boats. Park chose to strafe. Being the third flight, I had time to observe and identify the boats as small fishing craft, offering no meaningful military value. I completed a strafing pass, but did not shoot, nor did Brooks. As I flew over the bay, I could see most of the boat crews in the water seeking safety from gunfire.

The weather continued to worsen as Park, pictured right, turned for home base. I flew number three position on the right side of the formation, with Bill Brooks flying my right wing: low, just above the ocean, in rain, with poor visibility. After an extended period of time, Park started a hard turn to the right then quickly reversed into a hard left turn. To avoid overrunning the flight during the right turn, I, necessarily, reduced engine power. When Park reversed the turn, the airplane would not accelerate sufficiently for me to maintain visual contact, and I lost sight of the formation. Just feet above the water with no horizon, I could only start a full power climb on instruments. Brooks followed me long enough to get his power on and nose up, then lost sight of me. Once in a stabilized climb, I repeatedly radioed Park, but received no answer. Separated, on instruments Brooks and I both climbed above the weather. Brooks joined a flight of Marine F4Us and followed them to their home base.

Alone, low on fuel, and not knowing my position, I turned south to base course and began calling Mayday. Calls for help from other lost souls jammed the radio. Desperate, I prayed for help and an angle, code name "**Festival**," sent by God, answered my call and gave me a steer. I flew this steer while slowly descending until, through a small break in the clouds water appeared, I quickly ducked beneath the clouds to find continuous fifty foot ceilings, rain, and poor visibility. After about 30 minutes, I reached the north western coast of Okinawa, followed the western shoreline to a beached ship I knew to be due east of Ie Shima, turned west, and flew to the eastern coast of Ie Shima. Following Ie Shima's shoreline at about 50 feet in a counter clockwise direction until crossing a beached ship I knew to be just off shore from the end of Plum's runway, I dropped gear and flaps, turned left 90 degrees, and landed. Park and other members of his flight failed to return. Thirteen days later, Brooks failed to return from a night mission over Kyushu.

During mission debriefing, De Yonker reported that, upon losing visual contact with the formation, he had led his flight west some distance, turned south to parallel course, then turned east to find Ie Shima. His element leader, Wayne Duresmith, reported sighting a radar site on the hills above Amani O Shima's cove. I reported my flight experience and postulated that Park had drifted off course, had reached the northern coast of Okinawa, or one of the many islands south of Japan, and that his sudden turns were efforts to avoid hills on that land mass. My report judged that he and his wingmen, Duane D. Jones, right on opposite page,, and Albert W. Heilman at left, crashed moments after I last saw the formation, else they would have answered my radio calls. By climbing, Brooks and I had avoided the hills.

In the fullness of time, I would meet Duane's widow, Lorraine and their son. They came to a 318th reunion seeking some first-hand account of Duane's disappearance. I told them what I knew.

Years later, I came to know the voice of "**Festival.**" During 2001, Rob Reilly, an author seeking information on WWII combat air patrol missions flown by P-47 aircraft over Navy picket ships, contacted and corresponded with me. Through Reilly, I learned that Navy Destroyer DD579 named William D. Porter served on Station 15 with code name "Festival." Nine days after giving me the steer making it possible for me to find Ie Shima, a Kamikaze pilot flying a Val aircraft hit William D Porter with a mortal blow. The crew transferred to Gunboat 86, an escort vessel, and watched their ship sink beneath the waves. Below, see the destroyer's crew transfer to the gunship and, from a ringside seat, watch Festival sink beneath the waves.

Crew Transfers to Gunboat 86

And Watches Festival Sink beneath the Waves

Two days later, Friday 1 June, the weather over Ie Shima cleared, and the squadron launched another fighter sweep mission over Kyushu. Major Fojtik led the mission, and again, I led a third flight. In the queue, waiting for takeoff position, Lt. James Read's airplane failed to lift off, crashed and burned. Read, the only West Pointer in the Group is pictured right. In orbit above, after a long pause, Major Fojtik, waiting for the formation to form-up, radioed *"Get those airplanes off the ground – we have a war to fight."* With a  great deal of apprehension, I advanced throttle, and took off over the burning airplane. Again weather blocked our route to Japan, Fojtik aborted the mission and the squadron returned to base.

On Sunday, 3 June, and Tuesday, 5 June, the squadron launched missions to destroy the radar site reported by Duresmith to be on Amani O Shima. I flew each of these missions. We could not find a radar site. If, indeed, a radar site existed as reported, the Japanese had done a good camouflage job. We never found a radar site.

Wednesday, 6 June, the Group launched another large formation fighter sweep over Kyushu. Japanese fighters challenged the formation, and suffered a total of nine Japanese fighters shot down, including four Zekes destroyed, two by Captain Wolfe and one each by Lts. Harry Vaughan, and Robert Stone. Lts. Wayne Dureschmidt and Joseph Osner each destroyed one George.

The George, a new Japanese Navy fighter, designed to counter the P-47 and the P-51, first became operational in late 1944. A fine airplane with excellent performance, when flown by a well-trained, experienced pilot, it challenged  our best pilots flying our best American fighters.

On Thursday, 7 June, the 318th[th] sent 10 flights (40 airplanes) north to rendezvous with and escort 2 Navy PB4Y and 2 F-5 reconnaissance airplanes as they photographed the southern beaches of Kyushu, beaches intended as landing sites for the planned invasion of Japan.

The PB4Y, an Army B-24 modified by the Navy for recognizance and known as "Privateer," is pictured right. The F-5, a reconnaissance version of the P-38, flew low fast photographic missions. Karl Mulligan led one 333rd flight, Alfred Weeks flew his wing, I led his element, and Walter Peckham flew  my wing. Mulligan's flight flew high cover over one of the PB4Ys flying at 20,000 feet. Mission strategy placed Mulligan's flight above the Privateer at 28,000 feet, while two other 333rd flights flew at the Privateer's altitude.

Ahead and to the left, I saw three Zero fighters dive toward the photo ship. Mulligan signaled for me to go. Peckham and I followed the three Zeros down. In the dive, Peckham shot one down. Passing through the lower formations, I turned to parallel the Privateer's course and started a climb back to the high perch. The two remaining Zeros turned for a second attack. I turned hard right to intercept. After a few turns, one started a classic

Japanese tactic, a tight loop to end up on an opponent's tail. I shot him going up, and he began to burn. The airplane fell off into a diving turn.

I followed for a minute or less, hoping vainly to see its pilot safely swinging in a parachute. The third Zero ran for home. Our Squadron's Photo Lab gave me a portion of my gun camera's mission film which I sent home to my Mother. She included it in her war album. Two frames of that strip are pictured right.

The total 7 June mission score was eight Japanese fighters. Peckham's and my two plus six shot down by 19th pilots.

Note of interest: In the P-47's unpressurized cockpit, at 28,000 feet, there is insufficient atmospheric pressure for oxygen to transfer from lungs to blood, and one can breathe pure oxygen yet die for lack of oxygen. Pressurized oxygen masks forced oxygen into the lungs and blood, but to exhale one had to forcefully exhale as to blow up a balloon. Thirty minutes of this pressure breathing exhausted the most robust young man.

Three days later, on 10 June, the 318th launched a 40 ship formation to escort photo reconnaissance aircraft over southern Kyushu. Three 333rd flights flew a diversionary pattern intended to draw Japanese fighters away from beaches to be photographed. The day is well remembered.

Judge Wolfe, pictured right, led the 333rd lead flight. Fred Stephenson led the second flight. I led the third flight. Alfred Weeks flew my wing, David Brunner led my element, and Walter Peckham flew Brunner's wing. We flew north over the water until north east of

the beaches to be photographed. At the appointed time we turned west at 25,000 feet on a heading which would take us to Kobe, a major Japanese Naval Base. We opened canopies a tiny amount and began opening boxes of radar reflecting chafe. The airstream sucked the chafe through the canopy opening. The ploy worked, over Japan Brunner called seven Zekes, the Navy version of the Zero, behind at 23,000 feet. Wolf wheeled the flight into a descending left turn and came up behind the Japanese formation. All were shot down – one by my guns. I do not believe they ever saw us. Turning east, we saw 50 Jacks flying south at 25,000 feet toward us. Wolf started a maximum power, climbing, left turn, climbed to their altitude where a classic dogfight began. Our formation became scattered as aircraft paired off in individual duels. I saw Wolfe break off, out of ammunition, and attacked the airplane he had been chasing; a Jack, a new Japanese fighter similar to the P-47 recently introduced into Japan's air forces; flown by a veteran pilot with pilot skills sufficient to evade Wolfe, the 318th Group's leading ace. I concentrated on closing on the Jack until reaching a position to fly formation directly beneath him. I waited knowing that he could not see me, and that he would eventually level his airplane to look for me. He did. I reduced the throttle, drifted back, raised my nose, and hit him with eight 50 cal. guns. He exploded, and debris struck my airplane leaving two large holes in my right wing. Not knowing the extent of wing damage, I elected to withdraw from the air battle and headed south for home. Ahead, a flight of 12 or more fighters approached head-on at my altitude.

Uncertain whether friend or foe, and not wishing to fight with a damaged wing, I flew straight through their formation without firing my guns. They were foe and turned to chase, but could not catch me. As I approached Kyushu's southern coastline, in the distance to my right, I saw an airplane paralleling my course.

Cautiously, I drifted closer, identified it as a P-47, pulled up onto its wing, and recognized Peckham, pictured right. He had taken a hit in the engine, leaking oil covered the left side of his airplane, and I knew that the engine would fail and that he would go down. About five miles off-shore, his engine froze, and he bailed out. Remaining in orbit, I watched him go down, hit the water, get into his little survival raft, and start frantically paddling toward open sea. Air rescue answered my call for help on the emergency radio channel and instructed me to maintain the orbit over him and to continuously key my transmitter.

A Navy PBY Catalina, pictured right, homed on my signal, landed, and picked Peckham out of the water. As soon as the Catalina reported spotting Peckham, I again turned south heading for home – doubtful that sufficient fuel remained in my tanks to reach home. Persuaded by past fuel management briefings authored by Col. Charles Lindbergh, I believed that a hot engine is an efficient engine. I leaned the fuel-air mixture, reduced engine speed to lowest RPM, advanced throttle until engine temperature reached its red line and came home. Though fuel efficient, those power settings proved highly abusive to the engine and the engine had to be replaced.

On this mission, I flew Major Fojtik's airplane, Deloras III. Its damaged wing is pictured right. Back on Ie Shima, squadron maintenance opined that had I flown the airplane at high speed, air impact would have likely further opened the wing and ripped its skin away making the airplane unflyable. In the fullness of time, I would met Deloras, Fojtik's wife for whom he named the airplane.

The total 10 June mission counted 17 Japanese aircraft down. Over the primary target, the 19th shot down three. The 333rd diversionary formation shot down fourteen, 9 Zekes, 4Jacks, and one Betty bomber. On the deck, chased by two Japanese Zekes,

Lt. Robert Stone, by chance, flew over a Japanese air field. The two chasing Zekes collided with a Betty bomber flying the traffic pattern, and Stone received credit for two Zekes and one Betty.

The Jack, another Japanese Navy fighter developed by Japan as the war wore on, became operational in late 1944. Its performance equaled that of America's best. Though Japan produced a substantial number of advanced fighters during the war, it failed to plan for and train pilots needed to fly them. Had they been flown by well trained, experienced pilots such as he who evaded Wolfe on 10 June, these fighters would have made a significant impact on the war.

During June, the Kamikaze attacks continued. The squadron flew 207 CAP hours, approximately fifty four ship patrols. On patrol Lts. Otis Wayne Bennett, Robert Sadler, and Harry Vaughan intercepted and shot down four Zekes and one Nate. I led fourteen patrols. For hours on end, my flight orbited some northern point, usually Navy picket ships forming the radar net around Okinawa. Hours of boredom were often broken by the picket ship and their escort vessels misidentifying our P-47s and blazing away with all guns. This became a near certainty if Japanese aircraft entered the area. By one event, I learned how easy it is to make such a mistake.

While leading a patrol in orbit over a picket ship north-east of Okinawa, Fighter Control vectored me to intercept a bogie approaching from the North East. After about 20 minutes, below and ahead a large four-engine airplane came into view. From my perspective the airplane had the profile of a well-known Japanese aircraft, and I identified it as an Emily, pictured right. Fighter Control instructed me to shoot it down. Signaling the flight to arm guns and tighten formation, I dove to attack. Since Cadet Days on Matagora Island, my technique for establishing firing range continued to wait until I could read numbers and text on the target. When readable, I read "US Navy", dropped my nose, and flew underneath the airplane. Passing underneath, I could see the crew's expression of fear and apprehension. The airplane, a Navy Privateer, a Navy version of the Army B-24 having a single vertical stabilizer, used for photo reconnaissance, is pictured on page 99. Most likely inbound on a great circle route from Alaska with IFF off; it appeared hostile to Fighter Control. The split second decision not to shoot could easily have been different. Had I fired, smoke from my guns would have triggered the rest of the flight to shoot and thirty-two 50 cal. guns would have blown the airplane out of the sky. Since that day, upon hearing of friendly fire, I feel compassion not only for victims, but for the poor man who fired as well.

By Mid-June, 318th pilots were at the end of their string. Twelve months of constant over water flying, often hours from the nearest seashore, had exacted its toll. Parachute harness backpacks and seat packs contained an inflatable dingy  and survival gear, including a paddle and silk maps of ocean currents, but each pilot knew the paddle's futility and that downed pilots had little chance of being spotted and picked up. Each pilot had searched in vain for comrades known to be down in their dingy, yet never found.

On 13 June Lt. William Brooks, pictured right above, failed to return from a Heckler mission, and on 21 June Lts. James Clark and George W. Shulton, lower right, crashed  and burned on takeoff. Flying such unwise missions off an inadequate runway engendered a loss of confidence, both by pilots and Group personnel at large, in 10th Army Staff's ability to plan for and conduct an air war. The relationship between the ground echelon and the pilots became much like, but more than, that between loyal fans and their teams. A fighter group exists to gener-

104

ate and fly sorties. All personnel, crew chiefs, mechanics, house-keepers, cooks, and others play a necessary role in generating sorties needed for each mission. Returning from a mission, a low slow-row signaling a kill brought roars of cheers. Before evening outdoor movies began, often shown mission gun camera film also brought loud cheering. These cheers represented a sense of accomplishment for all. Contrariwise, a sense of ill-used sorties brought a sense of wasted individual efforts.

The last big battle for the southern half of Okinawa occurred on 17 June. On 21 June, after some mopping up, George Company, 22nd Regiment, Sixth Marines, raised the flag on the southern half of the island.

The 10th Army's Tactical Air Force Headquarters tasking began to assign targets located on Japanese home islands north of Kyushu. The distance to these targets exceeded the P-47's round trip internal fuel range – requiring wing tanks. With full internal and wing tank fuel loads, takeoffs on the available short runway, became a certain recipe for disaster. Headquarters assigned the first such mission to the 333rd. Major Fojtik made a courageous stand, and refused to launch his squadron on the mission. On Monday, 11 June, at 1:45 PM, Major Fojtik departed Ie Shima, destination Saipan. His departure came as an unexplained surprise. Relieved of his command the following day, Captain Judge Wolfe assumed command of the Squadron.

On Friday, 22 June, Hq. assigned Wolfe to the 318th Group Headquarters, and Major John Hussey, 73rd Squadron Commander, assumed command of the 333rd. Between the 22nd and the 26th June, orders transferred Wolfe and eleven other pilots, representing the squadron's leadership and persons most loyal to Fojtik, to Hawaii for subsequent return to the States with Harry Vaughan, Robert Sadler and me, three of the seven who joined the squadron on that Pearl Harbor dock in November of 1943, among the transferred group.

Though the runway had been extended to 4,200 feet, the takeoff problem continued. Group morale dropped, most every pilot had experienced the terror of a near fatal takeoff. Hq. requested assistance from Republic Aviation Company, the P-47 manufacturer. After my departure on 19 August, Joseph Parker, Republic's chief test pilot and Director of Operations, came to demonstrate proper takeoff procedures. Though advised by Lt. Col, Rasmussen not to do so, he attempted a takeoff with a maximum fuel load, crashed and burned.

In time, I learned more about Fojtik's departure. In the early 1950s, while stationed in the Pentagon; by chance we met, and occasionally lunched together and re-lived some of our 333rd experiences. He had left Ie Shima facing a Court Marshal for failing to obey a direct order. When Parker crashed and burned, the Army dropped all charges, cancelled the Court Marshal, and transferred him back to the States. I shall always have great respect for Fojtik. Standing firm against high command to protect his pilots took great courage. As a young man, about 25 years old, he possessed that courage.

I flew my last mission on 24 June. Though unknown at the time, my days of fighting wars ended on Okinawa. I shall always be grateful that I fought my war as a fighter pilot. A fighter pilot does not see the ugly face of war and is able to retain his humanity. He lives behind the combat lines in a relatively secure bivouac. Unlike the infantryman, the bomber crew, or the sailor, he does not see his comrades shot, suffer, and die. A comrade lost on a mission simply does not return from that mission. Only crash crews and medics see crash sites and remains when aircraft crash while landing or taking off. Nor does a fighter pilot see pain and suffering caused by his guns and bombs. He shoots at things; airplanes, tanks, locomotives, ships, designated enemy strong points on the ground, and other high value targets. Fortunately, he never knows for certain that anyone in those targets is hurt. A fighter pilot can fight a war and still respect the enemy.

The photograph on the opposite page pictures me sitting in Cheek Baby's cockpit for the last time. Its crew chief, Nolan Fredericks from Lakehurst, New Jersey, stands on the wing. A day or so later, a Military Air Transport C-54 took me to Guam.

From Guam, I rode a slow Navy PBM Mariner twenty-seven hours to Hawaii. The PBM had no seats, and only a catwalk at the bottom of the boat for standing, sitting or lying. It remains the most uncomfortable flight I have ever made.

Though military action during the Okinawan campaign, resulted in one of the epic battles of history, it has received little recognition, as such, neither by its contemporary generation nor by subsequent generations. The Okinawan invasion and battle exceeded the scope of the French invasion and battle. The Normandy invasion employed 284 capital ships, 150,000 troops, and 570,000 tons of supplies. The Okinawan invasion employed 327 capital ships, 183,000 troops, and 750,000 tons of supplies. Short supply lines across the English Channel and the Atlantic Ocean sustained the Normandy landing and the subsequent battle for France. Supply lines across the vast Pacific sustained the Okinawan landing and the subsequent battle for Okinawa. The highest ranking officers to die during WWII were General Simon Buckner, Commander of America's Tenth Army and General Mitsuri Ushijima, Commander of Japan's Thirty-Second Army. Incoming artillery killed General Buckner, and General Ushijima committed Hara Kiri. During hostilities, more than 100,000 Japanese soldiers died rather than surrender, only about 10,000 (1%) became prisoner. The Tenth Army experienced 7,613 deaths and more than 30,000 wounded. Thirty six Navy ships were sunk, 368 Navy ships were damaged, almost 5,000 sailors died, and an equal number were wounded.

In part, Okinawa lost its place in history because, at its time, the American public had grown weary of tales of battle and anxious for more national, more peaceful news. Five days after the 1 April 1945 initial landing on Okinawa, the Soviet Union joined the war against Japan. Seven days later, President Roosevelt died and Harry Truman became president. While Marines and Army troops were engaged in a fierce battle to capture the southern half of Okinawa, Germany's 8 May 1945 surrender overshadowed the news. On the morning of 6 August, an Atomic bomb dropped on Hiroshima, and three days later an atomic bomb dropped on Nagasaki. On 2 September 1945, the Japanese surrendered in Tokyo Bay aboard the battleship Missouri. No one remembers Okinawa.

THE FINAL MISSION

When the final mission is finished,
  And the compass reading is home.
Honor that worthy opponent.
  Be thankful his fate is unknown.

When the final approach is finished,
  And you cross runway threshold.
Thank your guardian angel.
  For guiding you home to the fold.

When the final landing is finished,
  And the birds are parked on the ramp.
Remember your missing companions,
  With eyes that are dry - not damp.

When the final mission is finished,
  And the last take-off is made.
Join-up with the great Commander
  In formation with glory arrayed.

Durwood B. Williams 1945

108

Chapter 7
INACTIVE RESERVE

During the week of 25 June 1945, I travelled, in comfort, to Guam on an Army Air Transport Command C-54 passenger airplane. From Guam, I travelled, as passenger, on a Navy PBM (an amphibi-
an aircraft, pictured right, landing on the blue pacific) to Hawaii, the most uncomfortable flight I have ever made.

About a dozen passengers had no place to sit. A catwalk, about five feet wide, extended along a portion of the hull. No insulation covered the hull's exposed inner skin and ribs. Crew cautioned passengers not to step off the catwalk – else their weight might punch a hole in the hull's skin. At flight altitude, the hull's interior became very cold and passengers, dressed for a tropical climate and acclimatized for tropical temperatures, suffered.

After ten hours, the airplane landed in the Marshall Islands on Kwajalein's beautiful turquoise lagoon. Kwajalein, located 2,400 miles southwest of Hawaii, is the largest of several islands in an atoll made up of coral reefs and small islands. Its shallow lagoon and surrounding waters display living coral which paints the area with beautiful white, greens, and turquoise. After refueling, we continued on another seventeen hours to Hawaii. During the twenty-seven hour trip from Guam, passengers sat, lay, or stood on the catwalk in near freezing temperatures.

The airplane landed on the waters of Kaneohe Bay and docked at a Naval amphibious installation located within the bay. Kaneohe Bay, not far from Bellows Field and about 3 miles in width, stretches about eight miles along the southeast coast of Oahu Island and at the time served as a major staging site for Navy amphibious aircraft patrolling the Pacific.

The Navy provided on site Navy quarters for arriving Navy passengers and transportation for Army passengers. I traveled to and reported to the Commander, Fort DeRussy, located on Waikiki Beach, one of several shore batteries built in 1911 to provide Hawaiian coastal defense.

In 1945, Fort Derussy shared the beach with large luxury hotels, including the Moana and the Royal Hawaiian. The Royal Hawaiian served as a Rest and Recreation Center for war weary soldiers fresh from battlefields on western Pacific islands. Although Waikiki Beach provided the Fort's best feature, after twenty months living on or near a beach, mostly in tents, Waikiki Beach held no appeal for me, and I moved to the familiar Bachelor's Officers Quarters (BOQ) on nearby Hickam Field which offered excellent quarters and fine dining in the Officers Club.

Hickam also offered the possibility that I might see Mary, and she did indeed arrive for a short Hickam layover while I remained on base, and I did see her. The loss of patients in the fiery crash on Eniwetok left its scar. She lost much of her zest for living – too quiet and too mature for a girl of her youth. I saw her for the last time on Hickam. After the war, by letter and Christmas cards, we remained in contact, but over time I lost contact with her.

During the week of 8 July, I received Orders to report to an Army Casual Depot to await shipment to the Continental US. It pleased me to see the names of sixteen other ex-members of the 318th Fighter Group on the orders, Including Robert Sadler, Harry Vaughan, Otis Bennett, and Carlton Berry, all close friends.

Thursday, 12th July, we boarded a Liberty Ship bound for the States. Hundreds of Liberty ships, mass produced during WWII and manned by the Merchant Marine crews, served a vital lifeline role by transporting men and material to battlefields

in Europe and in the Pacific. Powered by a single steam engine, they cruised at about ten miles per hour, and configured to maximize cargo capacity, they offered little creature comfort to either crew or passengers. The ship, dirty when we boarded, remained dirty throughout the voyage. The crew made no effort to clean, and the ship's Captain tolerated its dirty condition. After a few days at sea, passengers broke out brooms and hoses and cleaned the deck. Lower decks remained dirty throughout the trip.

Deep within the bowels of the ship, a stiflingly hot hold held a large number, perhaps as many as fifty, Japanese prisoners behind bars crowded into an area too small for their number. On two or more occasions, curiosity prevailed, and I went below to see them. Though dressed in a single garment resembling boxer shorts, they still showed signs of heat exhaustion. All, very young in their late teens or early twenties, represented the 1% of the Japanese soldiers willing to surrender on the battlefield. In the Japanese culture, surrender dishonored themselves and their families. Most fought to the death or committed suicide, often by the ritual Hara-Kiri. Obviously mentally deeply scarred by recent battles, they showed no emotion – their vacant eyes saw but did not seem to see. As a fighter pilot, I had not seen the ugly face of war, and held no enmity for the Japanese. I could and did pity them.

During the first few days of this long and tiresome voyage, flying fish and dolphins entertained passengers. Both, fish and dolphins, making a game of "race the ship," offered daily shows. Schools of dolphins would swim a short distance ahead of the ship's prow, slow their swim, let the ship overtake them, and, just before the ship overran them, accelerate and race forward. Growing tired of the game, the dolphins left the area, to be replaced by schools of flying fish which played the same game, except that when the ship came close, they would leap out of the water and fly forward.

Early Sunday morning, 22 July, California's coastal mountains appeared on the eastern horizon. During the afternoon our ship sailed under the Golden Gate Bridge, continued slowly up the

111

San Francisco Bay, and anchored near Fort McDowell located on Angel Island. At the time, Fort McDowell served as a detention center for Japanese prisoners of war. Showing relief and fear, the Japanese prisoners moved from the ship's hold to the island for continued incarceration. Their removal from the ship's hot hold brought both relief and fear to their eyes. Cool fresh air brought relief. An uncertain near future brought fear.

Though assigned to Fort McDowell, ship passengers remained onboard ship while the army arranged railway transportation east. However, free to visit San Francisco, Robert Sadler, Harry Vaughan, Otis Bennett, Carlton Berry, and I enjoyed a dinner at the Top Of The Mark, then San Francisco's most famous restaurant.

We learned that members of the Army's 27th Division also waited aboard ships anchored in the Bay. The 27th, New York's National Guard, federalized and transferred to Hawaii became the first Army Division shipped overseas following the 7 December 1941 Japanese attack on Pearl Harbor. It fought in the Gilberts, the Marshalls, the Marianas, and on Okinawa. The 318th Fighter Group fought in these same campaigns. Therefore, we felt a kindred spirit with troops of the 27th Division having flown air support over their battlefields, and air defense over their logistics and supply tail, both on land and on sea.

Since arriving in Hawaii in 1942, the Division had suffered 6,492 causalities, 1,512 KIA and 4,980 wounded. The Army considered many of the returning members shell shocked and mentally battle scarred. Unwilling to risk collateral damage to San Francisco's infrastructure and citizens caused by wild celebrating, the Army bundled 27th survivors into small groups, escorted them to the train station, and sent them home without having an opportunity to visit San Francisco.

Friday, 27 July, I boarded a troop train destined for the East Coast; assigned to a rail car destined for Fort Bragg, NC. The car contained two suites with two bunks in each suite. Robert Sadler and Harry Vaughan occupied one suite, and I occupied the other suite along with an Army Chaplain. Enlisted men, in coach seats, filled the remaining car space. In St. Louis, Sadler and Vaughan transferred to another train. In later years, I would maintain contact with both. Sadler would lead a civilian life. Vaughan would remain in the Air Force and I would see him and his family occasionally.

The train commander gave me a roster of the car's passengers and the responsibility to maintain order during the trip and to deliver all to Fort Bragg. A young Lieutenant did not impress these combat-hardened men. With little military training and no command experience, I needed help. Seeking out and asking, the senior NCO, a Master Sargent, agreed to take charge of the troops. He did an excellent job. He maintained order throughout the journey and all but one of the men reached Fort Bragg. The car stopped for a several hour layover in Atlanta, and departed with that man was missing.

My Mother, my Father, and my Sister met me at the Fayetteville, NC train station on Monday, 30 July. A Fort Bragg official also met me with orders requiring that, within two days, I report to the AAF Replacement Depot in Greensboro, NC. The following day, I drove my Father's automobile to Greensboro and reported. Granted 30 days of at-home temporary duty for recuperation, rehabilitation, and recovery, I returned home and began a month's long leave of absence from the Army. After two years and eight months of constant, risky, high pressure duty, those thirty peaceful, unhurried days of farm life were balm for my soul. A constant tension, long lived with, diminished, but remained, to some degree, for months to come.

In August I reported back to Greensboro to resume Army life, which included, among other things, an opportunity to fly AT-6 airplanes. In time, I faced another fork in the road. Given two choices: I could either accept another combat assignment, or accept a Reserve Commission and a release from active duty. I chose to accept a reserve commission knowing that the Army could recall me at any time it chose to do so. Choice made and granted a fifty-five day terminal leave, I departed Army life. En route home, I stopped at the North Carolina State College campus, registered for the 1945 Fall Semester, and began life as a college student majoring in Electrical Engineering. The Electrical Engineering Building is pictured to the right. Weeks later, I received a reserve commission dated 19 September 1945, and a discharge dated 14 November 1945.

NC State's 1945-1946 student population, augmented with newly released veterans, still lagged below pre-war levels. I found myself the single student assigned to Room 303, Berry Hall. Classes leavened with serious, mature, veterans, whose participation enhanced classroom discussion and the quality of professorial lectures stimulated all students. NC State recognized my Appalachian liberal arts course work, and, by carrying a heavy course load of math, physics, and engineering courses, I could graduate within three years. Another fork in the road presented itself, and I took the challenge, registered for a heavy class load, completed the year with a good grade point average, registered for, and completed the 1946 NC State College Summer Semester.

During WWII, my brother Rodney served as a B-17 ball turret operator in the 342nd Bombardment Squadron, 97th Bombardment Group, 15th Air Force, stationed in Foggie, Italy. A ball turret is pictured on the opposite page. After flying fifteen missions over East and West Europe, the Army released him from active duty in January of 1945. Having no High School Graduation Certificate, he stood for and com-

pleted a NC State entrance examination, registered for its spring semester and became my 303 Berry Hall roommate. After a first difficult semester, he became a good student and earned, with

honors, a BS Degree in Mechanical
Engineering. While at State, his
election to PI TAU SIGMA and
TAU BETA, both honorary engineering fraternities, made him, our
father, and me very proud.

Meanwhile in China, war continued between Chang Kai shek's
Nationalists Government and the Chinese Communist Party led
by Mao Zedong. Hoping to increase the likelihood of a Nationalists' win, the US Government gave the Chinese government a
large quantity of surplus P-47 airplanes. The Chinese, however,
lacked pilots to fly those airplanes. During early 1947, I received
a letter from the Chinese Embassy in Washington offering me an
opportunity to fly for the Chinese as a soldier of fortune. The US
Government sanctioned the offer, and the salary tempted me.
Another fork in the road, though sorely tempted to accept the offer, on advice of my father, I declined. Many American pilots
accepted the offer. When the Communist defeated the Nationalists in 1949, those pilots followed Chang Kai shek to Taiwan.
Many remained and lived out their lives on Taiwan. Some
founded the Flying Tiger Airline, and some flew for the French
during its war in Viet Nam. One of the more flamboyant, Earth-
quake McGoon, flew for the French during its losing fight with
the Viet Minh. In 1954, shot down while air dropping supplies
and reinforcements over besieged Dien Bien Phu, he crashed and
died.

While I attended the 1940-1941 school year,
Beattie Feathers, an American Indian,
coached Appalachian State Teachers College's football team. Coaching the NC State
team during the mid-1940s, he guided an
overachieving football team to the 1946 Ga-
tor Bowl – NC State's first-ever post season
game.

During the Summer of 1946, at home, on the dance floor of Williams Lake, my Cousin Mary Evelyn Williams introduced me to her East Carolina Teacher's College (ECTC) class mate, Rita Dawson. After a few pleasantries, I started to walk away saying something like *"Hope to see you around."* She shook her red hair, locked her big, brown eyes into my eyes and asked *"When?"* From that moment, Rita has been my love, my girl, and would, in time, become my wife, and the Mother of my children. Rita graduated from East  Carolina at the end of the 1945-1946 school year. Accepted as a Watts Hospital Medical Technician Intern, she moved into the Watts Intern Dormitory in Durham, NC.

To hasten graduation, I registered for NC State's 1946 Summer School and completed two prerequisite Electrical Engineering courses to qualify for certain Junior level classes. Completing these two courses made it possible for me to register for the 1946-1947 Fall Semester with hopes of graduating at the end of the 1947-1948 school year.

At the end of the 1947 spring semester I had completed all courses, except one, needed to register as a Senior in the 1947-1948 Fall Semester. Duke University offered that course, Field Theory, during its 1947 Summer School. I registered for and completed that course, taught by Professor Vail, who spent much classroom time discussing a novel concept to develop a Research Triangle Park which could generate a synergism between industry and nearby University of North Carolina, Duke University, and NC State College. In time that concept became reality.

116

Aided by the G.I. Bill, hundreds of ex-servicemen increased NC State's student population. Enrollment reached the 5,000 mark in 1947.

Three students now occupied Room 303, Berry Hall. At the end of the Fall semester, Dr. J. Harold Lampe, Dean of Engineering, called all rising Juniors to a meeting held in a large auditorium. With all assembled, he announced that *"Statistics, gathered over past years, show that one third of all entering freshmen drop out of school during their freshman and sophomore years. Over these years, NC State's staff and classroom facilities have been structured to account for these statistics. The current student population differs from those of years past. It is older, more mature, and more studious. Its performance does not match statistics of years past. Looking forward, the school cannot accommodate all rising juniors. They will be sorted by grade point average. Those having a grade point average below a cut-off, though qualified to rise, will have to find another college."* Fortunately, I made the cut. With much anger, those not making the cut did not return to the campus for the 1947-1948 school year.

For me, this became another heavy academically loaded school year. However the possibility of completing all course work needed for graduation during the 1948 Summer School became a reality. A job search began in early spring. At this time industry, transitioning from the production of war material to the production of material for the civilian market, offered few electrical engineering jobs. However, fully expecting to obtain a job in some unknown location, and not wanting to be separated, Rita and I married in March, in the Temple Baptist Church in Durham. In May, I accepted an offer from the South Eastern Underwriters Association – promising to report for duty after completing Summer School.

After the Summer Semester, Rita and I; traveled to Douglasville, Georgia, a small Atlanta suburb; moved into a furnished garage apartment; and I reported for duty as an electrical engineer to the Association's Headquarters located at 327 Trust Company of

117

Georgia Building in Atlanta. My task; inspect, evaluate, and write reports on water plants, pumping equipment, water distribution systems, and firefighting equipment of municipalities throughout Georgia, Alabama, and Tennessee, required much travel. Insurance companies used these reports to set insurance rates.

During the first few weeks of work, a senior engineer traveled with me, explained the drill, and verified my reports. The procedure required that I first meet with the town Mayor. He then accompanied me as I visited town facilities, or asked the town's Fire Chief to do so. In time, given a company car, I worked alone, and my work passed muster. Perhaps the greatest benefit derived from this work reconnected me to the calm, easy life of rural, small town America. For example, early morning in a small east Tennessee town, I found the Mayor absence from his office, and his staff seemed not to know his whereabouts. By asking, two old men sitting on a bench in front of a drug store, told me *"Go to that building, up those steps, and you will find him on the second floor in the first room to the right."* I did so and discovered the Mayor playing checkers. In a businesslike manner, I explained my purpose expecting a fast response. Instead he said *"Son, sit down. Let me finish my checkers game. Then, we will attend to this business."* The Mayor's priorities reflected the enriching lifestyle of 1948 small town America – a lifestyle much to be admired. Life is more than business.

In September, in the Douglasville Hospital, Rita gave me my firstborn, a fine, healthy baby boy given my father's name, Garthae. As a year old, he is pictured to the right. At the time, stressed with dire family finances, the infant made our financial status even direr.

In October, seeking additional income, I joined a local Air Force Reserve Squadron, the 327th Troop Carrier Squadron, located on Marietta Air Force Base, Marietta, Georgia. It flew the Douglass C-54 transport. I began flying on weekends and scheduled a C-54 check out.

The squadron also owned a few AT-6 airplanes, and I began flying the AT-6 in the local area. Only able to fly on weekends, C-54 checkout wore on and on. Pilots received pay only for making flights to distant airfields. I never completed the

checkout – too slow. Without checkout, I could not make such flights, and finances remained dire. Rita and I barely made ends meet.

Bad news floated on the 333rd Squadron's November News Circuit telling that Judge Wolfe died in an aircraft accident on my birthday, 24 November 1948. Shortly after takeoff in an F-80, an explosion in the engine compartment damaged his airplane's flight controls. At the time, Air Force fighters had no pilot ejection capability. Without control, he had no options. The aircraft crashed and exploded and the Air Force lost a good man, truly a leader of men – well respected by all. A great pilot, his glue held the squadron together during difficult missions.

In November, by letter, the Air Force asked me to voluntarily return to active duty – another fork in the road, a military or civilian career. The military option seemed most attractive. Firstly, it offered me the promise of flying high performance airplanes. This pleased me. Secondly, base pay plus hazard pay plus a housing allowance equaled $484 per month, high middle-class income in year 1948. Such pay would significantly reduce the family's financial stress. Rita and I both judged the military option to be our best choice.

In mid-December, orders signed by General Hoyt Vandenberg, AF Chief of Staff, requiring me to report for duty in Washington,

DC on or before 4 January 1949, arrived in my mail box. South-eastern Underwriters Association's management offered to, by its political influence, have the orders canceled. I declined the offer, and Rita and I packed our few personal items and departed Georgia.

We drove to North Carolina. Rita and Garthae remained with her Mother while I traveled by train to Washington. After a bus ride from Washington's train station, I rented a room in the Bachelor Officer's Quarters on Bolling Air Force. The following Monday, 3 January 1949, I reported to the USAF Central Control Group, Room 3D117, in the Pentagon. The Central Control Group acted as a carrying Unit that centralized administration for Air Force officers serving on Joint Boards and as members of various Committees in the Washington Area. The Central Control Group assigned me to the Aeronautical Standards Group with duty station located at 12th and Constitution in downtown Washington.

CHARACTER

A Reputation can be purchased or promoted
It may flower fleetingly...............and as fleetingly disappear

Character is what we are
And what we are evolves slowly but surely through the years

If the years have been rich in achievement and fine works
We are that much happier in a priceless and enduring sense.

Chapter 8
AERONAUTICAL STANDARDS GROUP

A two-man joint Board, Air Force Board Member Lt. Col. Lester M. Peters and Navy Board Member Commander Barton E. Day, commanded the Aeronautical Standards Group. The Army-Navy Aeronautical Board established the Aeronautical Standards Group in 1937 with a mission to develop specifications used by both Army and Navy as embedded parts of procurement contracts to buy airplanes and related aeronautical equipment.

Tuesday, 4 January 1949, I reported to Lt. Col. Peters, the Air Force Member of the Aeronautical Standards Group, located at 12th and Constitution in Washington, DC. The Group occupied Temporary U Building, a two story frame building architectural-

ly similar to the hundreds of barracks buildings constructed on military bases during WWII. Temporary U (Barton Hall), first in a row of such buildings extending from 12th Street to Navy's Bureau of Aeronautic in the Munitions

buildings located between 17th and 21st Streets, near the Washington Monument, faced Constitution Avenue, with the Washington Mall to its rear. These buildings show in the lower-left corner of this picture, taken from atop the Washington Monument. Twelfth is the second street from the bottom of the picture crossing the Mall. Barton Hall is the topmost building next to 12th Street. The National Museum of Natural History, the big building just beyond 12th Street remains, but the temporary buildings have long since disappeared. The National Museum of American History now occupies the site of Barton Hall.

Col. Peters assigned me to his Electronics Division and explained my mission; plan and execute an effective Air Force-Navy standardization program for aircraft and related aeronauti-

121

cal equipment, ranging in complexity from wire through connectors, relays, electro-mechanical devices, radios, radars, and autopilots. Recognizing my intimidation, he assured me that I would have time to learn and grow into the job. A tour through Barton Hall to meet staff members ended in Room 2-508. Here he introduced me to Major Garland C. Steen, my predecessor.

At the time, Major Steen held transfer orders; however, his departure date, four weeks following my arrival, provided a transition period during which time he helped me become familiar with office work and ongoing projects. During this period, I learned of background leading to my present position. Corresponding with a friend in Florida, Major Steen had initiated a transfer from the Aeronautical Standards Group to the 307th Bomb Wing, MacDill Air Force Base, in Tampa, Florida. However, the transfer depended upon Col. Peters' releasing him from his present assignment. Col. Peters would do so only if a replacement could be identified and placed on orders to report prior to Major Steen's departure. Major Steen persuaded Central Control Group's Personnel Officer to search Air Force records for a suitable candidate – a Major having an Electrical Engineering Degree. My name surfaced and Personnel selected me. Col. Peters accepted a 1st Lt. Selectee; personnel arranged my return to active duty, and published orders assigning me to the Aeronautical Standards Group. This story reveals the dearth of educated professionals within the Air Force 1949 active duty population.

For clarification, in 1947 Congress established the Department of Defense with a mission to manage the Navy, Army, and a new, hollow Air Force having no airmen. Following the establishment of this independent Air Force, the Department of Defense offered all Amy and Naval personnel an opportunity to transfer into the new Air Force. Few Army professional soldiers and few Navy professional sailors did so. The resultant Air Force population, therefore, became a product of WWII, made up of people who entered the Army Air Force during WWII, trained for a specific task, and performed that task on the ground or in the air. They were all young and ambitious, with limited military, administrative, or management training, and little academic background.

In mid-January, orders arrived in my office attaching me, for flight duty, to the1100 Air Base Group, located on Bolling AFB in Anacostia, Maryland, directly across the Potomac from the then Washington National Airport. Bolling offered me pleasing opportunities to fly first line airplanes. During January and early February, flying on weekends, I checked out in the C-45 Twin Beach, the B-25 Mitchell, and the P-51H Mustang. With weekends free from work and airplanes available, I took advantage of the opportunity and logged many flight hours. I found Washington life good.

The Aeronautical Standards Group, well-staffed and well organized, followed well written, easily understood, published policy and efficient and effective procedures. Good drafting and editorial staffs gave excellent support. The file structure allowed quick retrieval. Within a few weeks I realized that the Aeronautical Standards Group had a historic past – going back to the mid-1930s. Some files contained letters and other documents signed by an earlier generation, including Jimmy Doolittle and other boyhood heroes. Working with these files brought to my mind words from Longfellow's A Psalm of Life.

> *Lives of great men all remind us*
> *We can make our lives sublime,*
> *And, departing, leave behind us*
> *Footprints in the sands of time.*

In order, my foremost personal priorities were: save some money, buy an automobile, rent an apartment, and move Rita to Washington. Placing orders with several dealerships, I entered queues waiting for a new automobile. In the meantime, as a child of the Great Depression, living alone in Bolling's BOQ, driven by ambition, and thinking that I would have much free time, I registered for the Spring Georgetown Law School Semester as a night student. At the time, a career as a patent lawyer appealed to me, but not for long. Long office hours and frequent out-of-town travel left too little time for school work. After one semester I dropped out of law school, after being chastised by the school's Dean for poor class attendance.

Standardization activities demanded constant communication between three centroids: the Aeronautical Standards Group; the Air Material Command, Wright-Patterson Air Force Base, Dayton, Ohio; and the Navy Bureau of Aeronautics, at 18th and Constitution, within walking distance from my office. A ringing telephone and a full mail box kept me busy. Frequent interagency coordination conferences required my time. Some included representatives from the American Association of Aircraft Manufacturers. Our Group desired and respected the Association's advice, but did not require its approval. However, a standard specification's publication required Air Force, Navy, and Aeronautical Standards Group Board Members approval.

I quickly learned that my skills did not meet needs of the job. My inadequate writing skills generated frequent rewrites and an unnecessary workload for me, my secretary, and for the editorial staff. Within weeks after my arrival, I chaired a large conference held in a hearing room located in a Federal Building on Constitution Avenue. Not able to control proceedings, the conference came to a disastrous end without completing the agenda. At conference end, a Mr. Quackenbush, an executive from the Cannon Electric Company, stood and asked *"Lt. Williams, we have spent these many conference hours. Before we close, will you summarize what we have accomplished?"* Intimidated, embarrassed, and unable to do so, Mr. McGee, a civilian engineer from the Air Material Command, stood and answered for me. I shall always be grateful for his kindness.

Pleasantly surprised, not transferred out of the job, Col. Peters and Commander Day, both due to retire within the year and knowing that my poor performance could not hurt their careers, elected to help me. In particular, Commander Day became, somewhat, my coach. As Calvin Coolidge, he championed brevity, both the spoken and the written word.

Also, recognizing my inadequacy, I became an active member of the Toast Master's Club. The club offered an aspiring speaker a podium and an out-spoken critical audience – a magnificent learning experience. I also went home, retrieved my High School English textbook, and began an English self-study that continued throughout my career. That book, <u>Sentence and Theme, a Foundation for High-School Composition</u>, published in 1935, remained on a book-shelf in my office throughout my working days and remains in my office today. In time, my skills and self-confidence improved. I grew into the job and consider my Air Force career a success, due in large part to Col. Peters and Commander Day. My footprints in the sands of time will imprint, in part, their footprints.

Fortunate for me, frequent conferences and meetings required travel to Wright-Patterson in Dayton, Ohio. Wright-Patterson had long runways, adequate for high performance airplanes. Oft-time after work hours, when required, I left my office, flew a P-51H to Wright-Pat, and rented a room in the FADO hotel located on the second floor above Base Operations. The following morning, a staff car carried me to one or more day's work. Work complete, I flew back to Washington. The P-51H is pictured to the right-below sitting on Bolling's tarmac. Note the pierced steel plank surface, the runway surface I often took off from and landed on while in the Pacific.

These flights gave sheer pleasure. The P-51H, the last Mustang production model, and one of the highest performing fighters of WWII, looked like a fighter, flew like a fighter, and its Rolls Royce Merlin engine made music for fighter pilot ears.
A joy to fly, the flights gave balm to the soul. On the climb-out, as I approached Maryland's western border, glow from Pittsburg's Bessemer Furnaces became visible. As the flight progressed, the glow grew, became fire, and diminished. The fire

125

colored the entire flight with color, making each such flight a rich experience, particularly so for one beneath a bubble canopy. This experience, limited to few, is now available to none. Pittsburg's steel industry has long since vanished.

In mid-April 1949, a recently published AF Regulation arrived in my in-box. That regulation established procedures whereby certain commissioned officers of the civilian components of the USAF on extended active duty could make application for appointment in the Regular component of the AF and for their selection and appointment therein. This regulation included an age requirement – applicants must have passed their 21st birthday but not passed their 27th birthday. It also stipulated that applicants who served in the Armed Forces prior to 2 Sept 1945 and have not passed their 30th birthday could request a waiver.

A point of clarification, the Air Force, and other military departments, include a Regular component and civilian components. Civilian components include the Reserves, the National Guard, and WWII Army Temporary Appointees. In 1949, post war demobilization continued to rapidly remove members of the civilian components from active duty.

In May, ambition still burning hot, I requested and received a waiver, granted by a Hq. USAF letter dated 14 May. In June I submitted an application for a regular commission, and in November I met an evaluation Board in a room on Bolling Air Force Base.

Also in May, Detroit's automobile production lines began to deliver an occasional new automobile to dealer showrooms. On waiting lists of several dealerships, and in my office, a telephone call from an Anacostia dealer announced the availability of a new Chevrolet. Immediately leaving the office, and riding a bus to Anacostia, I purchased the automobile within the day. Now, freed from bus and trolley lines, getting to and from work grew easier, and I began looking for an apartment.

In 1949, housing had not recovered from limited construction during the war years. Few rental want ads appeared in newspapers. By word of mouth, renters learned of new properties coming on the market. I began to monitor construction sites and stood first in line when a two bedroom apartment, 3130 Parkway Terrace Drive in Suitland, Maryland, became available in late May. I rented the apartment, Rita joined me, and we purchased furniture for the kitchen and one bedroom, and moved into a near empty apartment. Additional furniture awaited healthier bank statements. During the first week in June, Rita and I traveled to North Carolina and returned to Suitland with Garthae and all possessions then resident in North Carolina.

Rita liked living in the Washington area. She quickly learned to navigate throughout the area in Washington's traffic, at the time quite light. As the budget allowed, she shopped the town for needed furniture. For her own clothes, she shopped on elite Wisconsin Avenue, and she patronized elite hair salons on Wisconsin.

The Aeronautical Standards Group's staff included four Air Force Officers, five Naval Officers and twenty-eight Civil Service employees. Among the staff, only Major Eager Brown and I flew, so, he and I often flew together. He had a bomber background and preferred long weekend flights in the B-25 Mitchell bomber, a work horse that performed well in all WWII war theaters. Often, during a long weekend we flew to San Bernardino, California, to visit his friend, and returned to Washington Sunday evening. In April of 1942, Lt. Col. Jimmy Doolittle's Tokyo Raiders launched sixteen B-25 aircraft off the Navy aircraft carrier, USS Hornet, deep in the Western Pacific to attack Tokyo.

The B-25, a powerful, stable, pilot friendly airplane, is pictured on the previous page. Major Eager Brown is pictured to the left below in the left seat of a B-25. Propellers and exhaust stacks just outside its cockpit generated high noise levels in the cockpit. Even with cotton in his ears, after a B-25 flight, a pilot remained deaf for a short period of time.

One Friday afternoon in November, I flew a P-51to Pope Field, Fort Bragg, North Carolina. My Father met me at Base Operations, and I spent the weekend with him and my mother. Returning home Sunday night, I took off from Pope's runway under a high overcast, in a southerly direction, over Fort Bragg's reservation. The runway, in poor repair, gave a very bumpy takeoff roll.

Radio-luminous instruments, standard WWII aircraft Instruments, glowed brilliantly when illuminated with an ultraviolet light. Ultraviolet light, often called black light, is barely visible. One black lamp, mounted with a swivel attachment on each side of the P-51 cockpit illuminated flight instruments. Shocks on the P-51's landing gear are normally stiff, and on take-off hard bounces rotated the two black lights downward. They no longer illuminated the instrument panel, and instruments lost their glow. There is no ground lighting on Fort Bragg's reservation; therefore, under overcast, with no ground lighting, no stars, no horizon, and no instruments, I had no reference needed to fly the airplane. Frantically, I searched for the black lights, finally found them, pointed them to the instrument panel, instruments slowly began to glow again, and I flew home.

The experience motivated me to propose a new project that would standardize airplane cockpits. At the time, and in years past, each airplane manufacturer had a free hand to design cockpit layouts as its engineering teams deemed good. As a result, cockpits differed between different manufacturers' airplanes, and often differed between models of the same airplane produced by the same manufacturer. The lack of a standard cockpit creates an operational hazard. While transitioning into a new airplane, if an emergency occurs, the pilot often cannot quickly locate a crucial instrument, switch, or control needed to cope with the emergency; resulting in a lost airplane and a lost pilot.

The idea received much headwind from Navy and Air Force engineers, few of whom were pilots. They postulated that a requirement to standardize cockpits would stifle innovation. I viewed innovation at the expense of safety a poor trade-off. Major Brown first endorsed the idea; followed by our Board Members. When our Board Members endorsed the idea, the debate rose to a higher level within Navy and Air Force bureaucracies, and, in time, the project earned approval. With approval, cycles of engineering, mockup construction, evaluation, and inter-service coordination commenced.

In June, I submitted an application requesting an appointment into the Regular Component of the Air Force. For references, I listed my three 333rd Squadron Commanders, my two Board Members and Major Brown. In October a letter from 1100th Air Base Wing, stated, *"You are requested to report for screening and procession at 0800 hours promptly, 14 November 1949, Room 1308 in Building, T-410, Bolling AFB. Processing will require your presence for one full day."* I met the Board and spent the day answering questions.

Christmas arrived, the historic decade of the forties ended, and the New Year ushered in the fifties decade. The telephone continued to ring, the in-box remained full, meetings and conferences continued to convene in Washington, and flights to Wright-Patterson continued. In June, a good month, the Air Force promoted me to Captain.

July, 1950 proved not a good month. An 8 July, Hq USAF letter responding to my application for a Regular appointment read: *"Your qualifications were carefully considered together with all other applicants. Your standing among the large number of applicants was not sufficiently high to include you among the number appointed, or to retain your application for further consideration."* Though disappointed at the time, in retrospect, I can understand the decision. My limited qualifications included those of a fighter pilot and only five months as an engineer in the Aeronautical Standards Group. With only five months engineering experience, my qualifications were judged solely those of a fighter pilot; and the 1949 the Air Force population included too many fighter pilots. That portion of the quote, *"...or to retain your application for further consideration"* captured my attention. It led to a later continuation of this story.

On the 25th, North Korea invaded South Korea, and a United Nations Security Council met in session to consider an appropriate response. China's UN membership representing the Chang Kai shek government then on Taiwan, caused the Russians to boycott the session. In the absence of a dissenting vote from the Soviet Union, the Security Council passed a resolution authorizing military intervention. The United States provided 90 percent of the resulting international response. Having greatly reduced 1945 Military Force levels, the United States did not have adequate active forces needed to repel the North Koreans. The Air Force withdrew fighter pilots from active duty organizations and recalled reserve pilots from inactive status. I fully expected to return to operational flight duty. It did not happen, pleasing both Rita and me.

In August, Rita gave me Larry, another fine, happy, easy to please, baby boy. Born in Walter Reed, he is seen here, after learning to crawl, reaching for my pocket slide rule. At the time, slide rules served as the engineer's calculator. With a twelve inch slide rule, a necessary office tool, or a six inch pocket slide rule, a necessary briefcase tool, the engineer performed addition, subtraction, multiplication, division, trigonometric, and logarithmic functions. The slide rule is a relic of the past, long since replaced by solid state, digital calculators. Yet the slide rule, seen above, remains in my briefcase today, and my twelve inch slide rule hangs today on a cabinet behind my office desk.

In November, orders arrived in my in-box directing me to proceed to Maxwell AFB, Montgomery, Alabama, to attend the Air University's Squadron Officer School's Class beginning 8 January and ending Thursday, 8 March, and to arrive not later  than 4 January. The Air University remains the Air Force's primary organization responsible for professional education of its enlisted men and officers. Among many other units and schools, it includes the Air War College, the Command and Staff School, the Squadron Officer School, and the AF Institute of Technology. In time, the Institute of Technology would play a part of my story yet to be told. Note my Chevrolet in the lower right portion of the picture above.

Rita and I traveled to North Carolina and spent Christmas visiting her mother and my family. Leaving Rita with her mother, I drove to Alabama.

I learned that the January 1951 class, the very first Squadron Officer School Class, served as the first class for the School Staff, for the Instructors, and for the Students. A great experience, Instructors and Staff invited, welcomed, and seriously considered student comment as the new curriculum played out. Mentors advised and counselled four students. My mentor Major Walter V. Gresham, leftmost and behind me in the picture above, advised and counselled me. An excellent officer, a true leader of men, he quickly gained my respect. In later years, our paths occasionally crossed, and we renewed friendship. The last time, we met I called him Major General Gresham.

Assigned C-45 Instructor while at Maxwell; to my satisfaction, I spent week-ends flying with and check-ing-out fellow students. The C-45, a small utility air-craft, shone right on Max-well's tarmac, seated seven passengers. Fast and easy to fly while airborne, but somewhat unstable on the ground, it needed much care and attention during takeoffs and landings – else it would embarrass its pilot with a ground-loop.

Completing all classwork, I returned to North Carolina, rejoined Rita and the boys, returned to Washington, and resumed the of-fice routine. Lt. Col. Peters assigned me, the junior officer in the Aeronautical Standards Group, the task of managing the Group's Red Cross 1951 fund raising campaign. I did so. In May, I re-ceived a letter of thanks and appreciation for my effort from Eu-gene W. Zuckert, Asst. Sec AF. Such letter could not but help enhance my resume.

Remembering the phrase, "...*or to retain your application for further consideration*." in the letter denying me a regular ap-pointment, I began thinking of a second application. Reading the authorizing Regulation again, I could find no bar to a second ap-plication. If indeed earlier denied applications were unavailable to the current Evaluation Board, then the likelihood that a second application would be considered seemed good.

During the latter part of 1950, American forces reached the Yalu River, bordering China. The Chinese entered the war and began to push American forces south. In January, the Chinese-Korean forces captured Seoul only to reach a stalemate. Contrary to na-tional policy, General Douglas MacArthur publicly recommended the use of nuclear weapons against the Chinese, and President Truman fired him. Returning to America, he spoke to a joint session of Congress in April of 1951 in a Washington overfilled by MacArthur supporters. I left my office mid-morning intending to hear his address, but on arrival found the Capital Building filled. Returning to my office building on Constitution, I staked out a spot, with my 35mm camera and cap-

tured his motorcade shown right. Two phrases in his address to Congress remain in American folk lore: *"In war there is no substitute for victory, and Old soldiers never die, they just fade away."*

I prepared another application for a regular commission emphasizing my experience with the Aeronautical Standardization Group and with the Squadron Officer School and included the AF Assistant Secretary's letter. References included Lt. Col. Hugh Masters, Lt. Col. Peters' replacement, and Major Gresham. I met the Evaluation Board (Lt. Col. Binnam, Major Byron, and Major O'Chancey) in September.

The cockpit standardization project progressed. I flew a Naval Air Test Center airplane, configured with a candidate standard cockpit configuration, stationed at Patuxent River in Virginia. Pleased with the layout, I realized that the project would bear good fruit. Not a part of our program, the airplane also came equipped with a radar coupled automatic pilot. During the flight I made several hands-off landings. Though anxious throughout these landings, I remain thankful for the experience.

In March, I received a Hq. USF letter stating *"You have been selected for appointment in the Regular Air Force, in the grade of 1ˢᵗ Lt. Subject to the following qualifications: Presidential Nomination, Senate Confirmation, and Physical Qualification."* I promptly went to Bolling, took the needed physical and mailed a medical report 17 April.

As the year 1951 approached its end, my thoughts turned to shaping my next assignment which would, in all likelihood, end twelve months hence. Remembering, from Maxwell days, that the AF Institute of Technology offered graduate studies for technically oriented officers, I asked the Institute to evaluate the adequacy of my resume for graduate school. A 5 February response certified eligibility for further studies in Guided Missiles, Weapons Systems, and Electronics. The study of Guided Missiles interested me. At the time the guided missile carrying weapons promised a new military weapon on the horizon. Few possessed science and engineering knowledge underpinning emerging missile research and development programs. In April I submitted, through channels, a formal application for guided missile graduate study to the Institute of Technology. In May orders arrived assigning me to the Institute of Technology, with duty station at the University of Michigan, to attend its Summer Session beginning 21 June.

Bad timing, on 28 May Rita gave me a beautiful, healthy baby girl. Born in the Bolling Hospital, she is seen to the right as a one year old who stole everyone's heart. With a newborn, storing household goods, travel to Michigan, finding a house, and setting up house-keeping within 24 days seemed unwise. With her mother willing, Rita agreed to live in North Carolina with her mother while I completed Michigan's Summer Semester, obtained lodging, and set up housekeeping. While Rita and Gail remained in the hospital, I carried the two boys to my mother's home and left them in her care. After release from the hospital, Rita and Gail went to North Carolina to join the boys and take up residence in her mother's home.

Three small children placed a heavy burden on Rita, but, a child of the depression, she too had ambition. Perhaps unwarranted, she had confidence in me, and believed that, together, we could make a secure life for ourselves and our children. Her support remains my blessing. She met the wifely standard set by Proverbs 31: 10-29.

Returning to Suitland, I packed and stored household goods, and during the week of 19 June drove to Ann Arbor.

Some ships drive east others drive west
With the selfsame winds that blow;

Tis the set of the sails
and not the gales
That tells them the way to go

Like the winds of the sea are the winds of fate
As we voyage along through life;

Tis the set of the soul
That decides its goal

And not the calm nor strife.

Ella Wilcox - 1916

History's winds blow unique
In each age and time

All must trim their lifelong sails
To match historic rhyme

As we journey along our chosen trails

Durwood B. Williams – 2013

Chapter 9
UNIVERSITY OF MICHIGAN

During the week of 9 June 1952, I drove from Washington to Ann Arbor, Michigan, and obtained a room in Fletcher Hall, the University's Graduate dormitory. Holding orders assigning me to Selfridge Air Force Base for flight duty, I reported to Selfridge, located near Mount Clemens on the western shore of Lake Huron and, on 12 June, checked out in the C-45 airplane. Returning to Ann Arbor, I began looking for a house to buy or to rent.

Friday, 22 June, I reported to the University of Michigan's Horace Rackham Graduate School pictured below.

The following Monday, classes began in a graduate program of study designed to give students a broad theoretical background in the sciences associated with the research, development, and production of guided missiles. *As a point of clarification: ballistic missiles are unguided,*

they fall where they wish; guided missiles include on-board intelligence that tells them where to go. All classes met in Michigan's

Engineering Building pictured above. The program included courses in aerodynamics, materials, structures, propulsion, servomechanisms, microwave engineering, and control and guidance of pilotless aircraft. Special course offerings, supported by excellent laboratory and research facilities, placed much emphasis on the control and guidance portion of the curriculum. Completion of the course normally resulted in the award of a master's degree in aeronautical engineering and a master's degree in electrical engineering. The course membership included one Canadian, Flight Lieutenant Richard P. St. John, and nine Air Force students: one Major, one Captain, and seven 1st Lieutenants.

As the picture of the Engineering Building suggests, the University, located within Ann Arbor's city limits, had little to no campus. Its stadium, pictured to the right, boosted 100,001 seats. During football season, Ann Arbor traffic became chaotic; making a drive across town near impossible,  and the wise chose not to drive downtown. Homeowners increased incomes by converting front and back yards into parking lots. Automobiles carpeted the entire town.

The summer semester, a fast paced, difficult study of mathematics, electronics, and electron tubes – yes electron tubes, proved difficult for one out of undergraduate school four years with additional needs to meet. During June, academics received priority; however, I made ten trips to Selfridge needed to maintain flight proficiency.

At the time, my friend and 333rd fellow pilot, Carlton Berry, stationed on Selfridge, flew operational P-51 fighters. I visited him, met his family, and somewhat envied him flying the P-51 while I sat in lecture and dormitory rooms in study. Months later, I learned that after his involvement in a mid-air collision over

Lake Michigan, search teams found no trace of Carlton. Like so many of my friends, he accepted hazards associated with flying fighters and lost the odds.

July weekends spent house hunting found a new Cape Cod, with an asking price of $10,500 located on the western edge of Ann Arbor, on the market in mid-July. It offered a full basement, two bedrooms on the ground floor, and an unfinished second level. A contract to buy the house closed Friday, 1 August, and the Cape Cod at 271 Sunset Road became available for occupancy. At my request, Selfridge arranged delivery of my household goods, then in storage on the Base, and I set up housekeeping in the little Cape Cod.

Activities; class attendance, at study, or unpacking and storing kitchenware, linens, and such into available drawers, closets, or elsewhere, made August a hectic month. When livable, I moved from Fetcher Hall to 271 Sunset. By the end of August, with the summer semester complete, and the Cape Cod ready to receive the family, time arrived for me to drive to North Carolina and fetch Rita, Garthae, Larry, and Gail.

An uneventful drive to North Carolina reunited my family, and allowed a few days to visit Rita's mother, Miss Ethel, and to visit my Mom and Dad. We found both families in good health and prosperous. The visit, a balm for my soul, reconnected my roots to the culture and good life of southeastern North Carolina. Nineteen-fifty-two, a good year for farming, had my father hard at work harvesting a good crop; making life good in Carolina.

For the return trip to Ann Arbor, storage space in the little Chevrolet could not accommodate two adults, three small children, and needed in-route accouterments. A luggage rack, strapped to the top of the  automobile, carried luggage exceeding automobile storage space.

Space within the little Chevrolet grew even smaller while driving to our new home. We welcomed the Pennsylvania turnpike as a time saver. The turnpike, at the time well maintained, afforded a high speed not possible on ordinary highways typical throughout the country. Stopping only for fuel, rest stops, and food, we reached Ann Arbor in about twelve hours. Gail cried throughout the trip, and two healthy little boys filled the car with activity. Rita reached our new home completely exhausted.

Rita and I spent the next few days rearranging furniture, sorting clothing, kitchen, and other household belongings into closets, drawers, and cabinets more suited to Rita's taste. Rita then shopped Goodwill and other such outlets; purchased an office desk, chair, and filing cabinet; and set up a study for me in the basement. Then back to a new semester's school work for me. A fellow student, 1st Lt. John Prodan and wife Ruth lived next door. John and I spent much of the fall and winter in my basement office studying together, and we carpooled so that an automobile became available for Rita and Ruth on alternate days.

For a family acclimatized to the relative warm southeast weather, Michigan's weather gave a new experience. Throughout the winter, ice on nearby lakes supported automobile traffic and fishing huts. Pictured right in the background behind Garthae, four fishing huts may be seen. In the spring, hopefully before sinking, owners dragged them ashore and placed them in storage for use during the following winter. One morning, blowing snow completely covered the little Chevrolet in a snow bank. Not remembering that Rita had a Doctor's appointment for one of the children, John and I attended classes on schedule, leaving Rita to shovel snow. In time, she forgave me.

To carry the 1952 Fall Semester's 15-hour academic load, all engineering and math courses, I sacrificed time with family and spent evenings in the basement, in deep study, yet my efforts earned only a 2.8 GPA. I became somewhat jealous of my neighbor, John Prodan, who found time for family life and time to finish the second floor of his house yet make a near 4.0 GPA. With a near photographic mind, he learned easily; yet forgot quickly.

The New Year promised a goodly life. Though still made up of engineering and mathematics, Spring Semester's 13-hour academic work load was less burdensome. Promoted to Major in April, my income increased to $668 per month, and family finances improved significantly.

Easter arrived on schedule. Rita dressed the children beautifully. In church on Easter Day, no father felt greater pride than me. With Easter, the warmth of spring also arrived on schedule.

We lived the good life: I enjoyed more family time, Rita adapted to my schedule, the children remained healthy, a nearby city park offered excellent play space for the boys, and Gail grew hair. The spring and summer semesters ended with respectful 3.4 grade point averages.

The warmth of spring brought welcome relief – making it possible to sit in the sun on the front stoop of the little Cape Cod. Note the stone restraining wall. An elderly black gentleman, who took great pride in his work, built the wall. On more than one occasion, I drove him across town for supplies; and along the way, with great pride, he pointed to

structures that he had built. He called them *"my monuments."* He taught me a great lesson; menial work well done can give great satisfaction and a good life.

With the 1953 Summer Semester completed, a visit to "Down Home, the Old North State" seemed in order. As expected; while there, the sun shined bright and the cotton bloomed white. A bumper crop of tobacco,

cotton, and corn stood growing in the fields. This photograph pictures my father's harvester gathering tobacco from the field, to be hung in barns and cured for market. At the time, with machines replacing agriculture hand labor, farming required less manual labor. In time machines replaced most farm workers who have yet to find steady rewarding work.

Knowing that my Rita needed a break from childcare, my mother suggested that we spend some time at the beach while she cared for the children. We accepted the generous offer, and enjoyed a good respite – a respite particularly good for Rita.

Back in Ann Arbor, we resumed our regimen of study and child care. Months came and departed rapidly. Winter brought deep

snow and cold howling winds. A twelve-hour academic work load during the Fall Semester and a fifteen-hour academic work load during the Spring Semester, all scientific and engineering studies, demanded much time in the basement office. I came to know and respect a fellow Air Force class mate, 1st Lt. William Harvey, and Rita bonded with his wife, Lorraine. From Las Cruces, located in the Rio Grande valley of New Mexico, they introduced my family to Mexican foods. Her tacos, served in Ann Arbor, have never been surpassed. We became lifelong friends who in later years would be our neighbors.

In spring, Selfridge offered the public an open house. Static displays of first line Air Force aircraft, including the Rascal guided

missile, covered its tarmac. The Rascal, pictured right, represented current missile technology, in reality a small airplane; powered by a small, air breathing jet engine, controlled by a computer, powered by vacuum tubes. A rocket launched ground-to-ground missile, it flew under computer control from launch to target. The Rascal captured public interest. Note the people in a queue waiting for a closer look.

Anticipating a transfer during the summer, Rita and I decided to buy an automobile having more space and better fitted to our family. We chose a big, new turquoise Oldsmobile.

General Dwight Eisenhower won the 1952 presidential race campaigning against Communism, the Korean War, and government corruption. During his first term, President Eisenhower introduced a new national defense policy giving priority to inexpensive nuclear weapons with less priority given to conventional military forces. At the time, a stalemated Korean War had UN forces and Korean-Chinese forces engaged in trench warfare along the 38th Parallel. Threatened by an US nuclear threat, North Korea, with China's blessing, entered into yearlong armistice negotiations beginning July of 1953. Negotiated results remain today: a cease-fire agreement and a divided Korea along the 38th Parallel.

Emphasis on nuclear weapons, known as "nuclear deterrence," materially changed the nature of Air Force research and development and introduced uncertainty into career plans of many Air Force members. In early spring of 1954, considering uncertainty introduced by the new policy and wishing to influence our next assignment, John Prodan and I drove the Oldsmobile to Washington and visited the Personnel Office in the Pentagon. The Personnel Officer quite willingly showed us worldwide Air Force positions needing to be filled and considered our preferences. I chose a position located on Eglin AF Base, Valparaiso, Florida. John chose a position located on Edwards AF Base, Muroc, California.

In May, I received orders from Hq USAF Institute of Technology, dated 25 April, reading: *"Major Durwood B. Williams is relieved from (Grad), Aeronautical Engineering (GM) course and assigned to Hq AF Armament Center (ARDC), Eglin AFB, Valparaiso, Florida. The officer is also assigned the 8696 Research and Development specialty as primary, yet retains 1121E Fighter Pilot and 8464 R&D Staff assistant specialties."* By different orders, John Prodan received orders assigning him to Edwards AF Base, and William Harvey received orders assigning him to Holloman AF Base, New Mexico.

The Canadian student and Air Force students at the University of Michigan in 1954 are pictured above. They include those completing the Guided Missile Course in 1954 and those who would complete the course in 1955. In time, all enjoyed successful scientific and engineering careers. Major William Green, right-most in the first row, as Program Manager, introduced the Hound Dog air-to-ground missile into the AF inventory. The Hound Dog, launched from the B-52, well served the nation during the early days of the Cold War, and my son Sgt. Larry Williams, as a Missile Systems Analysis/Specialist serviced and maintained the Hound Dog during the late-nineteen sixties.

William Harvey, right most in second row, is standing behind Green. In time, our paths would again cross and we would share the same office and would be neighbors on Long Island, New York. John Prodan, my Ann Arbor neighbor, stands third from right, at picture center, in third row. John and I remained corresponding friends until his death in the mid-80s.

Completing all classwork in June with a respectful 3.4 GPA, Michigan awarded me a Master's Degree in Aeronautical Engineering and a Master's Degree in Electrical Engineering. On 9 June, responding to a request from the Institute of Technology, I mailed the following "End of Course Evaluation."

"In general the curriculum is well-balanced and devotes the correct amount of time to each subject. The basic theme throughout the course is "Systems Analysis", and to this theme a large portion of the time is expended. The supporting subjects such as propulsion, aerodynamics, and electronics have been carefully selected.

I think that a math course in Laplace Transforms would be a helpful addition to the curriculum. However, I would hesitate to make the addition if it necessitated the deletion of one of the courses now in the curriculum. I also think that some business training would be helpful to the officers who complete this course, but again, I do not see how it can be fitted into the schedule."

With the Cape Cod leased, a moving van collected household goods, and the family departed Ann Arbor in the spacious Oldsmobile bound for sunny Florida. We chose to include some sightseeing and vacation along the way. Driving through Detroit, about twelve miles east of Ann Arbor, we entered Winsor, Canada and continued a leisurely Canadian drive north of the lakes to Niagara Falls, Canada and an overnight rest. A bright, sunny morning offered the family a view of the falls from the Canadian side. Afternoon offered a view of the falls from the US side. With the camera's light setting too low, my attempt to make a pictorial record of the falls failed.

After another leisurely drive through New York and Pennsylvania, we stopped again in Gettysburg for an overnight. Another sunny day offered a tour of historic Gettysburg Battleground. Though good for Rita

146

and me, the young children could not appreciate its significance, nor do they remember the visit.

Another day long drive and we arrived in North Carolina and visited parents and extended families. The families and farm life of the community, steeped in traditions centuries old, always buoyed and lifted my spirit.

MICHIGAN FIGHT SONG

Now for a cheer they are here, triumphant!
Here they come with banners flying,
In stalwart step they're nighing,
With shouts of vict'ry crying,
We hurrah, hurrah, we greet you now, Hail!
Far we their praises sing
For the glory and fame they've bro't us
Loud let the bells them ring
For here they come with banners flying
Far we their praises tell
For the glory and fame they've bro't us
Loud let the bells them ring
For here they come with banners flying
Here they come, Hurrah!
Hail! to the victors valiant
Hail! to the conqu'ring heroes
Hail! Hail! to Michigan
The leaders and best!
Hail! to the victors valiant
Hail! to the conqu'ring heroes
Hail! Hail! to Michigan,
The champions of the West!

Louis Elbal 1898

Chapter 10
AIR FORCE ARMAMENT CENTER

Arriving on Eglin Air Force Base in mid-July 1954, Rita and I chose to live on Base in guest quarters until permanent quarters became available. When available, we moved into an apartment located on Base at 5 Hatchee Street. Across the street lived a

young family. If my memory serves me well, the father, Captain Halburg, served as a medical doctor assigned to the base hospital. In later years, his mother became our neighbor in Michigan and a surrogate grandmother for our children.

Air Force Armament Center duty became my first experience with the Air Force Research and Development Command (ARDC). Motivated by a perceived Soviet Union bomber threat and an emerging Soviet nuclear missile threat, the Air Force established the Research and Development Command in 1950; with an assigned mission to accelerate development of weapon systems able to counter those threats. In 1951, ARDC established the Air Force Armament Center with Major General Edward P. Mechlin commanding. Located on Eglin AFB, the Air Force Air Proving Ground Command hosted the Armament Center as a tenant.

Eglin Air Base history began in 1935. From that time forward, Eglin has been home for one or more military test organizations, and its surrounding area has served as a test site for military aircraft. In 1941, the Army activated the Air Corps Proving Ground, and set aside a 384,000 acre military reservation known as the Eglin Gulf Test Range. In 1947, the Air Force became independent, gained control of the proving ground, and renamed it the Air Force Proving Ground Command. Customs and protocols prevalent on base in 1954 reflected this Old Army history. In the evening when Retreat bugle notes sounded; all outside stood at attention and saluted so long as the notes continued; automobile traffic halted, passengers stepped out and stood at attention; military passengers saluted and non-military placed the right hand over the heart. On New Year's Day, commanders held open house and protocol required each officer, with wife, to call, to leave his and her calling cards, and to leave within fifteen minutes. I am grateful that my Rita experienced these customs.

Only three years old on my arrival, with the Armament Center still developing strategies and practices needed to achieve its mission to integrate test operations and development so that a seamless test data feedback into the development process could be achieved, I could and did contribute to Center policies and procedures. Located on Eglin, the Center bordered on and had access to the huge, well instrumented geographic test area, the Eglin Gulf Test Range.

When I arrived on Eglin, items under test included three interceptor fighter aircraft, two tactical fighter aircraft; several target vehicles, and the M-61 Vulcan Gatling gun.

The interceptors, all-weather airplanes equipped with rocket powered missiles and radar, gave firepower to SAGE (Semi-Automatic Ground Environment), a nationwide air defense system designed to counter a Soviet bomber threat. They included: the F-86D Super Dog which would become operational and remain so through 1961, the F-89 Scorpion which would remain operational through 1969, and the F-106 Delta Dart which would remain operational through 1988.

The F-100 Super Sabre, a third generation, supersonic fighter-bomber designed to provide battlefield air defense and ground support, could be configured with a nuclear bomb capability, or four 20 mm cannons, and heat-seeking missiles. It supported American forces during the early days of the Vietnam War and remained operational through 1971. The F-105 Thunderchief, designed to penetrate enemy territory at high speed, at low altitude, and to delivery nuclear bombs, converted to carry conventional bombs, flew bomb missions against high value targets in North Viet Nam and remained operational through 1984. Captain Howard Leaf flew our F-105 test missions. In later years, we served together in Washington, and later he flew the F-105 in Vietnam and earned honors for destroying a high value bridge over the Red River connecting Vietnam and China.

The target vehicles, small gliders towed by aircraft, serve as targets for gunnery training for fighter pilots and training gunners aboard gun-ships and bombers.

The M-61 Vulcan, pictured right, is a power driven, six barreled, air cooled, electrically fired Gatling gun. In time, the gun became the weapon of choice for Air Force and Navy aircraft. It armed the C-47 gunships of the Vietnam War, the F-10 Thunderbolt (Wart  Hog) used extensively during Operation Desert Storm, and most post-Vietnam fighter aircraft.

Assigned primary duty as Chief, Fixed Systems Section, I worked for Major Jex Brigram, Chief, Fire Control Branch and, through Brigram Lt. Col. Henry B. Kuchman, Director of Test Operations. Both officers, with illustrious backgrounds, became friends and a joy to work for. My responsibility required me to design, monitor, analyze, and report the results of fighter aircraft tests. For each airplane, a System Program Office, managed by a Program Manager, located within the Wright Air Development Center, Dayton, Ohio exercised ultimate responsibility for successful development of these aircraft. Formal presentation of test results, using flip charts or overheads, required frequent trips to brief system Program Managers. Compared to today's PowerPoint presentations, such visual aides seem quite primitive. These trips afforded a continued acquaintance with Bill Green, my Michigan classmate.

Having no responsibility for target vehicles or Gatling gun tests, my experience with these test items became that of an observer. Tests of the Gatling, conducted on a firing range near the air base, when fired could be heard throughout the base as a continuous roar, rather than a sequence of individual shots. Some referred to the sound as that of their old grandfather's burp.

On one occasion, sitting at the end of the runaway waiting for takeoff clearance, I watched the launch of a target vehicle, having the configuration of a small unpowered airplane towed by a C-119 Boxcar airplane  with a long connecting cable. The C-119, a twin engine, twin boom troop transport, had a foreshortened fuselage between the booms. With the fuselage's rear end open, a photographer and a cable operator stood at the rear end of the C-119's interior. Late in his takeoff roll, the tow ship pilot aborted the takeoff. However, the un-braked target continued rolling and crashed into the rear of the tow ship giving the photographer and the cable operator a once in a lifetime experience. A C-119 is pictured above.

In September of 1954, Major Robert A. Taylor, newly assigned to the Armament Center, became Chief of the Fixed Systems Section, and my primary duty changed to that of a Project Officer. One month later, orders reassigned Taylor, and my duty changed back to that of Chief. We became friends, and later in life, our friendship strengthened while assigned duty in New York and Massachusetts.

Eager to expand my flying experience, I took every opportunity to fly. A next door neighbor, Captain Robert Lamb, the Center's Operations Officer, gave me many opportunities. During the summer, fall and winter of 1954, I checked out in and flew as first pilot the C-45 airplane and the VC-47 airplane. The VC-47, the standard C-47 modified to carry passengers, is comparable to the commercial Douglas DC3 that dominated the airways during the late 1930s and 1940s. In addition I made a few flights as co-pilot in B-29 and B-50 airplanes. I flew one flight as second pilot in the F-100 at speeds in excess of sound speed – about 760 mph or Mach 1. Captain Robert Ronca flew front seat. In 1965, shot down over Cambodia, picked up by Air America, he died before reaching a hospital. His name is on the Vietnam Wall: Panel1E, Line 93. I first learned of Ronca's death through Rita's brother Hartwell, at the time Personnel Officer for Air America.

In the fall of 1954, I checked out in the T-33 and the F-80, the Air Force's first operational jet fighter. Too late for WWII, the F-80 flew operationally in Korea and destroyed 17 aircraft air-to-air and 24 on the ground.

The T-33, a modified F-80, had a better engine and tandem cock-pits. It is pictured right; note the different wing tank locations. The F-80 wing tanks are attached be-low wing tips. The T-33 wing tanks are attached to wing tips. I flew F-80 chase missions to ob-serve flight tests and T-33 chase

missions with a photographer in the back seat photographing flight tests.

Eglin offered Rita the good life. All neighbors had young, small children who, at play, filled a highly secure neighborhood. A Post Exchange and Commissary, only blocks away, made routine shopping convenient. Base medical facilities provided care when needed, and the base offered, at little to no cost, recreation: mov-ies, a gym, and outdoor tennis and baseball courts.

Nearby Fort Walton offered
gasoline, fast food, and a few
small retail outlets. Serious off
base shoppers traveled to Pensacola, 40 miles of good road
west of Eglin. Pensacola also
offered excellent restaurants
serving great seafood dishes.

Nearby beaches, west of Fort
Walton and East, across the
bridge spanning the Choctawhatchee Bay inlet offered excellent sea shores. An Eglin
Beach Club offered good fast
foods and an outstanding beach.

Of all beaches that I have seen in the Pacific, on the West Coast,
and on the East Coast, the Gulf Coast beaches are best.

Experience with Eglin airplanes only whetted my appetite for
higher performing airplanes. At the time, the AF offered a short
training course designed to upgrade the
proficiency of behind-the-line pilots,
such as me, in the latest jet fighters. I
asked to attend this course, but Major
Brigram would not endorse my application.

In June of 55, Major Brigram received
permanent change of station orders.
Major William Sloan, Assistant Branch
Chief, became Chief, and I became
Assistant Branch Chief. Sloan drove a
like new British MG sports car, a per-
fect automobile for sunny Florida. After a few rides with him, I
needed one for myself and found one for sale in Pensacola.
It proved to be in poor condition, both mechanically and body-
wise. A simple automobile, I overhauled the engine and power

154

train, but found the body to be made of damaged wood, beyond my ability to repair. I sold the thing, and a few months later bought another MG in Washington, DC. This second one remains in my garage today.

A calm, wise and thoughtful Major George M. Walker occupied an office next door to my office. His experience included a P-40 crash as a young Lieutenant during a Mitchell Field, NY, takeoff and participation in the North African and European WWII Campaigns. Rita and I became lifelong friends with George and his wife Madora, known from childhood onward as Doda. They lived off-base, and our visits in their grand home gave us a taste of off-base living in the town of Fort Walton Beach.

Resident on Eglin, a large insulated, air conditioned hanger provided an opportunity to conduct tests in extreme cold. The hanger made possible tests of mechanical systems such as landing gear and flap retraction and extension while cold soaked in the hanger at -65^0 F. Radio, radar, and other electrical systems could likewise be exercised in the hanger. The finale tested the entire airplane. With a pilot strapped in the cockpit ready for flight, hanger doors opened, a tractor towed the airplane outside, and with engine quickly started, the airplane took off from a nearby runway, and with maximum power climbed into the stratosphere's lower boundary. At this altitude, outside temperature would again be -65^0 F, and all airplane functions could again be tested.

Scheduled to fly a T-33 chase mission early one hot, muggy summer morning, during preflight and cockpit check, I failed to notice that cockpit air conditioning sat at full cold. On takeoff roll, with the Sun peeping over the eastern horizon, air conditioned cold air condensed moisture contained in the outside warm air, and the cockpit began to fill with fog obstructing my view of the outside world. Concerned, but believing that I could climb out on instruments, I continued the takeoff. After lift-off, instruments became invisible – trouble. By placing my helmet next to the left side of the canopy, I could clearly see the left wing, the left external fuel tank, the horizon, and the Sun, and began flying the fuel tank as though it were remotely controlled. By keeping the tank's center on the horizon with its nose 30^0 above the horizon, the airplane remained in a slow climbing turn. After a reasonable time, judging that the airplane had reached a safe altitude, I found the air control, turned it to full hot, the fog vanished, and I completed the mission. A known truth relearned; small mistakes can lead to grave consequences.

In August of 1956, assigned to the Weapon Systems Plans Office as a Weapon Systems Planner, I began working for Lt. Col. Edward Hadfield, Deputy Commander for Plans. Well known within the Air Force, he flew as the test pilot for the XP-59, the first AF jet fighter. Though never produced for operations, the XP-59 paved the way for subsequent jet fighters.

Still wishing to expand my flight experience, I again applied for a Fighter Weapons Course designed to up-grade flight skills for behind-the-line Field Grade Officers, such as me, with high performing jet fighter experience. With the request approved through ARDC Headquarters, the Training Command placed me in the queue awaiting class assignment. Before my turn arrived, the Training Command cancelled all classes – another disappointment.

In the fall, a new on base ranch house became available, and Rita and I moved  our family into a larger, more luxurious home.

However, it's most striking feature, a back yard bordering on the north shore of Choctawhatchee Bay, gave a large, wide, white, sandy beach. It proved to be a great playground for the children, but Rita could not keep her house free of sand.

One day, shortly after moving into the new home, a hurricane passed directly overhead. For a few cloudy hours, a strong wind blew from the east. For an hour or so, the weather cleared with a blue sky overhead, as an island surrounded by a massive circle of dark, swirling clouds. Then a strong wind blew from the west. By nightfall, winds had subsided, but heavy rains continued. At twilight the following morning, Gail woke me with the news, *"water is in the house."* True enough, water indeed flowed through the carport, but sufficiently high house flooring elevation kept the water from the living area.

Such a beautiful backyard, bordering on a beautiful bay abundantly blessed with fish, oysters, and shrimp, demanded a boat. A boat, great for skiing, fishing, or just a boat ride for fun, met that demand.

The boat followed the family to New York and to Massachusetts. Later, it would long be stored in my father's barn, and would travel to Denver with Larry, and finally to Larry's friend as a giveaway.

Easter of 1957 remains one of my many good memories. Rita beautifully dressed Garthae, Larry and Gail. As always, with a hat and white gloves, she impressed me as a grand southern lady. In Church, my heart swelled with pride. Note the beautiful white sand of a Gulf Coast shoreline pictured below. While at Eglin, I made Christmas cards with such backgrounds representing snow scenes. No one could tell the difference.

In July, Rita gave me another son, Roger. As an infant, only days old, he exhibited a happy, cheerful disposition that would be his lifelong characteristic. That character is indicated by his smiling face pictured right as a two year old in Battery Park located on the southern tip of Manhattan Island.

In late December, I applied for assignment to the Flight Test School at Edwards AFB. Given a preliminary acceptance, my commander, General Mechling, would not release me from the Armament Center. With age, I have come to respect his judgment. He knew me, and knew that with four small children I should not continually accept the risks associated with flying high performance airplanes. They are risky. Too many friends of my youth died young in fighters – some with young families.

The Soviet Union launched Sputnik-1, the first artificial Earth satellite, during the Fall of 1957. A small, 23 inch diameter, polished metal sphere with four radio antennae, it could be seen, and

158

its radio pulses could be detected, as it passed over the US. It proved to be a "Sputnik Crisis" that shocked our Nation, began the Space age, and ushered in new political, military, technological, and scientific developments needed to compete in a more threating Cold War.

Likewise, Sputnik initiated changes within the Air Force; the Air Proving Ground Command's status changed from that of a Command to that of a Center; the Air Force Research and Development Command (ARDC) assumed command of the new Air Proving Ground Center, deactivated the Armament Center, and assigned its functions and personnel to the Air Proving Ground Center.

In February of 1958, my duty assignment changed from the Armament Center to the Air Proving Ground Center (APGC). Within the new Center, my assigned duty became R&D Administrator, Air Defense Plans, Test Requirements Office. In this assignment, I came to know Colonel David M. Jones then Air Proving Ground Center's Deputy Chief of Staff for Operations.

Col. Jones, one of the Doolittle Raiders, launched a B-25 from the aircraft carrier Hornet, bombed Tokyo, bailed out over China in Japanese controlled territory, and, with the help of the Chinese underground, returned to the US. Shot down during the North African Campaign, captured by the Germans, he spent two and a half years as a prisoner of war. He led the tunnel digging team used during a prisoner escape immortalized by the movie, Great Escape.

In March of 1958, orders relieved me from assignment Hq. APGC, ARDC and assigned me to Detachment #1, Hq. Wright Air Development Center, Wright-Patterson AFB, Ohio, with permanent duty station 220 Church Street, New York, NY. George Walker received the same set of orders.

Having no desire to move my family to New York, I called one of Lt. General Howell Estes' staff members asking that General Estes have my orders changed. General Estes, as Commander of the Wright Air Development Center, could wield much power. In recent past years, I had on several occasions briefed General Estes and believed that he could and that he would have my orders changed. Days later the staff member relayed a message from Gen. Estes saying that my orders had a number three Industrial priority – a priority beyond his pay scale.

Having no remaining option, my good friend Major George Walker and I jointly purchased a local fishing car and prepared to drive to New York. The fishing car, a fairly late model Dodge, after a lifetime on the beach, seemed in good mechanical condition, but showed an ugly, rusted body. We fitted plywood over rusted out rear seat floor boards to support our luggage.

A local machine shop converted a Chevrolet front suspension A-Frame into a tow bar fitted to my MG automobile, and in mid-March, leaving families behind; we departed for New York towing the MG.

Perhaps, my best Eglin work is summarized by a letter of recognition, written by Colonel William A. Kruge, received through channels a year and a half after leaving Eglin. I had known him as a Lt. Col. Since our last meeting, we both had been promoted; him to full Colonel and me to Lt. Col. While a staff officer in the Armament Center's Planning Office, I established an organization designed to integrate all tests conducted on the F-106 Interceptor and its armament, the GAR air-to-air missile. The organization included elements of the Armament Center, Convair, the F106 manufacturer, and the GAR missile manufacturer, Hughes. The organization proved to be successful, and later became a model for integrated testing of the F101B and other airplanes.

Ghost 333rd P-47s escort Concord home

THE AIR FORCE HYMN

LORD GUARD AND GUIDE THE MEN WHO FLY

Lord, guard and guide the men who fly
Through great spaces in the sky.
Be with them traversing air
In darkening storms or sunshine fair.

Thou who dost keep with tender might
The balanced birds in all their flight,
Thou of the tempered winds, be near
That having thee, they have no fear.

Control their minds with instinct fit
What time and adventuring, they quit
The firm security of land.
Grant steadfast eye and skillful hand

Aloft in solitudes of space
Uphold them with Thou saving grace.
O God, protect the men who fly
Through lonely ways within the sky.

Prayers for the Armed Services

162

Chapter 11
BALLISTIC MISSILE EARLY
WARNING SYSTEM

During the second week of April 1958, George Walker and I departed Eglin AFB, Fort Walton Beach, Florida, driving the rusty Dodge fishing car towing my little MG automobile. Stopping in North Carolina to store the MG in my father's garage, we continued on to New York and obtained rooms in Army Officer's quarters on Governor's Island, a 172-acre island in New York Bay. The island's name dates from colonial times when the British Crown reserved the island for exclusive use of New York's royal governors. George Washington fortified the island with cannon during battles for New York. Governors Island remained home for an US Army post until 1966.

The electronics industry grew up in New York City and nearby New Jersey. As it learned to apply many new electronic applications to military use, the Army built a sizeable research and development organization in New York City, the electronic industry's centroid; housed in an office building in the business District of Manhattan Island at 220 Church Street near Church and Worth, within walking distance to Ferry Terminals and to China Town. In 1947, the Department of Defense assigned various Army organizations to the newly established Air Force. During this reorganization, it transferred the New York organization from the Army to the Air Force. Westinghouse and RCA Companies also maintained offices in the 220 Church Street building.

Ferry boats provided access to Governors Island from ferry docks located at the southern tip of Manhattan Island near Battery Park – named for a battery of cannon installed here by George Washington. A commute to Church Street entailed a ferry ride to Battery Park and a subway ride to a subway station opposite 220 Church Street. Alternatively, a short walk from Battery Park, above ground in good weather or a short underground walk within the subway during poor wet weather required only a few minutes.

163

Monday, 14 April 1958, George and I reported to the Ballistic Missile Early Warning System (BMEWS) Program Office and sensed a level of urgency in the office. Motivated by the Soviet Union's Sputnik I earth satellite, the Air Force approved, funded, and initiated BMEWS with number three national priority and identified two senior Air Force officers, Colonel Walter Williamson and Colonel Leo V. Skinner, as Program Manager and Technical Director. Given access to personnel records in the Pentagon and authority to do so, they selected staff needed to flesh out a Program Office sized to manage the project.

George and I became some of the early arrivals. In time, a full complement of about fifty administrative, logistics, contracting, and engineering officers arrived. Twenty-one engineers, all highly trained officers – many having completed graduate school sponsored by the Air Force at the University of Michigan, the Massachusetts Institute of Technology or other prestigious universities, reported to Col. Skinner. They included Major James Early, a Massachusetts Institute of Technology classmate of George Walker, and Capt. William Harvey, my University of Michigan classmate.

BMEWS' mission, to provide the Strategic Air Command a highly reliable fifteen minute warning of a Soviet missile attack, imposed a high reliability system requirement. During the Cold War days, if attacked, national defense nuclear policy promised massive retaliation, most widely known as Mutual Assured Destruction, or MAD. The doctrine assumed that, if convinced that the US would launch its nuclear arsenal on warning, the Soviet Union would not launch a first strike.

Though in 1958 the Atlas and the Minute Man missiles were under development with national priorities of one and two, the Strategic Air Command's B-52 fleet constituted the only credible US nuclear strike force. Sputnik persuaded national authorities that the Soviets possessed a credible nuclear missile threat and that the US had no credible missile warning system. Hence a high priority program to build BMEWS.

164

Two requirements drove system design: a fifteen minute warning and warning reliability. Depending upon launch latitude in the Soviet Union, flight times of ballistic missiles impacting in the US, can be 20 to 30 minutes. When seen on the horizon from arctic sites, remaining flight times can be little more than fifteen minutes. Therefore, a fifteen minute warning requirement dictated an automatic computer controlled data processing and reporting system without human intervention.

A false alarm resulting in the launch of the B-52 fleet could result in catastrophic national consequences. Therefore, required reliability dictated that the operating system would generate only one false alarm within a period of five years. This required that the reliability of each alarm be five 9s. Stated differently, the probability that an alarm be false must be 0.00001. This reliability level dictated maintenance response times less than that available with current electronic technology. Therefore, to the best of my knowledge, the BMEWS system first employed self-diagnostics. It pioneered self-diagnostics. In later years, self-diagnostics became common in automobiles and other consumer products.

BMEWS included six major components: three radar sites, two display sites, and an interconnecting communications network.

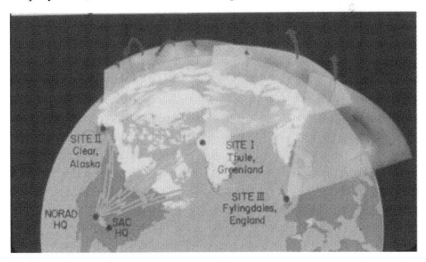

System configuration located radar sites, designed to detect ballistic missiles launched from the Soviet Union as they appeared above the arctic horizon, at Thule, Greenland, Clear, Alaska, and Fylingdales, England.

Output display systems, located at NORAD, the North American Air Defense Command, both within its Command Center on Patterson AFB and within the Alternate Command Center nuclear bunker deep within nearby Cheyenne Mountain, promised NORAD, a combined Canada and US organization, real time warning data needed to fulfil its mission to provide warning and air defense for both countries. Display systems, also located at the Strategic Air Command's Headquarters, Offutt AFB, Omaha, Nebraska, enhanced this Command's ability to launch, with little delay, the B-52 fleet on alarm. Later in time, General Curtis LeMay assumed command of the Strategic Air Command. A no nonsense warrior in the mold of General George S. Patton, his reputation enhanced the credibility of US massive retaliation nuclear policy.

An interconnecting communications network constituted the sixth major component. Duel parallel routes connected each radar site to NORAD and to the Strategic Air Command. Those parallel routes employed a different transmission media along sections of the routes. For example, a trans-Atlantic cable connected England with the US mainland. A parallel trans-Atlantic tropospheric-scatter link also connected England with the US mainland.

System design configured the three forward sites with detection radar, tracking radar, and site control subsystems. Site Control design included dual IBM 7094 computers programed to process radar data, calculate target trajectory, and generate impact point, alarm display, and diagnostics. Only by exercising BMEWS number three industrial priority, could we obtain the first six production IBM 7094 computers, IBM's first large solid-state computer model. Detection radars, using large fence antenna, designed to scan northern sectors, could detect missiles as they rose above the horizon, and report target position to Site Control.

Tracking radars designed to, receive detection radar returns, slew to lock on and track detected targets, and report high quality target position and dynamic data to Site Control.

Program Office organization matched major system components: a Radar Branch, a Communications Branch and a Systems Engineering Branch. Within the Radar Branch, Major James Early held responsibility for search radars and Major Henry I. Jones held responsibility for tracking radars. The Communications Branch, headed by Major Robert A. Taylor, a friend from Eglin days, held responsibility for the Communications Subsystem.

A Systems Engineering Branch held responsibility for the Site Control Subsystem. Branch Chief, George Walker, held responsibility for signal processing, missile impact prediction, and alarm generation. I held responsibility for all sub-system interfaces, and William Harvey held responsibility for displays and system diagnostics.

During the last three weeks of April and May, system requirements study and office procedures development occupied working hours. After checking out in the T-33 and the old reliable C-45, Mitchell AFB's Base Operations designated me T-33 flight instructor – making me happy with the promise of much flight time. In the old rusty Dodge, George and I house hunted in New Jersey and on Long Island during weekends. The Dodge's appearance tended to cause sellers and agents to discount us as serious buyers. Eventually, George purchased a house in Seaford on Long Island. I purchased a house, pictured on the following page, at 501 Pacific Street, Massapequa Park, on Long Island.

During the last weekend in May, Capt. Donald Messmore, my 1951 Squadron Officers School roommate then stationed on Mitchell, flew me to Eglin in a T-33 and returned to Mitchell solo. During the following week, with household goods packed and loaded in a moving van, Rita and I packed needed travel items and departed Eglin 6 June 1958. We first stopped in Tallahassee, Florida, home of Florida State University, to visit my old squadron mate Harry Vaughan and his family. At the time Harry, on

167

active duty as a weather officer, attended the University completing meteorology graduate studies sponsored by the AF Institute of Technology.

We next stopped at family homes in North Carolina – always a soul rejuvenating place. Earl, my brother-in-law, agreed to travel with me to New York. Stopping in Washington, we enjoyed a fine dinner in Bolling's Officer's Club and spent the night in the Officer's Quarters on Bolling Air Force Base – an unique experience for Earl. The following day, we arrived at 501 Pacific Street, Massapequa Park on Long Island. He helped me meet the moving van, arrange furniture, unpack and store kitchenware, clothing, and other household goods in appropriate drawers, chests, and closets.

With the house setup complete, we returned to North Carolina to fetch Rita and the children. At Earl's suggestion, we traveled the Eastern Shore of Maryland and Virginia to cross the Chesapeake Bay Bridge – Tunnel connecting the Eastern Shore of Virginia with Virginia Beach. Earl's suggestion proved wise. For both, the drive down the Eastern Shore, crossing the bridge, and passing through the tunnel made a good memory.

Note the absence of yard landscaping above. In order to reduce our mortgage closing cost, Rita and I agreed to landscape the yard. We leveled and seeded the lawn, and set shrubbery. The task, much greater than expected, persuaded us to mutually agree never again purchase a house without landscaping. While on a business trip to Long Island years later I drove past 501 Pacific Street and found the lawn green and shrubbery that Rita and I set grown to cover the lower third of the windows.

Pacific Street dead-ended on Violet Street, a street one address to the right of our house. William Harvey and James Early pur-

chased houses on this
street. Both homes,
visible from our bay
window, created a
small Air Force com-
munity. Bill, Loraine,
and son Jerry are pic-
tured to the right. Vio-
let Street is seen in the
upper-left background.

In order of installation priority, Site I (Thule) enjoyed first priority. Site preparation and construction commenced in late 1958.
Concrete foundation pads, necessarily poured on permafrost,
created a unique problem. Anticipating that concrete curing,
weight pressure and building warmth would thaw the permafrost
causing installations to sink, construction design embedded refrigeration pipes in concrete pads as they were poured.

System design configured Site I
with four AN/FPS-50 fairly well-
developed detection radars and
one AN/FPS-49 tracking radar.
At the time, a prototype AN/FPS-
50, operating in the Caribbean on
Trinidad Island scanning Cape

Kennedy's down range, promised reliably detection of missiles
in flight. A prototype of the less well developed tracker, installed
in the parking lot of RCA, the BMEWS' prime contractor, in
Moorestown, New Jersey, promised test data needed to confirm
its design. The tracker's radome, visible from the New Jersey
turnpike, could be photographed while driving past on the turnpike. The tracker operated at UHF just outside the amateur band
and could track targets beyond 3,000 miles.

Massapequa Park offered two options for commuting to or from
the city. A commute by carpool traveled Sunrise Highway and
connecting highways to Brooklyn Bridge, crossed the bridge,
traveled city streets, and parked in a an expensive rented parking

space near the office. Slow traffic, both on Long Island and in the city, placed the carpool on the Bowery in the morning as night movies ended – as the carpool slowly crept along the Bowery, street people, having spent the night in movie theaters, populated sidewalks scratching and preparing themselves for another day of panhandling.

The Long Island Railroad offered a second option. A commute by rail required a drive to the Massapequa Station, a train ride to Grand Central Station, a Subway ride to 220 Church, and a walk to the office. The railway option costs differed little from the costs of the carpool option. Initially, I chose the carpool option. Typical for middle class families of 1950s, Rita and I owned but one automobile. Using the train option, if Rita needed the car during the day, she drove to and from the train station early mornings and late evenings – periods most busy with our small children. Shopping for a good, reliable used second car, a salesman remarked that good, reliable, used cars remained on dealer lots for only hours – that weekend shopping would prove fruitless. On promise that he would select and hold one for me, I trusted him with a small down payment on a car yet to be identified. In the office a few days later, I received a telephone call from the salesman. He held a 1953 Ford coupe in excellent condition, with another buyer, on the lot, wishing to buy it. I agreed to buy it without seeing – a good decision. This purchase, a brown coupe, served me well for seven years.

From this time forward, the train-subway option became my commute choice. Among other things, it gave me an opportunity to know New Yorkers better. Contrary to a widespread belief, I found them not always rude and short tempered. Early in each week, alert, friendly, fellow passengers talked to fellow commuters, or read newspapers. As the week progressed, their energy diminished, and they became ever more irritable. Departing Grand Central Station Friday evenings, weary, sleeping men and women filled passenger cars. I found it best to leave them alone.

Likewise, during the latter days of the week, New Yorkers in the public square could be rude. Early one morning in Grand Central

Station, a friend, Major Charlie Bayless, and I stopped at a small retail stand within the station. As I watched, he paid for a small item with a twenty dollar bill. With an expression of rage, the clerk reluctantly accepted the large bill for the small item. Charlie then picked up another item, a cigar, from the counter. As the clerk returned change, Charlie gave him the cigar, and as we walked away, the clerk asked *"What shall I do with the cigar?"* – mistake, Charlie answered *"Stick it where the Sun doesn't shine,"* and metagrobolized the clerk.

The New York area offered many attractions including nearby Jones Beach. Though crowded, its clean beach provided pleasant afternoons by the seaside. In years past, George and Doda Walker had lived in New York City and still knew how to navigate the town. Rita and I enjoyed stage plays on Broadway and dinners in some fine restaurants with them.

Mitchell AFB Officers Club offered good Sunday after church lunches with a familiar AF atmosphere.

171

Though not old enough to remember, Rita and I took advantage of the opportunity to show the Statue of Liberty to the children. To the left above, the Statue is pictured as seen from the Statue of Liberty Ferry Boat. To the right, Rita, holding Roger, is resting on steps leading to the Lady's head. New York City's skyline shows in the background.

In April of 1959, my promotion to Lt. Col. created an awkward situation. I now outranked my Branch Chief. Normally in this situation, the Air Force offered two options: the Lt. Col. could be transferred and replaced with a more junior officer, or the Major could be transferred to another assignment. At George's request a third action followed. I became Branch Chief, and George became a staff officer within the branch. This arrangement worked without rancor. George possessed a gentle character, without a trace of envy – more with the soul of a poet or philosopher than that of a Cold War warrior. He often hummed or quoted the lyrics of The Impossible Dream. In later years, I heard The Impossible Dream sung at his funeral.

The Air Force assigned a C-54, equipped with long range fuel tanks, two bunks for crew rest, comfortable passenger seats, and a maintenance crew chief to the Program Office.

Hangered on Mitchell AFB and flown by pilots assigned to the Program Office, it made regular staff visits to the three radar sites time efficient, and as comfortable as possible.

172

Greenland is pictured to the left below as the C-54 approaches the Greenland coast near Thule. Thule Air Force Base of late 1959 is pictured right.

Two of the four Site I detection radar fence antenna pictured below in a photograph, made during the winter of 1959, shows the mid-day sun on the horizon at picture center. Construction lights on antenna and buildings make work possible in the twilight of a polar winter day.

As BMEWS system engineer, my duty gave me an all-encompassing view of the system, and I became the program's voice. I used the above picture to introduce periodic status briefings given to NORAD, to SAC, and to the Pentagon. This color slide presents an eerie, bluish image. With an audience assembled, a technician turned off all lights. After a few seconds as the audience became restless, he projected this color slide. It never failed to get full attention from any and all audiences.

Fuel aboard the C-54 made possible a flight from Thule, Greenland, along a great circle route over the polar region, to Fairbanks, Alaska. Pictured right is a small island near the North Pole. In these regions, the mag-

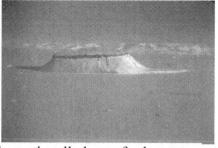

netic compass is of no value; it continually hunts for but never finds the North Pole. Navigation depends upon a gyro stabilized compass manually set to some reference heading.

At takeoff, the navigator set the gyro compass to runway heading; an accurate compass reading. Without a magnetic compass, this setting became precious – not be altered along the route. Throughout the flight from Thule to Fairbanks, the navigator stood behind pilot seats on guard to insure that no one touched his gyro compass.

After making landfall, our route crossed miles of Alaska's tundra, some portion pictured left above. After an overnight in Fairbanks, our party traveled about seventy miles southeast to Clear by helicopter. BMEWS Site II is located in the valley beyond the mountain range pictured right above. At the time of our visit, in progress site preparation offered little to photograph and no overnight accommodations.

Returning to Fairbanks for another overnight, we departed the following morning for a 4,400 mile, 20 hour, non-stop flight to Mitchell Field. Though several pilots took turns flying the airplane, the flight exhausted all before reaching Mitchell.

Russia's Sputnik earth satellite not only sparked BMEWS, it also sparked extra-terrestrial flight into the national consciousness, created what would become the National Aeronautics and Space Administration (NASA), enhanced the ongoing Mercury project to put an American in earth orbit, and planning for future Gemini and Apollo projects. Anticipating a future need, the Air Force began planning for future space flight missions. At my request, the AF Institute of Technology evaluated my AF record, determined me academically qualified for graduate training in Astronautics at the Ph.D. level, and noted that availability for the course would be a Hq. USAF decision. On 23 September, I forwarded and Col. Skinner indorsed my request for an availability determination.

By chance, I met Mr. George P. Aldridge in a hallway of the 220 Church Street office building. Mr. Aldridge, a retired President of RCA, still held an office in the building. With no assigned tasks, lonely and needing to talk, he occasionally visited my office. When asked *"What characteristic leads a man to a successful career as president of a major corporation?"* he quickly answered *"Vision: long before the advent of radio, in 1915 a young engineer, David Sarnoff an RCA executive from 1919 to 1970, proposed radio as a household utility such as the piano or phonograph."* He further remarked that a copy of Sarnoff's 1915 proposal resides in his files. A few days later, his secretary came to my office and gave me a copy of Sarnoff's three page 1915 memorandum. Mr. Aldridge and David Sarnoff were friends from the days of their youth when both served as observers in back seats of Army aircraft flying over German lines during WWI telegraphing German positions to Army intelligence.

In brief, Sarnoff's memorandum envisioned radio as we know it today. It estimated the cost and selling price of Radio Boxes, the cost of constructing a transmitting station, operating cost, revenue from advertising and sales of Radio Boxes, and profits. In time, his company, an RCA predecessor, executed his proposal, and we have radio today. Sarnoff can truly be called an early technological prophet.

In 1959, the Air Force decided to consolidate management of all Air Force ground electronics systems research and development activities within the Command and Control Division, a newly established division, commanded by General Kenneth P. Bergquist, located on L. G. Hanscom Field in Bedford, Massachusetts. As a captain in the late 1930s, General Bergquist managed the installation of a radar aircraft warning system in Hawaii. On 7 December 1941, the system barked, but no one noticed.

On 6 January of 1960, our Command reassigned all persons, presently assigned to the Wright Air Development Center with duty station at 220 Church Street, to duty station Laurence G. Hanscom Field for the purpose of forming a standard System Program Office. This changed our duty station without a change in assignment. Such orders required movement of equipment, files, and people while maintaining program management continuity. Management continuity required a careful phased move of all elements. The need to hire replacements for Civil Service employees not willing to move to Massachusetts received first priority.

Secretaries, all Civil Service employees, chose not to leave New York. Col. Skinner asked me to go to Massachusetts and hire replacements. Prior to my arrival, Civil Service advertised open positions, selected applicants, set up interviews, and arranged a temporary office for me. Arriving in that office early morning, a line of applicants stood from office door, down a long hall, around a corner and down a second hallway.

Civil Service required me to interview all or none. Clearly, my interview preparations, including set questions, dictation, and typing skill demonstration, did not allow time to interview all. Instead in a shortened interview, I evaluated, graded, and recorded the appearance and speech of each. From these notes, I hired the needed number of secretaries. A good selection, those chosen joined a growing organization, and, in time, earned positions in offices of the Commanding General and other Senior Staff positions. In later years, when needing a staff car in Massachusetts, I called one of these ladies, and Motor Pools gave priority to my need.

Returning to New York, moving preparation commenced. We put the house on the market with an undetermined future occupancy date. The old fishing Dodge remained available. Expensive automobile disposal in New York persuaded George to keep the Dodge. Again, George and I left families behind and drove to a new duty station. In very cold January weather, with no cabin heat in the Dodge, two large cans filled with hot water carried between the driver's seat and the passenger's seat provided some warmth. When the water cooled, we stopped at a Service Station and refilled the cans with hot water.

Reaching Hanscom, we obtained rooms in Bachelor Officers Quarters and began organizing offices in an office building set aside for BNEWS. In time, as equipment, files, and people arrived, the Program Office became operational with business as usual. As in New York, the old Dodge provided transportation for weekend house hunts. In contrast to New York, Bedford, a small town, offered a buyer's market. I purchased a house on the east side of Bedford. George and Jim Early purchased houses on the western side of Bedford. Bill Harvey and Henry Jones purchased houses in nearby Billerica, a small town on the old Boston through Lexington road. Returning to New York in June, a move to Bedford commenced. A moving van collected household goods, a house buyer accepted house keys, and the family departed New York.

Historic Bedford is only eighteen miles west of Boston. Paul Revere's historic ride traveled along a route, now abandoned, passing through nearby Hanscom Field. At Lexington, to the east, militiamen fired the first shots of the Revolutionary War.

They fired those shots on Lexington Commons. Pictured left on the following page, Garthae and Roger stand on the Commons, now well-kept and known as Lexington Green. Nearby stands Buckman Tavern.

On 19 April, 1776, Buckman Tavern, the busiest tavern in town, housed Lexington's first village store, and served as Headquarters for militiamen gathered on Town Commons awaiting British troops. Now its 18th Century tap room opens to the public, but no longer serves pints of beer as in the days of old.

At Concord to the west a few miles, a reconstructed Old North Bridge spans the Concord River. Arched and supported by six wooden piers, its height above the river permitted boats of colonel days to travel up and down the river. British and Americans fought the first Revolutionary War battle on this bridge. It is now a National well-kept, historic park site. Regrettably, my children, too young to appreciate the experience, have no memory of their visit to the bridge.

As expected, winter snow brought challenging yards and roadways. Large front and back Jonathan Lane yards offered beautiful picture card snow scenes.

As winter wore on, the beauty became less appreciated as streets, driveways, walkways and steps required constant snow removal.

Unlike Ann Arbor, Rita now had a snow crew. Pictured right, Gail and Roger preferred shovels. Rita, not shown, preferred a broom.

By letter dated 29 January, the Commandant of the AF Institute of Technology advised me that Hq USF had made me available for an Institute of Technology program and that my application for admission to the Ph.D. Astronautics program was under consideration by the Board of Admissions for a September 1961 entry.

In February, an AF Selection Board selected me for promotion to Major in the Regular Air Force. In March, a major AF reorganization; renamed the Research and Development Command the AF Systems Command; renamed the Command and Control Development Division the Electronic Systems Division; and reassigned all persons, presently assigned to Wright Air Development Division in Ohio, to the Electronic Systems Division for duty with the 474 System Project Office. The reassignment united our duty station and duty assignment.

Spring's warming enticed the family to visit historic sites in Boston and surrounding towns and villages. USS Constitution, Old Ironsides, graced Boston harbor. Rita and the children show standing on Old Ironsides forecastle to the right.

Nearby Sturbridge Village, designed and constructed to recapture the colonial period, offered glimpses of colonial homes, tools, and lifestyles.

Typical housing architecture pictured left above shows window panes of hand blown glass. Fully transparent, they lighten the home but distort images seen through windows. Pictured right, Rita watches over Gail as Gail endures punishment in stocks on the village square.

Thule became operational in September of 1960. Coached by Col. Williamson and Col. Skinner, I prepared an Initial Operational Capability Briefing that described system performance parameters. Once satisfied with the presentation, we made a briefing tour, and I briefed NORAD, in Colorado, SAC Headquarters in Omaha, Nebraska, and the Pentagon. The briefing emphasized system reliability and a false alarm rate of one in five years. On 5 October, less than two weeks after our briefing tour, a false alarm occurred. Bad news – I now had the responsibility to prepare a second briefing that restored some system credibility.

The system had interpreted radar returns from the Moon to be a missile destined to impact in continental America. An antenna side lobe had detected the returns. Every antenna transmits and receives signals through a main beam and several side lobes. Antenna design maximizes main beam signals and minimizes side lobe signals. A well designed antenna will not see targets of interest in side lobes. Consider your hand. Imagine the middle finger to be an antenna's main beam. Consider the thumb, the second finger, the fourth finger, and the little finger to be side lobes.

A fist with the middle finger pointing straight ahead makes a simple illustration of antenna side lobes.

Radar cannot distinguish side lobe returns from main beam returns, so the system processed moon returns as though they were seen by the main beam. Given position and dynamic data, as reported from the side lobe, the system properly calculated a missile rising within its main beam scan sector on a path to impact within the US.

Our second briefing tour, in mid-October, encountered skeptical to hostile audiences. An argument that the false alarm incident provided a great, realistic test of the system provided sufficient traction for me to get off the stage with some credibility. A true argument; geography prevented system tests using real missiles; the moon accessing the system via the side lobe presented data equaling that of a true missile rising within the main beam's scan sector. The system properly analyzed and reported received data. Equally beneficial future tests, scheduled by the moon, could be repeated.

By letter dated 6 January 1961, the Institute of Technology's Commandant informed me that I had been selected by the Board of Admissions for training in astronautics. In April, I received orders assigning me to the Institute of Technology with duty station at the University of Michigan for the purpose of attending a Post Graduate Doctorial course in astronautics beginning Thursday, 22 June 1961. The orders also attached me to Selfridge AFB for flying.

School start date gave Rita and me eight weeks to prepare for a move. We put the Jonathan Lane house on the market, but could find no buyer. Again, I left the family behind and traveled to Ann Arbor alone.

Pilots are plane people
With special air
About them

181

TODAY

With every rising of the sun
Think of your life as just begun

The Past has cancelled and buried deep
All yesterdays. There let them sleep.

Concern yourself with but today
Grasp it, and teach it to obey.

Your will and plan, since time began
Today has been the friend of man.

You and Today! A soul sublime
And the great heritage of time.

With God himself to bind the twain,
Go forth, brave heart! Attain! Attain!

Anonymous

Chapter 12
SCIENTIFIC FRONTIERS

After leaving Bedford, Rita, and the children Wednesday morning, 7 June 1961 and driving twelve hours, the little brown Ford and I reached Ann Arbor during the late evening. The following day, I obtained a room in Fletcher Hall, a dormitory for graduate students. In some sense a homecoming, I had lived in Fletcher Hall during the University's Summer School nine years earlier in 1952. On Friday the 9th, I reported to Selfridge AFB; checked out in the T-33 airplane, flew during the weekend, and spent the following week looking for a house rental.

The Summer Semester commenced Thursday, 22 June, offering a challenging, difficult academic work load of advanced mathematics and physics. A poor abode choice, Fletcher Hall mostly housed school teachers satisfying a periodic Michigan State requirement to upgrade their education. Not serious students; Fletcher Hall seemed more like an Animal House than a dormitory. Classes and study absorbed much available time, leaving little opportunity for house hunting.

Summer School raced along. Return to academia, a department and a group of professors little changed since I left the University in the spring of 1954, felt seamless. Limited available time made house hunting unproductive. Without adequate inspection, I rented a house being vacated by a fellow Air Force student expecting to complete his studies at the end of the Summer School.

Swiftly passed the days, June turned into July and July turned into August. Rita sold the house in Bedford, and at the end of Summer School in mid-August, I returned to Bedford to fetch the family. Returning to Ann Arbor, with one quick look at my rental choice, Rita said, *"I will not put my family in that house."* With me obliged to attend classes, Rita searched for and found a more pleasing rental, a very modern design with many large windows, both upstairs and downstairs, on the elite side of Ann Arbor. Mrs. Halberg, the mother of our Eglin neighbor, who lived next door became a surrogate grandmother for my children. Apprehension that the house would be cold during winters proved ill founded. A very comfortable house, it made a great home. A Ford Company Vice President for advertising lived in the neighborhood. His daughter became Gail's friend and playmate. Driving to and from Church, we drove past an early home of Gerald Ford.

A rigorous Fall Semester kept me in class or in a study set up by Rita in a small room next to the master bedroom. In addition to continuing studies of physics and mathematics, the semester introduced me to astrophysics, the study of the physics of the universe, and to computer programming. My limited knowledge and experience with FORTRAN offered little to no help. The university required students learn and use Michigan Algorithm for Decoding (MAD,) a programming language developed by the University hoping to compete with and replace FORTRAN. Not competitive, MAD made no impact beyond the campus and in time the university scrapped MAD along with my time learning the code.

Occasional trips to Selfridge, not only necessary to maintain flight proficiency, they also proved therapeutic. The semester induced stress and a few hours airborne, particularly at night, relieved stress. Words cannot fully describe the experience of observing the universe at night from under a bubble canopy at 25,000 feet. Feeling suspended in space, the star's faint song may be heard above the hum of the engine's steady drone.

In reason's ear, we all rejoice,
And utter forth a glorious voice.
Forever singing as we shine,
The hand that made us is Devine.

National authorities believed that a Soviet bomber fleet still poised a serious threat, and NORAD maintained a constant air defense alert. Occasional exercises tested air defense readiness. Selfridge often flew missions simulating Soviet bomber attacks, and when possible I participated. Usually on weekends, I flew to a Canadian air base in northern Canada and landed. The following morning, I joined a formation simulating a bomber attack on some credible target in Canada or the US. Most often, NORAD fighters intercepted the formation before it reached the would-be target. Once intercepted, the exercise ended, and I returned to Selfridge and to more study.

The Fall Semester offered a rigorous but fascinating study of advanced mathematics, physics, and MAD programming. Advanced calculus Professor, William Kaplan, a widely known mathematician, taught heavily subscribed classes held in a very large room with seating progressively raised from front to back so that all students could see and be seen. Kaplan well earned his reputation. Though challenging, he made mathematics come alive, and each class a joy. Physics studies focused on the physics of the atmosphere, its structure and elements. Programming studies remained an exercise in logic – always a challenge. Passing doctorial preliminary examinations at the end of the Spring Semester opened the door to doctorial study and thesis selection.

The year's winter, characterized by blowing snow, gave winter fun for the family. By flooding a level portion of our back yard, we created a skating rink that needed little maintenance, and the children learned to ice skate. Ice on a nearby lake remained clear of snow and offered a larger field of ice for skating by neighborhood children and some parents. I skated with a kitchen chair for stability. To have her father seen by friends skating with a kitchen chair embarrassed my daughter Gail. A nearby hill offered great sled and toboggan rides.

Summer and Fall 1962 Semesters brought studies of Astrophysics, Variational Calculus, and the definition of a thesis satisfying University requirements. Astrophysics is the study of the physics of the universe, the physical properties of celestial objects, their behavior, and their interactions. A typical spiral galaxy is pictured at right above.

185

Variational calculus is a branch of mathematics useful for finding minimum energy paths between two points in n-dimensional space. While ordinary calculus studies small changes around a point, variational calculus investigates small variations along a path. First conceived in 1696, mathematicians of the 18th century further developed variational calculus as a mathematician's curiosity and published tomes for storage on dusty shelves of great universities for study by PhD candidates.

Motivated by President Kennedy's 15 May 1961 national challenge to land a man on the Moon and to return him safely to Earth before the end of the 60s decade, Mercury and Apollo programs launched an active space decade. The idea of space travel, in turn, launched a paramount need to define routes in space that required the least fuel, a classic variational calculus problem; textbooks, long on dusty book shelves, became required study for application by scientists and engineers associated with Mercury and Apollo, both military and civilian. I anticipated future involvement in these programs.

Reading the textbook's introduction to variational calculus gave me a better understanding and appreciation of the near environment, the earth, the universe, and its creation. The words below recreate the introduction as remembered.

> *A Monk living in a Monastery in the French Alps during the early 18th Century hypothesized that God, in his infinite wisdom, would have designed the world so that all natural processes would operate on a minimum energy path. Further, developing and using then existing variational calculus, he demonstrated that some natural processes do indeed operate on minimum energy paths. Some examples: the catenary exerts less stress on a rope, a drop of water contains the maximum volume of water that may be contained by water surface tension, and the tree tends to form a spherical shape so as to grow the maximum foliage in available sunlight.*

Anticipating clear lake ice, during early winter my sons and I built an ice boat, similar to that pictured to the right. Runner blades removed from skating boots attached to each apex of a triangular wood frame served as boat runners.

With her sewing machine, Rita made a canvas sail. Unfortunately, heavy 1962 snow storms, with little wind, covered lake ice with a blanket of snow throughout the winter. The sailboat rested on snow. Its blades could not reach ice, and the sail could not make the boat move. The boat traveled with the family during two station changes to be finally abandoned in the attic of a house in Albuquerque, New Mexico.

A second, more successful, project cut blocks from yard snow and formed an Eskimo Igloo constructed on the front yard. After enduring a freezing rain, the snow blocks welded into a single frozen structure that retained its integrity until late March. It provided a playhouse, surprisingly warm, for the children until late March.

I devoted my 1963 Spring Semester entirely to a thesis titled Mars Minimum Energy Voyage having an objective to find a minimum energy path from Earth to Mars with a soft landing. The first task, write a computer program that could define a minimum energy path to Mars' gravitational field, required software code written on punch cards using machines located in the University's Computer Laboratory. At the time no personal computers existed. Typically, one spent days coding a program module to produce a card deck for delivery to the Computer Laboratory's code receiving desk. The following day, sometimes the second day, the deck of cards and a computer run print-out became available for pick-up. More often than not, the print-out offered little more than *program did not run.* After more days troubleshooting and punching code, a revised card deck returned to the computer desk. Eventually the module ran satisfactorily, and the process continued with the next module.

Jeffrey, the youngest son born on 23 April of 1963, completed our family – one daughter and four sons. They, in time, would give me nine grandchildren. Rita and I consider this family our greatest achievement.

In late May, the Air University denied my request for an extension to my University of Michigan assignment so that I could complete my thesis, and orders arrived assigning me to the Office of Aerospace Research (OAR) located at 4th & Independence Avenue, SW, Washington 25, DC, with a reporting date not later than 18 June. This came as a disappointment. To my knowledge, the only computer conversant with MAD software existed on the University of Michigan's campus. I needed that computer to complete my thesis. This bad timing created another fork in my journey offering two options. One option included retiring from the Air Force, retaining student status, completing the thesis, and seeking civilian employment. My five year service commitment, in order to attend the University, made this option problematic. As a second option, I could accept an Aeronautical and Astronautical Engineering Degree, and continue an Air Force career. The degree, known as a Professional degree, is above the Masters level, but below the PhD level. Rita and I chose to remain Air Force.

Fearing that a move in early June would impose excess stress on baby Jeff and his mother, with Rita's agreement, I again left the family, traveled alone to Washington to report for duty, to buy an appropriate house, and return to fetch the family. Departing Ann Arbor Thursday, 6 June, the little brown Ford and I reached Washington around midnight to spend a needed rest in a Bachelor Officer's Quarters (BOQ) room on Bolling Air Force Base. Saturday, Sunday, and the following week I spent house hunting; to find a seller friendly market and few houses available for immediate occupancy.

I reported to my new duty station, located in Temp D Building at 4th and Independence, on Monday 17 June 1963. Temporary D's architecture did not match temporary buildings constructed in Washington during WWII. I understand that it dates from WWI. Old but sound and on the Mall two blocks from the Capital Building and across the Mall from the Mellon Art Gallery, it occupied a choice location. A short walk made the Capital Cafeteria's famous bean soup a luncheon delight, and the art gallery featured frequent art exhibits that could be viewed during a long lunch period.

OAR at the time, a separate operating organization exercised functions and responsibilities of a major command. Its genesis dates from efforts during WWII to find new scientific knowledge needed to build advanced weapons of war. Its mission, plan, program, and manage basic research of interest to the Air Force, positioned it on the frontiers of science. Organizationally, OAR included Headquarters at 4th & Independence in Washington, the Cambridge Research Laboratories in Massachusetts, the Aeronautical Research Laboratory, Wright-Patterson AFB, in Ohio, and the Frank J. Seiler Laboratory at the Air Force Academy in Colorado.

Major General Ernest Pinson commanded OAR. His high regard within both military and civilian scientific communities derived from contributions to the knowledge of aeromedicine, nuclear weapons radiations hazards, and crew safety. He played a major role during the development of the modern aircraft ejection seat.

Reflecting his great confidence in early designs, he ejected from high speed sledges racing across a California dry lake bed.

Assigned duty as Chief, Physical Sciences Division, I reported, through channels, to Deputy Chief of Staff for Plans and Programs, Colonel Thomas Love, with a responsibility to manage physical science research conducted by in-house laboratories and to grant financial support for research conducted by non AF national and international civilian laboratories. Tasks included: review of ongoing research, recommend levels of financial support for ongoing research, recommend new research projects, evaluate new research proposals, and budget for ongoing research and for new research in planning stages.

House hunting continued during second and third week of June. On Saturday, 22 June, I signed a purchase agreement to buy a house, then under construction, for $25,000. The agreement promised a 27 August 1963 occupancy date. My residence remained a Bolling BOQ room until late August when I returned to Ann Arbor to fetch the family. During the first week in October, a moving van delivered furniture and household and goods, and the family moved into our new home at 3319 Albion Court, Fairfax, Virginia, 22030, a comfortable, four bedroom Garrison Colonial house located about one mile, as the crow flies, from Fairfax Circle. The home of General George Pickett, who led Pickett's Charge at Gettysburg, stood nearby.

Basic research explores the unknown, and no objective criteria exist for judging its worth. Should a particular research project prove without merit, its OAR staff officer's subsequent Effectiveness Report would reflect his accountable. The principal investigator's background, personality, enthusiasm, the quality and appropriateness of his staff and laboratory, and his peer reviews offered the basis for judging the worth of his research. Therefore, this assignment demanded that I travel to and visit government, university, and other laboratories, both domestic and foreign, and spend much time reading scientific journals.

I visited: laboratories in Spain and saw bull fights, laboratories in Italy and saw Rome, laboratories in Switzerland and saw Lake Geneva. When arrived in-country, protocol required a report to the US Embassy, so I met the Ambassador and/or Staff members of several US Embassies.

On Friday, 22 November, someone came to my office telling that President Kennedy had been shot. Quickly walking to the conference room, I found Lt. Col. John Fowler, my boss, practicing a speech in a darkened room. I turned on a television set. John gave me an evil eye, but as he began to understand the news, he joined me and other staff members to watch throughout most of the afternoon.

Daily tasks embedded me deeply into the scientific community of the day and made me conversant with scientific literature of the period. I learned that science tells how the world works, but cannot tell **why**. Gravity, a major pillar supporting science, still evades understanding. Science cannot explain why an apple, when detached from the tree, falls to the ground. Ask a native deep in the Amazon jungle *"Why does the coconut fall from the tree?"* and the answer is likely to be *"because."* Ask a high school student, and the answer is likely to be *"gravity."* Ask college physics majors, and the answer is likely to be *"mutual attraction between two masses."* Ask a scientist working at the boundary of scientific knowledge and the answer is likely to be *"because."*

In the early sixties, scientific literature postulated the existence of a Higgs particle that could give birth to mass, and given mass gravity is born. The CERN La-  boratory in Switzerland began a project to confirm the particle's existence. At the time, I had the opportunity to visit Switzerland and the CERN laboratory. Lake Geneva is pictured above.

In 2012 the CERN Laboratory reported an experimental result consistent with the postulated Higgs particle. The experimental result suggests a particle yet to be positively identified as the Higgs particle.

Taking a broader view, western society defines the existence of the Universe by two concepts. The scientific and secular concept postulates a Big Bang beginning with an ever expanding debris field in which, by gravity, stars, galaxies, and the solar system coalesce, and over time life is formed by random processes. A philosophical and theological concept is found in Genesis – *In the beginning God created the heavens, the earth, and all living things.*

Note that the Big Bang theory must be accepted by faith and by faith alone. Likewise the Genesis story must be accepted by faith and faith alone. Each must therefore, by faith and faith alone, choose. Is the miracle of our life given by a random process or by an intelligent God?

The OAR tour coincided with the height of the Viet Nam War. In October of 1965, the Air Force's operational pilot "well" began to dry up, and the Air Force invited approximately 700 behind-the-line pilots needed to fly combat missions to volunteer. National policy decreed that no two family members could serve in Viet Nam at the same time. Garthae and Larry approached draft age, and knowing that I could keep them from the jungles of Viet Nam, I volunteered. For this same reason, Bill Harvey served two tours in Viet Nam during his sons' window of vulnerability.

Garthae graduated from Woodson High School in June of 1966, and joined the NC State University freshman class in the fall. Leaving my first child on a distant campus became an emotional moment.

In early 1967, I received orders to report to Fairchild AFB, Washington, on 24 April for two months of survival training, then to report to the 363rd Tactical Reconnaissance Wing, Shaw AFB, in Charlestown, South Carolina, for five months of F-101R reconnaissance mission training, and to expect a departure from a port of Aerial Embarking for shipment overseas on 6 December 1967. The F-101R, a McDonnell supersonic fighter designed for long range bomber escort missions, modified for the reconnaissance mission, carried no guns. Mission survival depended on speed. Approaching target at high speed at treetop level below radar, it begin a maximum g vertical climb with cameras mounted on the fuselage's bottom operating through a 45 degree partial loop. The high g turn continued over the top and rolled out heading home again at treetop lever. Surprise, short exposure, and high speed enhanced survival.

Scheduled to depart Washington by commercial air on Sunday, 23 April destination Fairchild AFB, by telephone on Thursday, OAR's Personnel Officer, with no reason given, told me to not leave town. This news overjoyed Rita. Understanding came the following week by letter dated 25 April with news of my presence on the Colonel's promotion list. I had been promoted out of the cockpit.

Though, with an effective date months later, my promotion created an awkward situation within the Command. Promoted, I outranked others, in the command's hierarchy, who outranked my current rank. The solution created a new position, Assistant for Limited War, reporting to OAR's Chief of Staff. At General Pinson's suggestion, considered as an order, I initiated a conference designed to present ongoing research, relevant to the Viet Nam war, to a broad military and civilian audience. The National Academy of Science agreed to host the conference.

For my own peace of mind, I required the Principal Investigator of each selected research project to come to Washington, give his intended presentation, and consider suggestions from OAR staff members. The format sat selected staff members along the sides of a long table. The speaker stood and spoke from one end of the table. Still a Lt. Col. and junior member in the room, I sat at the other end of the table. Except for one by a Nobel Laureate from Stanford University, all presentations, well presented, contained pertinent content, and good organization. When finished, I said to him, *"If I was a professor and you were my student, I would give you an F for this presentation."* Staff members were aghast. The speaker looked surprised for a moment, then smiled and said *"Col, I agree with your grade. If you will reschedule me, I will give you a good presentation."* I did, and he did. The conference successfully completed on schedule, and I received some acclaim.

In mid-June of 1967, Command orders transferred me to the AF Weapons Laboratory, Albuquerque, New Mexico. For this move Rita and I purchased a travel trailer that could sleep the family while we traveled to New Mexico. Its downsides, driving all day, finding a campsite, and connecting utilities, exhausted me. The family, having slept in the automobile during the day, not ready for bed, filled the trailer with activity until late evenings.

For the first time, Rita selected our next home located at 1311 Constitution Court, in Albuquerque – her favorite for all time. Her choice proved great. The yards, professionally landscaped, included an underground watering system that kept shrubs and grass well watered. Its front yard beauty is pictured below left, and a dream back yard, pictured right, offered ripe cherries and other fruits for picking.

I reported for duty 26 July 1967 and served as Research and Development Director in the Laboratory's Foreign Technology Division. Colonel David Jones, the Laboratory Commander and

Colonel Walter Beckham, the Laboratory's Chief Scientist gave me space and time to learn the demands of a new job. I came to enjoy the work, particularly debating with Beckham mathematical foundations for analytical studies performed within the Laboratory

Beckham, a European WWII fighter ace, flew a P-47D named Little Demon. We had much in common. I flew a P-47D on Hawaii and on Saipan. A model of my airplane, named The Witch, is pictured right.

All enjoyed New Mexico. Larry and I overhauled the MG engine, and a professional painter painted the MG red. The Base Hobby Shop provided clean space and excellent tools needed for engine overhaul. At the time Al Muncy enjoyed success as a driver on the Indianapolis speedway. His brother, an Air Force Captain, frequented the Hobby Shop repairing an automobile he raced on nearby dirt tracks. A fine mechanic, he greatly helped Larry and me with our engine.

From her kitchen window, Rita could see morning sun rise slowly above the Sandia Mountains into a clear blue sky. Looking left, perhaps five miles, she saw cable cars climb the western slope carrying skiers to ski slopes on the eastern side of the mountains where Jeffrey

learned to ski. Beyond the edge of watered yards, desert and tumble weed appeared dry and barren when compared to Virginia. As time wore on, with Rita's aid, the desert took on a beauty of its own.

New Mexico offered much. Foods offered new experiences. The La Pinto Restaurant offered great after church lunches. Rita and I took cooking classes. She learned to cook Sopapillas, Huevos Ranchros and other dishes that the family enjoyed for years to come. Bite the sopapilla, pour the honey – good. I cooked true Chile Relleons – good.

New Mexico exposed family members to American Indian culture. Left above Larry stands by a doorway of ancient Anasazi Indian cliff dwellers. A very old Indian Pueblo, still occupied, is pictured right. In the foreground flows the Rio Grande River. Note the half dome in the center of the Pueblo's yard beyond the river, a mud-brick oven for cooking Indian bread.

Through the Kirkland Wives Club, Rita met a lifelong dear friend Dee Ford. In time, I met husband John and their children. We would know them on a subsequent AF station and in Washington, DC, after retirement. Later in time, I saw Dee and John buried in Arlington National Cemetery.

Rita enjoyed her favorite home for only a short year. A year after our arrival in Albuquerque, a nomination for the National War College 1968 -1969 class presented another fork in the road – I could decline or accept the nomination. Still ambitious, I accepted, and the travel trailer traveled back to Washington.

I remain always grateful that the Air Force gave me an opportunity to visit the frontiers of science. That visit expanded my wonder of life, and caused me to greater appreciate scientists of ages past who have given us a great understanding of the world in which we live. Just hours ago in historic time, our forefathers stood on western European shores wondering what dragons lived beyond the watery horizon and how far the earth's edge.

With a globe model of the Earth, a Pacific island native can today know what lies beyond his watery horizons. Likewise, scientists preceding ancient Egyptians and onward have modeled the Universe so that we better understand life surrounding us and the skies above. Incomplete and needing patches such as anti-matter and black holes to accommodate experimental data not fitting the picture puzzle, the models will serve us well into the future until some now-unknown scientists find missing pieces.

QUESTIONINGS

Hath this world, without me wrought,
Substances other than my thought?
Lives it by my sense alone,
Or by essence of its own?
Will its life, with mine begun,
Cease to be when that is done?
Or another consciousness
With the self-same forms impress?

Doth yon fireball poised in air,
Hang by my permission there?
Are the clouds that wander by,
But the offspring of mine eye?
Borne with every glance I cast,
Perishing when mine eye is past?

And those thousand, thousand eyes,
Scattered through the twinkling skies,
Do they draw their light from mine,
Or, of intrinsic beauty shine?

Now I close my eyes and ears,
And creation disappears;
Yet if I but speak the word,
All creation is restored.
Or – more wonderful – within,
New creations do begin.

F. H. Hedge 1841

Chapter 13
NATIONAL WAR COLLEGE

Knowing that our tour would last for only a year, Rita and I chose to rent a house near our previous Albion Court home. Larry at right sits in the red MG, pictured in grayscale, in front of 1941 Santayana Drive located near Fairfax Circle.

I reported to the National War College 19 August 1968, and began a most delightful year studying national and international political, economic, and military affairs in context with military history, current force levels, and military strategy. The War College, pictured right, is located on Fort McNair, a few blocks southeast of the Capital Building in Washington, DC. Students included Defense, State, and other

Government Agency officers. Study format included reading, lectures, and debate. Guest lecturers included Chairman of the Joint Chiefs of Staff, Military Chiefs, major Department Secretaries, members of Congress, and prominent leaders from industry, and news media. Notable lecturers included Henry Kissinger, Barry Goldwater, Art Buchwald, and Rosco Turner.

I skipped class and spent an afternoon in Ft. McNair Officer Club's bar listening to Rosco Turner, a contemporary of Charles Lindberg, Howard Hughes, Wiley Post, Amelia Earheart, and other famous pilots – all heroes of my youth, relive races, barnstorming days, and memories of his colorful pet lion Gilmore. An occasional scotch kept him talking.

199

The college offered student wives, considered associate students, special lectures. Rita, bottom left, wears the big white hat in the picture to the right and listens to Senator Clara Booth Luce speak.

A field trip during the Spring of 1969 gave class members an opportunity to visit Austria, Yugoslavia, Germany, England, and France. In each capital city, senior government officials received class members and briefed prevailing political, economic, and military issues of their respective country. The trip gave me a great lesson, not only in current international affairs, but also in history of years long gone.

Vienna, capital of Austria, located on the shore of the beautiful blue Danube River, once served as the border of the ancient Roman Empire. Senior Austrian officials briefed our Class in a large conference room having many doors. The Congress of Vienna, held in this room in1814, led to 100 years of European peace. Attended by royal officials from all European countries, no agreement could decide on the protocol question, *"Who enters the conference room first?"* The solution made a door for each country official, and all entered at the same time. Those doors remain today.

Expansion of the Ottoman Empire reached Eastern Europe in the 16th century. City walls of ancient Belgrade in Yugoslavia still stand bearing cannon balls received

during a siege by an Ottoman Empire army in 1521. Yugoslavia, populated by both Muslims and Christians, occupied a buffer ar-

200

ea between the Muslim East and the Christian West. Conflict within this buffer zone has continued throughout centuries following Ottoman Empire's decline. Consider the ethnic cleansing of Muslims during the recent Bosnian War of 1992.

Come forward in history; consider two Yugoslav partisan groups, one led by Josi Tito and one led by Draza Mihailovc. During WWII they united to oppose German occupation; yet, divided by ethnicity, religion, and ideology, they simultaneously opposed each other and sought post war dominance. A covert Allied team, including a Yugoslav expatriate, visited both camps in 1943. Returning to England, the team recommended that Tito be given Allied support. With Allied support Tito prevailed and served as Yugoslav's President until his death in 1980. Major Radovich worked for me during my OAR tour of duty. The following story comes from those OAR days.

> *"Tito considered Radovich, that expatriate team member, a traitor for being a Mihailovc partisan during the early days of German and Italian occupation of Yugoslavia. Randolph Churchill, Winston Churchill's son, led the Allied team. German initial attacks defeated the Yugoslav Air Force and Radovich, a Yugoslavian Air Force pilot; had continued to fight with Yugoslav Army ground forces and partisans; had escaped to England; had flown with the Royal Air Force and with the US Army Air Forces; and had been given a post war US citizenship and a US Air Force commission. He had recently received a letter from his father telling that he could return to Yugoslavia without fear. He decided to do so with a promise that he would call me each day. He gave me a telephone number and asked that I inform the State Department if his daily calls ceased. He visited his father and returned without trouble."*

Tito's reign, that of a benevolent dictator, forced an era of peace between ethnic groups. Under his leadership, Yugoslavia's economy thrived. At the time of our visit, clean city streets and well maintained infrastructure suggested prosperity. Government officials gave our class excellent briefings and presentations – the best received during our tour. Tensions between groups emerged after Tito's death in1980, the economy collapsed, and unrest and civil war followed.

The Class tour included Bonn and Berlin in Germany. An Allied agreement at the 1945 Potsdam Conference, divided Germany. It remained divided into East Germany and West Germany until 1990. During that period, Bonn served as the Capital of West Germany.

In Bonn, German Minister of Defense officials joined Class members, and senior German staff officers briefed the Class in the Minister of Defense's conference room, a large room with a table extending its full length. Drawn drapes, able to cover a full wall, revealed a wall map of Europe. That map presented a pre-war Germany. Without words, the map spoke a very clear message; *a divided Germany will not stand.* If officially announced, European and American governments would have rejected this 1969 politically incorrect message. In effect, the Germans were testing – probing for an American reaction to the idea of a unified Germany.

Among others, we met General Johannes Steinhoff, a leading German WWII fighter pilot who in the later days of the war; crashed a ME 262 jet fighter, was badly burned, and still showed facial burn scars. He served as Germany's Luftwaffe Chief of Staff and later commanded all Allied Air Forces in Central Europe.

Berlin, divided into a British Sector, a French Sector, an US Sector, and a Russian Sector, accessed the West by air or by road traffic through a fenced neutral corridor, through East Germany, connecting Berlin to West Germany. In time the Russian Sector became part of East Germany, and Berlin and the conduit to the West served as a pathway for 3.5 million Germans to escape socialists East Germany.

To stop loss of human capital, East Germany sealed its West Berlin boundary in 1961 with what became known as the Berlin Wall. At this wall in 1963, President Kennedy's remark, *"ich bin ein Berliner"* (I am a Berliner) cheered the world, and in 1987 President Reagan's remark *"Mr. Gorbachev, tear down this wall"* hastened its destruction in 1990.

The above picture, made from a popular viewing tower inside West Berlin, shows a portion of the wall. Note the windowless building to the right with WWII bomb damage yet to be repaired in 1969. Note the two rows of black obstacles bordering a space clear of all buildings. That clear space extended beside the full length of the wall. Firing from towers, snipers shot anyone entering this "Kill Zone." Hitler's suicide underground bunker lay below the empty, flat area just beyond the obstacle rows.

By treaty, western officials had a right of free access to East Germany. To protect and maintain that right, the US Commissioner encouraged US visiting officials to exercise that right and to visit East Germany. Class members did so. From the American Sector, Check Point Charlie, pictured right, served as our point of entry.

Passing through Check Point Charlie and a walk in East Berlin offered a stark contrast between East and West. A more prosperous portion of East Berlin at mid-day is pictured right. Note the absence of people on the street and the absence of economic activity. In contrast, West Berlin showed a beehive of busy people in office buildings, banks, prosperous retail outlets, and shoppers buying

goods. A strange experience; when meeting East Berliners on the street, they looked in all directions, seeing no police they made eye contact and smiled. With police nearby, they passed looking straight ahead without eye contact.

Pictured right is one of several impressive Russian War Memorials in East Berlin celebrating Russian soldiers who fought and died during the battle for Berlin. A total of 5,000 soldiers are buried here. Each square in the foreground is a mass grave for 1,000 soldiers. Note the statue standing in the distance.

In a closer view shown right, some of our Class members can be seen climbing steps leading to the statue base. The white hat, low center, is the uniform white cap of a War College staff member, a Navy Admiral, traveling with the Class. At lower left stand two Russian soldiers. Surprisingly, several Russians saluted as I walked within the memorial. Receiving and returning their salute

gave me an experience few Americans receive during a lifetime.

In England, during a visit to the Tower of London, a site of torture and death during the darker periods of English history, I viewed tools of ancient executioners. Within the castle's walls,

executioners beheaded seven or more royal personages, including Queen Ann Boleyn. Identities of others of lesser rank have long been lost to history. The rack remains within its walls. Strapped to the rack, it literally pulled prisoners apart. Common throughout England during days of old, thresh, the name given to wheat threshing straw, covered castle earthen ground floors. Those earthen floors served as burial ground for many executed. As I walked these now tile floors, torsos, heads, and limbs still slept below.

The tower houses the Crown Jewels of England on exhibit for public viewing. Pictured right are the Chair and some of the Regalia worn by Kings and Queens during coronations. These represent but a few crowns, scepters, and jewels on display.

The tower also houses armor worn by knights of old. Most suits clearly fitted small men, much less than six feet. One suit, worn by Henry VIII, stands heads above the crowd.

Piccadilly Circus of-
fered multiple, simul-
taneous, and strange
presentations. Here a
mummy wiggles and
turns promising to
escape from his
mummy wrap. I
watched for a while,
but my schedule did
not allow me to stay
to see that he escaped.

Perhaps the most awkward moment of my career occurred in
England. Our British briefing occurred in the Headquarters
building of a British Military Base outside of London. An American Army bus transported Class members from our hotel to the
British Base. An American staff car transported the senior member of our party, a Navy Admiral. Our bus arrived on schedule
with no staff car in sight. Protocol required the Admiral to lead
the class into the building, so we remained in the bus parked
about fifty yards from the building's entrance and waited, and
waited for perhaps thirty minutes.

The British welcoming group, seeing the bus, came out of the
building onto a portico and stood as a formal group and waited,
and waited. As time wore on, I and others needed a pit stop.
Eventually in ones and twos, we walked to the portico. Among
the first, as I approached the British group, the senior officer
asked *"Admiral?"* I answered *"No, Colonel Williams needing a
bathroom,"* breaking the formality, but the awkwardness remained. Eventually, the Admiral arrived and the briefing began. I
later learned that shopping had caused the delay. In my judgment, the Admiral had disrespected his Navy, the British, and all
Class members. Others held the same opinion.

In June Larry graduated from W. T. Woodson High School – the
school from which his brother Garthae had graduated with the

class of 1966. Pictured right, his mother stands proudly by the graduate. In August, he entered the freshman class of St. Andrews College in North Carolina. Though proud to see our children progress in life, an emptying nest saddened Rita and me.

All good things end; and in the Summer of 1969, the National War College Class of 69 approached its end. I received notification that my next duty station would be the Electronics Systems Division in Bedford, Massachusetts, a station from which Rita and I departed in 1961. Major General Henry Kushman, then a member of the Air Staff in the Pentagon, offered me a position in his office. I had worked for Lt. Col. Henry Kushman while at Eglin. With his rank and position, he could have my duty station changed from Bedford to the Pentagon.

Another fork in the road, a tour of duty on the Air Staff could be a career enhancement, and another promotion would need such an edge. A new Air Force Chief of Staff, General John D. Ryan, opined publically that the Air Force needed no new Air Force Generals from the WWII era. Though Promotion Boards made independent decisions, a known Chief's opinion would have a negative influence on my selection.

A Pentagon tour would require another four years in the Washington area; an area troubled by drugs in the neighborhoods and in the schools. Within the past year, a teenager in our neighborhood had died from a drug overdose in a nearby large drainage culvert. For the first time, Rita and I suppressed ambition and chose to move Gail, Roger, and Jeffrey out of the Washington area. Was the choice wise? No one ever knows what lay on a road not taken.

A long vacation allowed a visit to North Carolina followed by
Maryland outer shore camping on an undeveloped beach. Unfortunately, houses, condominiums, hotels, restaurants and retail
outlets now cover that beach, like so many Eastern shorelines.
Too bad.

In late Fall, we reported to the Electronic Systems Division before Bedford schools began.

Chapter 14
ELECTRONIC SYSTEMS DIVISION

A day's drive from Maryland's beach towing the travel trailer returned the family to Bedford, Massachusetts, in late July of 1969. The family moved into an on-base housing Cape Code, small but adequate for our diminished family, at 133 Patterson Drive on Hanscom Field. Within a few days Gail, Roger, and Jeffrey attended school classes. John Ford's family, living behind us on a street to our rear, brought Rita enjoy and a happy reunion with Dee and her family.

The family, again living in winters of heavy snow, enjoyed a big back yard that provided ample space for making snowmen. Across the street, directly in front of the home, a steep hill equipped with a rope tow provided front yard skiing.

Above Roger, to the left, and Jeffrey, to the right prepare for a downhill run on a most convenient slope.

Orders assigned me Director of several System Programs, all mature programs approaching full operational status. They included elements of my old friend, BMEWS, and a Sea Launched Missile Warning system comprised of radar sites along US east and west coasts. Fort Fisher, one of the radar sites designed to warn of missiles launched from submarines beneath off shore Atlantic waters, remained operational into the 1980s. In a later time, after retirement, my family vacationed on Fort Fisher in North Carolina. My office, located in Billerica, a twenty minute commute in good weather, could be an hour or more on a snowy morning.

Five months later, in December, my assignment changed to Director, Terminal Control System Program Office with offices conveniently located on Hanscom Field. The Terminal Control System's design promised a mobile radar system able to provide guidance, called ground-controlled approach, to pilots landing airplanes during conditions of low ceilings and poor visibility. The system's military nomenclature, TPN-19, will be used hereafter when referring to the system.

A ground-controlled approach (GCA) requires three major components; surveillance radar to provide aircraft position data within an airport local area; precision approach radar to provide runway alignment and glide slope elevation data during final approach; and a control unit to provide radar scope display, ground-to-air communications, and air-traffic controllers. Using surveillance radar data, controllers maintain local air control and sequence aircraft to final approach. Using precision approach radar data, controllers monitor final approach and give voice corrections to runway azimuth and glide slope elevation deviations. If necessary, a good controller and a good pilot can make a successful GCA approach in a near zero-ceiling and near zero-visibility weather condition.

GCA first came to my attention during the Okinawan Campaign with the installation of a GCA system on Ie Shima to provide Plum Field air traffic control. At the time, the 318th Group operated off Plum Field, but Group pilots had neither confidence in air-traffic controllers nor instrument flying skills needed to make the system work. To my knowledge, none of our pilots made an instrument approach under GCA guidance. The Plum Field GCA model, nomenclature AN/MPN-14, later installed on all Air Force Bases with up-grades and modifications, remained in service throughout the 20th Century. Not designed as a mobile system, the MPN-14 did not meet mobility needs of the Viet Nam War or the needs of a subsequent National Defense Fast Response Strategy.

The TPN-19, designed to meet this mobility need, configured the system in three shelters for transport on trailer flatbeds, for quick set up, and full operational status in a short period of time. Solid state technology made the needed downsizing possible.

The three shelters are pictured above deployed on Grenier Air Force Base in New Hampshire. The search radar shelter is pictured right. The precision radar shelter, without its antenna deployed, is in the foreground. The air traffic control shelter is in the rear.

The interior of the control shelter is pictured right. Radio equipment and radar scopes are arrayed along the left side of the shelter. Air-Traffic Controllers, from here, control local air traffic and give voice guidance to pilots during final approach and landing. Successful landings during periods of low ceilings and poor visibility require that: the system operates properly, the Air-Controller is proficient, the pilot has complete confidence in the controller, and the airplane is flown by a proficient instrument pilot.

Self-interest of others within and without the Air Force made the TPN-19 a controversial program. In 1970, wearied by war, the American public gave little support to the Viet Nam War or to large defense costs. Reduced funding for the Department of Defense forced Air Force R&D budget cuts. The multi-million dollar TPN-19 budget, secured by prior year appropriations, became a target for underfunded projects such as the F-15 fighter and AWACS, the Airborne Warning and Control System. TPN-19 critics abounded within the Pentagon, the Systems Command, and others within the Air Force seeking enhanced budgets from TPN-19 funds.

Historically Gillfillen, an ITT subsidiary, manufactured, provided spare parts, and maintained the MPN-14. ITT, the International Telephone and Teletype Company, viewed the TPN-19 as a threat to a lucrative business and joined the critic's choir. An ITT Lobbyist, Dita Beard, had access to the highest levels of government and to Congress.

A typical development includes a design phase, a prototype development phase, a test phase, a redesign phase, a production phase, and an operational phase. No one can expect the prototype development phase to produce a perfectly designed complex system. Initial program plans include defined tests, test funding, and redesign funding. A program is vulnerable during its test phase. Ever present critics seek, find, magnify, and use any test failure to discredit the system.

My role became more that of an advocate, rather than that of a manager. During my stewardship, with the TPN-19 program in its test phase, somewhere within the Hanscom community a mole existed. Critics learned test results by the time they reached my desk. I have never known who leaked those results. My friend John Ford knew, but he would never tell.

Officials, at Command level, at Air Staff level, and by Congress questioned the system's viability. Senior Air Force officials, fearing damage to their careers, chose not to become involved. In Congress, the House Armed Forces Committee became an actor. Correspondence prepared by Committee Staff, signed by Committee Chairman, Mendel Rivers, addressed to Air Force's Congressional Liaison Officer, floated to my desk for action. At times, action required my briefing the Command and/or the Air Staff. At one time I briefed a House Armed Forces Committee Sub-Committee.

At other times, action required my visit to the Liaison Officer's office in the Pentagon to prepare a letter, to be signed by the Liaison Officer, in response to Congressional correspondence. By and large Chairman Rivers, informed by two decades of experience, knew the critics' motivation and supported me. At times, I visited his staff and prepared a response to an AF Congressional Liaison Officer's letter for Chairman Rivers' signature.

One issue achieved much traction. When operational, the new GCA system would operate in areas populated with the old existing MPN-14 system. Critics charged that signals transmitted by the old system would generate noise in the new system, making both inoperable. I prepared a highly technical briefing based on solid state filter theory, passed it through my Commander, through the System Command's staff in Washington, and briefed Major General Pascal in the Pentagon. His entire staff rejected my argument and insisted on a redesign. Giving some credence to my argument, yet unwilling to oppose his staff, General Pascal postponed a decision.

Returning to Hanscom, on inquiry I learned of an MPN-14 in operation on Grenier Air Force Base in New Hampshire, the location of a prototype TPN-19, then undergoing test. I called General Pascal and invited him to visit Grenier to see the new system in operation. He came. I sat him down in front of a radar scope and asked, *"What do you think of that display?"* He answered, *"Great – great clarity."* I then pointed to an occasional tiny streak across the screen and explained that it came from an MPN-14 located on base directly across the runway. He said, *"I will be dammed."* From that point forward, the interference issue never arose again.

During the Summer of 1972, a Systems Command inspection team visited Hanscom, inspected my program files, visited Raytheon, the Prime Contractor, and prepared an Inspection Report. Protocol required the team to present their findings to my commander, General Joe Cody, before leaving Hanscom. Using hand drawn flip charts on an easel, the team chief briefed General Cody, his staff, and me. He described a poorly managed program heading for disaster.

The briefing ended – followed by a long period of silence. Finally General Cody asked, *"Durwood, have you anything to say?"* Answering *"Yes,"* I walked to the podium and asked the team chief, *"May I use your flip charts?"* With a look of surprise, he answered, *"Yes."* Turning all flip charts over, I answered one-by-one with another briefing. Another long period of silence followed. Finally, General Cody asked, *"Durwood, are you going to tomorrow's briefing?"* I answered, *"Yes."* General Cody stood and walked out of the conference room. Nothing more was said.

General Cody had referenced the team's schedule to brief the System Command's Staff the following morning in Washington. I attended and heard the team chief give my briefing. Nothing more was heard from the inspection.

During April of 1972, a briefing tour included, in order: the Air Force Communications Service, the Air Force Air Material Command, and the Air Force Systems Command. At the time, the TPN-19 approached its production and deployment to the Communications Service for operation and to the Air Material Command for logistic support. Only the Communications Service offered positive program support. While briefing the System

214

Command's Senior Staff, tired and frustrated, I remarked that senior Command Staff members and Air Staff members should take a position and either cancel the program or support the program. Otherwise their responsibilities remained unmet.

Though true, my comments were not tactful and proved to be unwise. When entering my office the following morning, an urgent message waited asking me to report to General Shielly, my then commanding officer. I reported.

> *He advised me to get out of the Systems Command immediately. Else, I would be assigned to the most undesirable location within the Systems Command. He had already talked to General Stoney, Commander of the Air Force Communications Service, who was willing to give me a safe harbor.*

I agreed, and Special Orders A-283, dated 3 May 1972 transferred me to the Communications Service. Thus, my career with the Air Force's research and development community ended.

Until recent days, I never looked back to wonder what happened to TPN-19. While writing this chapter, curiosity prevailed; and with little research learned that the program ended successfully, systems were deployed and remained in operation throughout the 20th Century and into the 21st Century. The MPN-14 likewise remains in use into the 21st Century.

In May of this 2013 year, the Air Force awarded Raytheon a $50 million contract for the development of a new, highly mobile control system that will replace both the TPN-19 and the MPN-14 systems. A normal development cycle is three to four years, depending upon priority. Therefore, both TPN-19 and MPN-14 systems will likely remain in service through year 2016 or beyond.

Radio conversation between GCA ground controllers and pilots is standard and highly stylized. Airway flight paths are standard. A holding pattern is an oval racetrack anchored on a radio fix.

Published letdown procedures, known by controllers and pilots alike, are standard for each airfield. Therefore, radio traffic is minimized. On the following page a typical radio sequence begins as a flight from Dayton, Ohio, to Andrews AFB in Maryland approaches a radio fix over Dulles, Virginia. The active Andrews' runway runs north-south. The first 4 exchanges are initiated by a Washington Traffic Controller. Sequences 5 through 8 are initiated by an Andrews GCA area traffic controller. The remaining sequences are initiated by an Andrews GCA final approach controllers. Bold letters represent a controller's voice.

TYPICAL GCA RADIO TRAFFIC

1. Air Force 456123 – This is Washington Control
Washington Control – This is Air Force 456123
Air Force 456123 is cleared to Dulles VOR – maintain 25,000 feet
Roger Washington – cleared to Dulles at 25,000
2. Air Force 123 – Washington Control
Washington – Force 123
Air Force 123 – Hold 180 radial at 25,000
Roger Washington – Hold 180 radial at 25,000
3. Air Force 123 – Washington Control
Washington – Force 123
123 Cleared to 20,000 feet – hold 180 radial
Roger Washington – hold 180 radial at 20,000
4. Air Force 123 – Washington Control
Washington – Force 123
123 cleared to Andrews's outer marker at 2,000 feet –
Contact Andrews Channel 5
Roger Washington – 123 cleared to Andrews's outer market at 2,000 –
Going to Andrews Channel 5 – Thanks and goodnight
5. Air Force 456123 – This is Andrews control
Andrews – This is Air Force 456123
Air Force 123 – I have you on radar –
Nearing 360 – maintain 2,000
Roger Andrews
6. Force 123 – Turn left to 360 – maintain 2,000
Roger Andrews – steering 360 – holding 2,000
7. Force 123 – drifting left of course steer 06 degrees
Roger – 123 steering 06 degrees
8. Force 123 – on course steer 03 degrees
Roger Andrews – 123 steering 03 degrees
9. Force 123 – You are on course steer 02 degrees
Roger Andrews – 123 steering 02 degrees
9. Air Force 456123 – This is your final controller – how do you read
Force 123 – loud and clear
10. Force 123 – you are on course and on glide slope – begin your descent
Do not respond to further transmissions
Roger Andrews
11. Force 123 drifting right – steer 360 degrees
12. Force 123 – on course – steer 01 degrees
13. Force 123 drifting below glide slope – decrease rate of descent
14. Force 123 – on course above glide slope – increase rate of descent
15. Force 123 – on course – on glide slope
16. Force 123 – Crossing threshold – takeover and land
Thanks control – good run – good evening

High Flight

Oh! I have slipped the surly bonds of earth
And danced the skies on laughter-slivered wings;
Sunward I've climbed, and joined the tumbling mirth
Of sun-split clouds – and done a hundred things
You have not heard of – wheeled and soared and swung
High in sunlit silence. Hov'ring there,
I've chased the shouting wind along, and flung
My eager craft through footless halls of air.
Up, up the long, delirious, burning blue
I've topped the wing-swept heights with easy grace
Where never lark, or even eagle flew –
And, while with silent lifting mine I've trod
The high untrespassed sanctity of space,
Put out my hand and touched the face of God.

RAF Pilot Officer John Magee – 1941

Chapter 15
AF COMMUNICATIONS SERVICE

A hurried departure from Bedford left the travel trailer in a Hanscom boat storage lot. Rita, Roger, Jeffrey and I departed in mid-May. Gail, having graduated from Bedford High School in June of 1970, resided in Greenville, North Carolina, completing her second college year at East Carolina University. Garthae still attended North Carolina State University in Raleigh, North Carolina.

Larry, an Air Force Sergeant assigned to Wurtsmith Air Force Base, resided in Oscoda, Michigan. The Wurtsmith main gate is pictured top right. Below, alert B-52s sit ready for launch.

Larry served as a Missile Systems Analyst tasked to insure that Hound Dog missiles loaded on strategic B-52 bombers, if launched, could destroy their targets. William Green, my

1950s University of Michigan classmate, served as the Hound Dog missile's system program manager. His children, rock-and-roll teenagers during Elvis Presley's performing days, named the missile Hound Dog.

219

Reporting for duty 21 July 1972, after an extended vacation in North Carolina, I became Director of Programs, HQ, Air Force Communications Service (AFCS) on Richards-Gebaur Air Force Base. Richards-Gebaur, located in Missouri 17 miles  southeast of Kansas City, offered on-base housing on Bong Street. So! The move required no house hunting.

However, the house offered no garage space for the MG automobile. Unwilling to let it endure the ravages of weather, I constructed a small custom shelter, and the sheltered MG happily rested in a Base storage lot for boats and travel  trailers. The MG remained in storage throughout our Richards-Gebaur tour of duty.

AFCS organizational components residing on Richards-Gebaur included its Headquarters and the Headquarters of its operational organization, the 1842 Electrical Engineering Group. Though relatively a young command, AFCS commanded the 1842 Electrical Engineering Group, a very old organization in earlier days known as GEEIA, the Air Force Ground Equipment Engineering and Installation Agency. The Director of Programs, a  member of the Command Staff, planned, budgeted for, and authorized installation programs. I served in this role until assigned in1974 Commander of the 1842 Electrical Engineering Group.

This, my first command assignment, brought a new experience. A Commander is not only responsible for mission performance, but is also responsible for the wellbeing of all men and family members within his command. I was blessed, however, with senior Civil Service staff members who willingly helped me survive.

During my tour, we managed hundreds of active installation projects, both domestic and foreign: cable, microwave and tropospheric transmission system projects, air traffic control system projects, and air defense system projects. Most overseas projects promised to satisfy country-to-country Foreign Military Sales agreements between the US and England, Germany, Spain, Iran, and other countries.

AFCS gave me a new experience. Heretofore, my work community had been Pentagon, Command, and Center staff officer and contractor personnel. Exposure to military equipment had been limited to prototype testing prior to production. Current duty included responsibilities for installing and operating production equipment. The physics of signal transmitting and receiving systems demand siting in remote locations, away from highly populated areas. Visits to project installation and operating sites, often necessary, gave me a view of remote England, Germany, Spain, and Iran.

On German farms, I saw turnip storage techniques in use much like sweet potato storage techniques I saw, when a boy, use by North Carolina farmers. Piled in a pyramid, covered by straw, covered by earth, accessed by a small tunnel, potatoes survived the winter's cold. In Spain, hams hanging in small bars mimicked hams hanging in my father's smokehouse – both in look and taste. My father's ham curing method dated from Spanish culture left by early Spanish explorers who roamed from Florida to North Carolina.

In rural England, the English Cottage with a thatched roof still provided shelter for English families. This architecture and roof technology is centuries old. Ancient castles appear in unexpected places, and portions of Hadrian's Wall still stand.

Richards-Gebaur, a small base, offered a united community with a good spirit and healthy, inspiring activities available for all ages. Jeffrey, a Pop Warner football team member, pictured right, wears his football togs. For each league team, a cheer-

leading team of little girls gave sideline support. Jeff stands by our second car, a red Ford, purchased from the Command's chief scientist.

During game time, Jeff's cheering team cheer as the game plays out.

Early into the tour, the AFCS Commander, General Stoney, called me into his office and told me to go to Spain and resolve a Spanish complaint concerning an AFCS project to upgrade Spain's air defense system. By country-to-country correspondence, Spain had expressed great dissatisfaction with a US Foreign Military Sales contract performance. A US Navy destroyer delivery required a tow into a Spanish port. A recent Spanish news article pictured a senior Spanish Air Force Officer welcoming delivery of US airplanes while standing beside one riddled with bullet holes – embarrassing the Spanish Air Force.

At the time, Francisco Franco, head of the one man ruled Spanish State and a devout Catholic, held strong convictions and much power. Tossing litter subjected one to a long jail term picking up trash from clean city streets and highways. He demanded citizens follow a high moral code. Selling or buying Playboy constituted a serious crime; equally so if caught reading a black market issue.

The AFCS Project purposed to upgrade Spain's air defense system: radars, control centers, and an interconnecting communications network. Although behind schedule and over cost, Spain's major complaint concerned a radar site located near Barcelona close to the Mediterranean Sea. Project team members, consorting with Norwegian blonds on the Mediterranean Costa Dorado coast, conflicted with Franco's moral code.

Travelling as Military Airlift Command passengers, a team of three, including two senior staff members familiar with Spain, and me, arrived on Torrejon, an US air base located near Madrid. Here, we rented an automobile and drove to Madrid. As we drove, my first view of Spain's countryside reminded me of New Mexico.

The following day, after a visit to the US Embassy, the team commenced a tour of each project installation site, the first being the office of the in-country Project Manager. On arrival, he presented a well prepared presentation: status, schedules, budgets, in-country policy constraints, and other project issues.

The tour continued from east to west. Pictured right, a tropospheric transmission site located on Spain's northeastern coast scans the Atlantic talking to the Azores. By and large, the team found dedicated technicians and high quality installation work at each project site.

The tour's last site, located in northeastern Spain near Barcelona, is close to the Mediterranean Sea. The route from Madrid to Barcelona initially follows a dry riverbed between two low mountain ranges. The landscape might persuade New Mexico or West

Texas natives that they had returned home and that they traveled along the Rio Grande. The sense of being in Spain, perhaps, persuaded early Spanish explorers to continue up the Rio Grande

The team's out briefing noted that the project faced three problems: behind schedule; over cost; and technicians consorting with women on nearby beaches breached Franco's moral code. The team judged the third to be the most serious. Disapproved by Spain's highest levels of government, Spain's government-to-government correspondence included it as a major complaint. Unless corrected, the problem would fester, grow, and become public. If allowed to continue, it could put at risk the careers of the technicians, the in-country Project Manager, and senior AFCS staff members.

The team recommended a six day work week and longer weekday work hours until the project returned to schedule. This would correct the schedule problem and stabilize costs. The team also recommended that technicians working the radar site near Barcelona learn that their conduct, known by high level US and Spanish government officials, may go public. The team also recommended restricting the technicians to the installation site until site project completion. The in-country project manager agreed with the team's assessment and recommendations. The team returned home and submitted a report to the Commander. I heard nothing more from Spain.

Rita enjoyed a strong and active Officer's Wives Club. Club activities included regular luncheons at the Officer's Club and visits to Kansas City sites of interest and elegant fashion shops. Periodic fashion shows, sponsored by the Club, highlighted Rita and other club members serving as fashion models.

224

Light traffic in our neighborhood made the entire neighborhood, streets included, serve as a large playground. Roger, riding his unicycle, made the street in front of our home his racetrack.

A 150 mile drive west across Kansas plains placed the family in Abilene, Kansas, for a visit to General Dwight Eisenhower's boyhood home and Presidential Library. Pictured right, Rita and Jeffrey stand in front of the Library, Rita carrying her white pocketbook and Jeffrey standing beside her.

I had expected General Eisenhower's home in early life, pictured right, to be quite modest. Born in 1890 into an improvised family in Denison, Texas, when but an infant, he moved with his family to Abilene, Kansas. The plaque, pictured low-right, declares this his family's home from 1898 to 1948. Clearly, at some point in time, the family became well-to-do.

The Von Stubben Hotel, located in Stuttgart, Germany, served as home base while visiting installation sites in Germany. Operated by the US Army, it has provided a German home away from home for US Military since the end of WWII.

Aircraft, ferrying service members home after long years in Viet Nam prisoner of war camps, often landed on Richards-Gebaur for fuel. The Richards-Gebaur stop gave the POW's their first emotional step on American soil since leaving Viet Nam. Given a large formal welcome as they

deplaned for a short on-base visit while the airplane refueled, many kneeled and kissed the tarmac. As spectators, Jeffrey, Roger, Rita and I found ourselves, in a real sense, first touched by the Viet Nam war.

A 1974 agreement between the US and Iran initiated a new Foreign Military Sales project with a mission to modernize Iran's national telecommunications, air defense, and air traffic control systems. Leading another team of three, I traveled to Iran charged with a mission to discover and document the technical configuration of existing systems and the operational requirements that new, modernized systems needed to meet. These data would provide; a basis for an engineering design of the new systems: a request for industry proposals, and a contract to upgrade current systems to meet Iran's requirements. This mission generated two tasks. One task required visits to control centers, visits to telecommunication transmit sites, and receive sites, and visits to radar sites scattered across the whole of Iran. The second task required discussions with Iranian senior military and government officials to define and document new-system requirements.

Traveling by commercial air to Teheran, the team set up home base in a modern Teheran hotel having all amenities found in US and European hotels. Protocol required a visit to the American Embassy. Learning that we would travel throughout Iran, the Embassy staff cautioned that away from Teheran, we could expect poor hygiene. The staff identified the better lodging throughout the country and recommended we drink buttermilk as a health sustaining drink, and that we could buy bottled butter-milk throughout Iran wherever soft drinks where sold.

Conferencing with senior Iranian military officers and senior government officials, we selected system site locations to visit and developed a travel itinerary. The Iranians assigned a comfortable twin-engine passenger airplane, a crew, and an Iranian Air Force Major to the team. By and large, all sites selected were located in remote locations, some road distance from the nearest airport. The itinerary included cities and towns having airports from which we could reach one or more sites of interest by automobile. During the tour, the Major served as interpreter and as logistician to arrange for security, staff cars, and reservations for lodging, and meals.

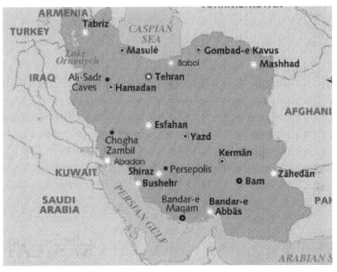

The aircraft's itinerary included towns marked by a bright sun in the above map. In the west they included: Tabriz in the north near the Soviet Union and Turkish borders, Abadan bordering Iraq near the upper shore of the Persian Gulf, and Bushier bordering the Persian Gulf opposite Saudi Arabia. Mid-east sites included: Babol to the north near the Caspian Sea, Esfahan south of Teheran, Shiraz and Bandar Abbas near the Straights of Hermuz. Sites in the east included: Meshhad in the north east near the Soviet Union and Zahedan near the border between Afghanistan and Pakistan.

The Major proved a good logistician. At each town, a staff car and lodging reservations waited. In smaller, remote towns, small two story inns having perhaps 25 rooms offered primitive lodging accommodations. Room occupants shared a common bathroom that often had no running water – only large water urns and circular holes in the floor served as toilets. By and large, they served good food and buttermilk. I do not recall any team member becoming sick.

Iran-Iraq border disputes have continued for centuries and continue today. Travel and visits to western sites along the Iraqi border incurred a notable sense of anxiety among the crew and those we met during our site visits. A hot dispute concerning the border along the Tigris River near Abadan, ongoing while we were in-country, motivated armed Iranian military vehicles to escort our road trip to and from Abadan and our visit to a nearby radar installation.

The tour offered some delights, such as inexpensive caviar from the Caspian Sea available in Babol and a weekend spent in a luxurious Bandar Abbas hotel on the shore of the Straights of Hermuz watching a stream of tankers carrying oil pass through the straights. Built for tourist's trade, the hotel offered all amenities found in US and European hotels.

While in Shariz a non-working side trip to the ruins of Persepolis gave me, one who likes history, a great experience. The site of ancient Persepolis, the capital of early Persian empires, is about eighty miles northeast of Shiraz – see map on previous page. Persepolis, served as the ceremonial capital of the first Persian Empire. This empire, founded by Cyrus the Great, extended from western India to Egypt and Greece. As the Empire expanded; it destroyed the Babylonian Empire; captured Babylon where Jews lived in captivity and Darius befriended Daniel; and destroyed the Acropolis in Athens, Greece. Kings, often mentioned in the Bible, ruled here. They included Cyrus, Xerxes, and Artaxerxes. Cyrus allowed the Jews to return to Jerusalem. Alexandra the Great captured Persepolis in 330 BC, and to revenge the destruction of the Acropolis, he destroyed the city.

Flying above the Iranian desert teaches old history and history in the making. While over the desert I noticed what appeared to be spall thrown up by a string of bomb impacts. Rows of craters extended for fifty miles or more from highlands across the desert to small green cultivated areas. Evenly spaced and of identical size they formed a straight line across the desert. By inquiry, I learned that the craters are footprints of Qanats, water systems centuries old, dating back to Biblical time.

Finding a water source at an elevation above desert floor, a tunnel dug between successive shafts connected the source to an exit in the desert miles away downhill. Still existing, water flows through these tunnels from their source to make possible garden spots in the desert. The tunnels require constant upkeep – making constant work for a profession long held by generations of family members.

Likewise, viewed from high above the desert, large sections of desert appeared light green – showing signs of new plant growth. This new growth resulted from the White Revolution, a reform program initiated by the Shah in 1963 to modernize Iranian society, by among other things, educating the peasantry, redistributing land, and reclaiming the desert. By centuries of overgrazing, much of Iran once verdant with grass and forest, became desert. By making sections of the desert off limits to goat, sheep, and cattle grazing, the land began healing.

An unbelievable primitive society still exists in eastern Iran. Roads, not much more than sheep and goat paths, make travel by automobile difficult. Traveling from nearby towns to visit one or more sites, the driver, anticipating flats, carried several extra tires already mounted on wheels ready to roll. Often, one or more tires required change. During one trip, during a tire change, a family appeared from out the desert, crossed the road about the length of a football field before us, and disappeared into the desert.

A donkey, a man, and a woman carried large loads. Children carried small loads. That family, living a nomadic life not different from that of Biblical times, travel day by day, carries all of their possessions. They walk slowly from water hole to water hole as their flock of goats and sheep graze. They camp each night at a water hole. Overnight, the family and flock quench thirst, rest, and prepare for another day's journey to the next water hole.

Returning from another site, with the last extra tire running on the road while yet some distance to town and hotel, the driver stopped in a small village to have flats fixed. While waiting, a villager, I understood to be the village Police Chief, invited the team to attend a show in a small local theater. We accepted.

Leading us into the theater and down an aisle to the front row of seats, the Chief shouted some commands. All seated on the front row stood and left. We sat. With some help from the Major, I understood the gist of the story line. The story compared village life existing before the White Revolution, to village life after the White Revolution. Each time the audience heard the term "White Revolution" they cheered with much enthusiasm. The cheering convinced me, and I remain convinced, that I heard authentic cheering, and that the Shah's reforms had indeed improved the people's lives. However, I still wonder if I experienced a staged bit of propaganda.

With the site tour completed, meetings began with senior military and government officials with a purpose to define all functions the new system need perform. These requirements became drivers during system design. Iranian officials quickly stated, agreed to, and documented all functions except educational television, a requirement to make education by television available throughout Iran, even into the most remote areas.

The religious leaders of Iran, fearing loss of control over an educated citizenry, vehemently opposed educational television. Their opposition divided Government officials. Some argued to include educational television in the set of requirements. Some, fearing an uprising of Islamists provoked by their religious leaders, argued against including the television requirement. The debate continued for several days.

Extended debate offered the team an opportunity to visit Tehran as tourists. A huge Bazaar, a unique market in tents common in the Near East, offered many things. I purchased jewelry for Rita and odd items for my children.

One evening, the American Embassy called and advised the team to remain in the hotel throughout the following day. We did so and watched a day long parade of men marching on streets below our hotel patio. As they marched, they rhythmically beat their backs; some with leather straps, and some with chains. They blooded their backs by repeated strokes. I later learned that the day celebrated "Day of Ashura," a day of mourning for the death of Muhammad's grandson during a battle in Iraq during the seventh century. Advice to remain in our hotel proved wise. With streets of Tehran filled with a frenzied mob of irrational men, both young and old, I remained happy to avoid the mob.

Final, approved system requirements included the educational television function, and the team returned to Richards-Gebaur. In time, the team's report would inform a Request for Proposal, Industry would bid, and a Foreign Military Sales contract would be consummated. My faint memory tells me that International Telephone and Telegraph (ITT) won the contract. When the Iranian revolution of 1979 disposed the Shah, the building housing the contractor's in-country program office became the first to burn, and the Mullahs of Iran won the educational television argument.

The Crown Jewels of Iran remain my most astonishing experience in Iran. The jewels open for public viewing in a large two-story building, fill both floors with row-after-row of display cases filled with beautiful jewels, many mounted. Many others, not mounted, fill jewel encrusted bowls. Pictured on the following page is a miniscule sample of the jewelry and artifacts on display. One cannot touch the throne of early kings without touching a ruby, a diamond, or some other precious jewel. Pearls, the size of eggs, display labels in ancient Arabic script with names of Xerxes and other ancient Persian kings.

The family returned to North Carolina in May of 1974 to participate in two family milestone events. Gail graduated, in the rain in the football stadium, as a Physical Therapist from East Carolina University. Pictured right, graduates are marching

eventually to fill all available seats. Note umbrellas in stadium stands.

After the graduation exercises, Rita and I walked Rita's memory lane on the campus and Greenville streets. As we walked, a young man, running as a deer, approached, ran by and smiled as he passed. Later that evening, we met that young man, Gail's friend Barry Johnson.

The trip offered an opportunity to visit Rita's mother and my parents. Time spent with them rewarded all. However, their farm life had changed. No longer a close community of tenant and farmer families working together for a common harvest, machinery had replaced manual labor and farm life, though more efficient, seemed somewhat sterile.

Garthae's June marriage to Sheila Hodge in Charlotte became the second family milestone. In Charlotte, the Williams family attended a wedding rehearsal and a wedding. Pictured right, my family includes a

new daughter. In time they gave us a grandson, Nicholas, and granddaughters, Crystal and Amber.

For Christmas of 1974, the entire family gathered on Richards-Gebaur. Larry drove his Corvette from Denver. Gail, Garthae, and Sheila came from North Carolina by commercial air. A skiing trip to the Steamboat ski resort followed a family Christmas celebration.

While siblings graced mountain tops, Sheila skied bunny slopes. All family members skied except Rita. After years of trying without success, she remained content in the apartment or in the ski lodge.

Resulting from an early 1975 Air Force reorganization, the AF Communications Service lost its command status, became an agency of the Military Airlift Command, and initiated plans to move to Scott Air Force Base located in Illinois 20 miles East of St. Louis. Rita and I faced another fork in the road: should we make another military move or should we retire? The loss of my organization's command status further reduced my already slim chance of promotion. After twenty-seven years living as tumbleweeds, Rita looked forward to a more stable life. We chose to retire.

On Saturday, 27 June, a retirement parade honored me and six other retiring men.

Rita sat in bleachers and watched as AFCS marched in review.

Preparation for a move commenced with first order of business: to choose a permanent home location. Back to Sampson County, NC, or to some other location? With Roger in high school and Jeffrey in grade school looking forward to college within a few years, we chose Raleigh and its proximity to great universities.

The MG, removed from its cocoon and placed on a trailer, prepared itself for the road. A moving van arrived on schedule and our active Military duty ended.

During my military career, the Army and Air Force together awarded me the Legion of Merit, the Distinguished Flying Cross, the Air Medal with three Oak Leaf Clusters, the Asiatic-Pacific Campaign Medal, the WWII Victory Medal, the American Campaign Medal, the AF Commendation Medal, the National Defense Service Medal, the AF Outstanding Unit Award, and the Longevity Service Award with one Silver and one Bronze Oak Cluster.

The first eight medals listed are pictured on the opposite page in order of rank from left to right and from top to bottom.

Breathes there a man with soul so dead,
Who never to himself has said:
"This is my own, my country land!"
Whose heart hath ne'er within him burned,
As home his footsteps he has turned
From wandering on a foreign strand?

Sir Walter Scott

237

Do you thrill when the marching feet
Of jubilant soldiers shake the street,
And the bugles shrill, and the trumpets call,
And the red, white, and blue is over all?
Do you pray, amid starting tears,
May it never be furled through age-long years?

A song for our flag – our country's boast,
That gathers beneath it a mighty host;
Long may it wave o'er this goodly land
We hold in fee 'neath our Father's hand.

For God and liberty evermore.
May that banner stand from shore to shore,
Never to those high meanings lost,
Never with alien standards crossed
But always valiant and pure and true
Our starry flag: red, white, and blue.

Margaret E Sangster

Chapter 16
RETIREMENT

A Williams' caravan departed Richards-Gebaur during the first week in July. Driving her Lincoln, Rita towed a U-Haul filled with clothes, personal items, and household goods. Driving the red Ford, I towed a trailer carrying the MG.

Arriving in Raleigh, we met Gail at her apartment at The Lakes, an apartment complex in North Raleigh. In the same apartment complex an apartment, rented by Gail some weeks before our arrival, waited for my family. The U-Haul load provided household goods needed to set up light housekeeping in the apartment.

The first order of business, to find and chose a house, gave Rita another opportunity to shop and select a house of her choice. It pleased me that she could to do so, but weeks passed with picky house hunting unable to find a satisfactory house. In May, Carolina Power and Light Company delayed construction of Shearon Harris, a nuclear power plant 20 miles southwest of Raleigh. The delay forced a nuclear engineer, now without a job in Raleigh, to sell a recently purchased Raleigh house and relocate to some other area.

Rita liked the house, and we bought it. A wise choice, the house pictured right after a snow storm, had the master bedroom on the ground level. In time, that became a godsend when Rita lost her mobility and became confined to the first floor.

Moving in and setting up housekeeping in our new home, Rita and I looked forward to easy living, playing golf, travel, and doing other fun activities. Rita purchased a new set of golf clubs and began golf lessons. A golf instructor stood too close behind and, on her back swing, Rita knocked the instructor to the ground. The event so disturbed Rita that she no longer played golf.

After years of challenging, productive work, retirement became a bore. I welcomed a job offer by the Computer Sciences Corporation (CSC) located in Falls Church, Virginia, within the Washington DC beltway. However, informed by experience during previous Washington area duty, Rita and I chose not to return Roger and Jeffrey to a drug infested neighborhood. Bored, with skinny bank accounts and with Roger's and Jeffrey's college expenses looming, Rita and I chose to accept the job offer. I rented a small apartment located in Falls Church near CSC and began to commute; to Falls Church Sunday evenings and to Raleigh Friday evenings. Such commuting continued for seven years by carpool, surprisingly always full with others on standby hoping that someone might drop out of the pool so that they might join.

CSC, an old and large company, provides information technology services and professional services to foreign and domestic customers, including consulting services to the Department of Defense. At the time, two satellite communication systems, one to be operated by the Defense Communication Agency (DCA), the other by the Navy, in their infancy contracted for professional services. My work assignments included consulting work for DCA and the Navy relative to these systems.

Within the first year, needing a hardware item, I entered a hardware store located directly across the street from CSC's office building and surprisingly met John Ford. He owned the business, a franchise store. After greetings and "how are you?" he remarked that, by low sales and cash register skimming, his company earned no profit, rather it lost money. I suggested that he sell his business and work for CSC. He did. As a CSC Branch

Manager, I persuaded CSC to hire him and assign him to my Branch. The by-chance meeting reconnected Rita and me to John and his family.

Occasionally, visiting me in Falls Church, Rita shopped and lunched with friend of old, Dee Ford. Dee, a great equestrian, owned Bell, a lovely Arabian, and rode in horse shows in  and around Washington. Dee sat her horse well.

Another family milestone passed in February of 1976 when Gail married Barry Johnson, her friend since college days, in Raleigh and we gained another son. In time, they would give us a granddaughter, Amy, a grandson, Bradford, a great grandson James, and a great granddaughter, Piper. Among the wedding guests, pictured left above and seen from left to right Gail's: Uncle Dallie Baggett, Grandfather and Grandmother Williams, and Aunt Jewel Williams Hawley.

Another pleasant surprise, while having dinner at nearby Fort Myer, I met Richard Bennett, an old friend since our days at the Office of Aerospace Research. Divorced, recently back from a tour in Vietnam, he needed a friend to talk to, and I spent time with him listening. Our friendship deepened and continued until he died. Requested by his son, Toney, I wrote a portion of an eulogy read during his funeral at the Arlington National Cemetery.

Rita's personality began to change in 1978. She lost her self-confidence, initiative, and interest in daily activities, both in the home and outside the home. After visits to and treatment by Psychologists she improved, but not back to earlier days. Hoping to bring back her zest for living, I rebalanced my work, commute, and home life schedule, in an effort to enrich her life. CSC allowed me to work some weeks at home on unclassified material; a common practice now, but unheard of in those days.

Taking leave from work in the spring of 1979, she and I visited Israel with party members who came from our church and from other North Carolina churches. Dr. Scoggins, a Wake Forest Seminary professor and a Biblical Scholar who had for years studied and lived in Israel, led the party. He lectured during an educational tour of the Holy Land that visited Biblical sites ranging from Beersheba in the south to Jerusalem, from Jerusalem to Hazor in the north, from Caesarea on the Mediterranean coast to Capernaum on the Sea of Galilee, and from Capernaum to Jericho.

A flight from New York landed us in Tele Aviv on Israel's Mediterranean coast. In a hotel at dinner during the evening, General Moshe Dayan, with his black eye patch, sat at a table near Rita and me. I knew of him. In years past he had served with distinction as Chief of Staff of the Israel Defense Forces during wars with the Arabic states.

The ancient city of Jerusalem, a first priority site to visit, is pictured on the previous page as viewed looking north-west. Note the south-eastern corner of the ancient city wall as seen in the center-right portion of the picture. The bright dome, upper-center, is the golden dome of a Muslim mosque; it dominates the Old City. This Mosque, the Dome of the Rock, sits on the site of the Jewish second temple, destroyed by the Romans in 70 BC. The dome covers a large rock from which the Muslims believe the Prophet Mohammed ascended to heaven in the company of the Angel Gabriel.

Photographing the Mosque is forbidden. Pictured right, a scaled construction model of the Mosque still stands on the Mosque courtyard. Encouraged to reverently enter the Mosque, Rita and I did so holding hands, a no-no. An attendant politely separated our hands. He also pointed out a depression on the rock believed to be Mohammed's footprint.

An ancient Roman amphitheater is pictured above left. Sitting in the stand looking toward the stage, the Mediterranean Sea shows in the background of the picture to the right, and in the foreground stand members of our tour party. The location, the site of Caesarea by the Sea, represents the remains of a major Roman seaport. St. Peter preached here and the Romans imprisoned St. Paul here for two years.

Throughout history, water has been a precious commodity west of the river Jordan and eastern mountains. Portions of an aqueduct, built by Romans to carry water from eastern mountains to Caesarea, still stand as a monument to the skills of Roman engineers.

By nature, desert covers much of Israel and looks much like west Texas. In ancient times the camel, the work animal of choice,

traveled for days without water and survived by grazing sparse desert vegetation. Pictured right Rita rides a standing camel with adequate style, not so as the camel stood. One mounts a camel as it squats on the desert. Getting up, the camel's back legs rise first; placing the saddle at forty-five degrees with the rider facing the desert floor. However she hung on, without needing the watchful camel driver's help.

The tour included a visit to the site of ancient Caesarea Philippi located twenty-five miles north of the Sea of Galilee at the southeastern base of Mount Herman. Spring water flowing from a cave is the largest Jordan River water source. Throughout ancient time Pagan, Jewish, Greek, and Roman cities thrived on this site. Carvings from ancient time remain on the vertical mountain cliff. The site is within the northern portion of the Golan Heights near the Lebanese border. To reach Caesarea Philippi, our party crossed a bridge over the Jordan River and traveled through the disputed Heights. At Caesarea Philippi, Jesus said to Peter, *"You are the rock on*

which I will build my Church." Standing next to the cliff and looking east, one sees the distant desert littered with large rocks. Those rocks could well have prompted Jesus' choice of words.

"Matthew 16:17 – And Jesus answered and said unto him, "Blessed art thou, Simon Barona, for flesh and blood hath not revealed it unto thee, but my Father which is in Heaven. 16:18 – And I say also unto thee, that thou art Peter, and upon this rock I will build my Church; and the gates of hell shall not prevail against it."

Pictured left above Rita stands by the flowing spring water looking east over a rock strewn desert. To the right, she wades in the Sea of Galilee.

The tour next stopped at Jericho, also located in the West Bank a few miles north of the Sea of Galilee. Free flowing springs around the site have attracted ancient cultures for thousands of years. In the Old Testament, it is known as the "City of Palms." The place is also known as the Israelite's point of entry, led by Joshua, into the Promised Land to see the walls come falling down. As the above picture shows, palm trees still grow in Jericho.

Masada pictured above, an isolated rock plateau overlooking the Dead Sea, remains the highlight of my Israeli visit. Between the years 36 and 30 BC, a period of Jewish unrest, Herod the Great fortified the mountain and built palaces on its top as a secure retreat for himself and his family. Ruins of his palaces remain and show above on the leftmost portion of the plateau. An ingenious system for catching and storing rain water insured a continuing water supply. Warehouses on the top plateau stored food sufficient to survive an extensive siege. In the dry desert air, those food supplies could survive for years without spoiling.

A Jewish revolt in the year 66 AD flared into a countrywide war between Roman and Jew that raged for four years. Early in the war, a group of Jewish warriors destroyed the Roman Masada garrison, and with their families, occupied the site. Titus, a Roman general, conquered Jerusalem in 70 AD, sacked the city, destroyed the Temple, and expelled Jews from Palestine. Some who survived the war and subsequent round-up and expulsion joined the group atop Masada. With Masada as their base, the group raided and harassed the Romans for two years.

In the second year, the Roman Governor's Tenth Legion commenced a Masada siege. The Legion camp's footprint on the desert floor remains visible from atop the mountain and shows, bottom center, in the picture on the previous page. The siege continued for a year. During that year Roman soldiers constructed an earthen ramp, also pictured, up against the west side of the mountain. One afternoon, Roman soldiers marched up the completed ramp, breached Masada's defensive wall, and retired for the day.

Overnight, the Jewish defenders had no hope. Tomorrow, the Romans were certain to overrun all defenses. They faced two options: surrender or death. They resolved *"that a death of glory was preferable to the loss of freedom and to a life of slavery."* Rather than become slaves, all chose death. A chosen number killed all others then committed suicide. When the Romans reached Masada's top the following morning, they met the silence of 960 slain men, women, and children.

The Masada story is an honored part of Jewish history. While on Masada's top, a Masada tour guide told that when Israeli Air Force cadets are commissioned, their oath to defend Israeli includes the statement: *"Masada shall not fall again."*

The HP-85 computer, a precursor to the Personal Computer, made by Hewlett-Packard, came on the market in the early 1980s. It had 32 kilobytes of internal memory, a small 4 x 4 inch screen, a small magnetic tape cassette for storage and retrieval of off line memory, a small four inch paper tape printer, and software applica-

tions limited to Basic programming and simple graphics.

The computer promised to fill a need to solve an ongoing problem connected to my work. I purchased one, and it became a major attraction in CSC's office building. Then, and now, secure communication systems coded multiple small signals, transmitted them through a wideband nonlinear (hard limited) channel, and decoded the signals at the receive site. Hard limiting suppresses signal strength and suppression increases as the number of signals transmitted through a single channel increase. To efficiently load a channel, one needs to calculate suppression levels as additional signals are added.

Using Bessel functions, suppression can be calculated, but done manually calculation time can be weeks. When programmed, the HP-85 completed the calculation in hours. The hours increased with increasing numbers of signals transmitted by a channel. Though slow, the computer solutions became a welcomed giant step forward. Such small computers pioneered the desk top and lap top computers, today sitting on desks and in laps.

Another family milestone passed in 1983 when Roger married Michelle Matuskowitz in Raleigh and the family gained another daughter. Friends during student days at Louisburg College in Louisburg, NC, and North Carolina State University in Raleigh, in time, they would give us a grandson, Zachary, and a granddaughter, Natalie.

Barry, still running as a deer, crosses Raleigh's Half-Marathon finish line at right below.

In 1985, John Ford and I attended an air show in Northern Virginia that featured a P-47D named the Little Demon, flown by Captain Walter Beckham in Europe during WWII. I knew Beckham from earlier days at the AF Weapons Laboratory as the laboratory's Chief Scientist while I managed the laboratory's Analysis Division. Beckham stood beside the airplane as John and I approached Little Demon sitting on the tarmac as a static display. As the three of us stood beside Little Demon hanger flying Frank Stranad, an author who wrote of early aviation history on Long Island, walked up and introduced himself. At the time, he belonged to a team of volunteers preparing a P-47N airplane for display in a Long Island museum.

Few N models, the last P-47 model built, reached a combat zone. At the airshow, Stranad hoped to meet someone who had flown P-47Ns in combat during WWII who could help configure an airplane with authentic markings to represent a combat P-47N. My group flew the N model over Japanese Pacific Islands and over Japan. I agreed to help and solicited additional help from Robert Rieser, Arthur Bowen, and David Brunner, all fellow pilots of my WWII 333rd Fighter Squadron. Good artists, they drew nose art on squadron airplanes.

The project successfully configured P-47N, Serial Number 44-89444, the very last P-47 to roll off Republic Aviation Company's production line. It is a true image of Cheek Baby, an airplane, named for my mother that brought me home from some difficult missions. In addition to my mother's name, it displays my name and Nolan Fredrick, its Crew Chief. Pictured above, I stand on its wing as it sits in an old Mitchell Air Force hanger. That hanger, restored and modified, serves as today's Cradle of Aviation Museum.

The squadron emblem is very symbolic. The three die represent the 333rd Squadron The squadron flew the Bell P-39 Airacobra during early war years and still flew the P39 when I joined the squadron. The flying snake's wings are P-39 wings. The P-39 fired a cannon through its propeller hub, and the snake breathing fire represents cannon fire. The snake is a Coral Cobra found on Pacific coral islands, and the cloud represents navigational aids. Missions often required long over-water flights to targets on distant small islands. Limited data from few weather stations produced poor weather and wind forecasts. Typically, navigating by clock and compass alone flights by-passed targets. Approaching estimated time of arrival, flights steered to the largest cumulus cloud. That cloud, formed by differential heating between island and water, identified the island's location.

The airplane, now exhibited in the museum, shows in a gallery of sixteen pictures on the Cradle of Aviation's web site. The above picture is one of the sixteen. At war's end, not worth the cost of transporting it back to the States, the original Cheek Baby, dumped over a cliff into the sea, rests in a watery grave in the

Pacific over which it had traveled so many miles. It has been resurrected in the body of the last P-47 to roll off Republic Aviation Company's production line.

Slowly, Rita's melancholy worsened, requiring a visit to Duke Hospital's Psychiatric Ward. After a two week treatment, she returned home improved but needing more support. I resigned from CSC in December 1982, and set up a home office configured to have attributes of a government secure facility. The Department of Defense authorized the office to receive and store material classified up to and including the secret level. For two years, I worked as a consultant for CSC as an independent contractor.

Working in Raleigh, I joined a Fort Bragg flying club. When Fort Bragg's Commander closed that club, I joined a Franklin County Airport club near Raleigh. Flying, though in small airplanes, remained fun and therapeutic. Among other joys, my grandsons Brad and Nicholas flew with me.

Rita's mental health improved, stabilized, and she became competent but, from this point forward, I remained in the home for her when needed. To add spice and variety to our life we traveled frequently. Places visited include Hawaii, Prince Edward Island, Nova Scotia, and Germany. Rita particularity enjoyed the German visit. She saw the Wall between East and West Berlin, Checkpoint Charley, and the walled off Brandenburg Gate. A West Berlin church, preserved in its wartime state as an iconic reminder of war, gave her a small taste of war. Shopping in Berlin gave her a joyful experience.

We traveled the international corridor from Berlin through East Germany to West Germany and saw firsthand the poverty of socialist government. Villages and farm houses in East Germany, damaged by war, still needed repair. Large sections of farm land lay fallow. Cultivated land, poorly cultivated, promised poor harvests. In contrast, once in West Germany we saw houses in good repair and crops flourishing in fields beside the corridor.

In West Germany we attended a concert in a concert hall designed by Beethoven. The seated audience faced a stage configured as the mouth of a large horn. The horn rolled back, down, and under the audience. The orchestra sat and performed below the audience. The conductor, alone on the stage, faced both his orchestra and his audience. The concert hall is perhaps one of a kind.

Another family milestone passed in the winter of 1989 when Jeffrey married Kathryn Davis Leonard in Charlotte and we gained another daughter. Kathryn and Jeffrey met in Raleigh as students, Kathryn at Peace College and Jeffrey at North Carolina State University. In time, they would give us a granddaughter, Madison, and a grandson, Dawson. Kathryn expected Doctor Ballantine, Pastor of Hayes Barton Baptist Church in Raleigh, to conduct the service. A heavy snow storm prevented travel from Raleigh to Charlotte, but a frantic search secured a timely substitute pastor.

Two years later in 1991, Rita and I traveled to Hawaii to visit the islands during the 50th Anniversary of the Pearl Harbor Attack and to attend a reunion of the 7th Fighter Command. Little to no attack damage remained in the harbor. However, tears in the form of oil droplets seeping from the battleship below floated on the water below the Arizona Memorial.

Sunrise, sunset, quickly passed the years. Grandchildren grew into adults, even as we gazed. As the years passed, Rita performed routine, daily tasks with ever increasing difficulty, yet bravely soldiered on. Finally, after hours of effort, she could not prepare lessons for her 1997 Summer Bible School class. Her Raleigh Psychiatrist diagnosed Alzheimer. Duke Hospital's Psychiatrist diagnosed Dementia. Regardless the name, during the following year she became, and remained, a charming four year old girl requiring the care of a four year old.

Rita's physical condition, appetite, and sleeping habit remained good. Ever content, she never tired of watching old movies seen in her younger days. So much so that she often voiced the dialogue before movie characters spoke. My daily schedule, dictated by her needs included: morning dressing, feeding, stimulating, and putting her to bed. Occasionally, she came from out her foggy world and faithfully recalled events that we shared in our youth. Those moments were balm for my soul. Most evenings, when put to bed, she looked up at me and said *"You are a good husband."* Those remarks turned my days into good memories.

My flying days ended. Driving time to the airport, airplane pre-flight time, flight time, airplane securing time, and drive home required the better part of a day. I could not justify such time away from Rita for two hours of fun. However, I did continue visits to the Racquet Ball court. An hour on the court earned a good workout needed for physical and mental health, and kept me away from home for only a short period of time.

Annual extended family reunions in my back yard became yearly highlights, giving Rita an opportunity to see family, relatives, and friends. Each year's reunion sponsored a golf match, The

"Mama Sudie Classic," named to honor my mother, privileged the winner to keep a MSC Trophy during the following year.

In May of 2004, Nicholas completed ROTC training at NCSU earning a commission in the US Air Force. His ROTC commander gave me the privilege of administering his oath of office and signing his commissioning certificate for the Air Force.

Pictured left above, his father and his grandfather Hodge pin his 2nd Lt. bars on. Following graduation, Nicholas attended pilot training at Laughlin Air Force Base in Del Rio, Texas. Shown right above, his mother is pinning his wings.

While stationed at McConnell Air Force Base near Wichita, Kansas, Nicholas, as a distance runner, helped organize a funding campaign for a Wichita veteran's memorial. After construction completion, he helped dedicate the memorial as a keynote speaker. Among the patio pavers, shown on the opposite page, there are three pavers that honor his two grandfathers, and his Uncle Rodney.

I attended the last two reunions of my old Fighter Group. In years past, each of the three squadrons held an annual reunion, but as illness and the Grim Reaper took its toll, attendance declined and squadrons formed a single 318th Group reunion. The Grim Reaper's toll continued and Group reunion attendance dwindled to a precious few.

The 318th Group held its 2007 year reunion in Washington, DC, during March. It gave the old timers an opportunity to visit, among other things, the Air Force Memorial. Pictured below the group of old 318th Fighter Group veterans placed a wreath at the base of the Memorial. Only sixteen were on hand to lay the wreath.

The Memorial symbolizes the spirit of flight with three spires that soar 270 feet high. They symbolize contrails of the Air Force Thunderbirds as they perform their climatic bomb burst maneuver.

The following year, the 318th Group held its reunion in Dayton, Ohio. The principle event unveiled a plaque, standing on Air Force Museum grounds, to honor the 318th Fighter Group. Presented to the Air Force Museum for care and eternal safekeeping, the plaque is pictured right above.

The still active 333rd Squadron, based on Seymour-Johnson AF Base located near Goldsboro, NC, flies the F-15 Fighter. I invited the Squadron Commander to have his squadron participate in the reunion. He agreed to do so.

During the dedication ceremony, two 333rd F-15s made a low pass overhead with all afterburners burning. They landed and set up the airplanes as static displays in a Wright-Patterson AF Base hanger for our group to visit.

The pilot and weapon operator crew members joined our banquet. A total of seventeen members of the WWII 318th Group attended. They are pictured above. The F-15 crew members kneel in front.

Among the group, only seven old 333rd Squadron members attended. They are pictured right from left to right: Walter Peckham, Otis Wayne Bennet, me, Jack Flanagan, Marsden Dupuy, Charles Schmidt, and Victor Peterson.

The age contrast between the F-15 crew members is evident. Generation after generation of young men and women serve to keep the Air Force strong and robust, able to defend our great Nation.

Jack Flanagan designed the 333rd emblem. He is pictured right standing beside a today's young 333rd Squadron pilot wearing the emblem as a shoulder patch. Jack too wore the shoulder patch sixty-nine years earlier. Again, observe the contrast between young and old.

The Triangle Flight of Honor flew its first mission in October of 2010. The mission chartered a large airliner and flew a full load of North Carolina WWII veterans to Washington, DC. In Washington, chartered busses carried the group for visits to memorials including: the WWII Memorial, the Iwo Jima Memorial, the Viet Nam Memorial, the Lincoln Memorial, and others. The trip, the best organized activity that I have participated in since Aviation Cadet Days, ordered Veterans into groups of four, with each group assigned a Guardian tasked to help those needing help and to watch over all four.

Veterans included my brother, Rodney, and my friend and fellow commuter to and from Washington in earlier years, Tom Holmes. Rodney, stationed in Italy, flew the ball turret position on B-17 bomb missions over Germany. Tom flew the B-24 waist-gun position; also out of Italy. In addition to gunnery duty, Tom served as mission photographer. My grandson, Bradford, then living and working in Washington, joined us.

Above they are pictured from left to right: Rodney, me, Bradford, and Tom. Landing at Reagan Airport, deplaning passengers met approximately 500 people waiting in the terminal cheering and waving American flags to greet the old veterans, then in their late eighties or nineties; some in wheel chairs, some with walkers, and some with canes. That welcome was special for all.

A waiting tour bus transported the Group to many Washington Memorials including: Jefferson, Lincoln, Viet Nam, Korea, Iwo Jima, and WWII. The Viet Nam Wall is particularly moving. Over the years, it has become a  place of healing for those hurt by our most divisive war. Day after day, artifacts dropped at the wall's base heal someone's heartbreak.

As I walked along the Wall, a broken bracelet caught my attention. I picked it up. A note, written by hand on a shipping tag attached to the bracelet, read *"Over all these years, I have worn this bracelet in remembrance of you. It broke and fell off my arm, telling me that it is time to let go."* Reading the note, I carefully returned it to its proper resting place.

Of many pictures made during the tour, the best is that of the Iwo Jima Memorial. Pictured right, the rising flag centers the scene with no tourist present.

A visit to the WWII Memorial provides a moving experience. Constructed on the Washington Mall with funds contributed by the public, shaped as a north-south ellipse, the west side looks toward the Lincoln Memorial. A northern tower inscribed "Atlantic" represents the European Theater of War. A southern tower inscribed "Pacific" represents the Pacific Theater. Fifty-six columns, named for 48 States and eight Territories, form the ellipse. The centerpiece, a pool with water fountains rising to freely fall, symbolizes freedom.

The center portion of the west wall contains 4048 golden stars; row on row. Each star symbolizes 100 deaths, representing 404,800 WWII dead. Below the stars a small pool of still water symbolizes death. On its side is engraved *"Here we Mark the Price of Freedom."*

The Memorial could not be complete without a calling card record of a Kilroy visit. Wherever the WWII GI traveled, in Europe or the Pacific Theater, this calling card on vehicles, houses, fences, and other structures recorded his passing as *Kilroy was Here.*

Rita continued life as a contented four year old. Content, she often began to sing for no apparent cause "God Bless America," or "I Walk in The Garden Alone." In March of 2010, she suffered a

259

mini-stroke, was hospitalized for several days, and returned home with little apparent mental damage but with reduced mobility. Not understanding the need, she refused to cooperate with physical therapy routines recommended by our Physical Therapist daughter, Gail. Believing that professional care would serve better than that received in the home, I placed her in a Nursing Home. Not so. I brought her home after a twenty-six day visit needing treatment for bed sores by Rex Hospital.

With the help of Certified Nursing Aids, she received more than adequate care at home, but her ability to walk continued to slowly decline. Able to walk shorter and shorter distances; she walked for months in the home holding my hand, or an aide's hand, for support. More months passed and she walked in the home holding two hands of someone walking backward. Movement outside the home required a wheelchair. For months when required by medical appointments, I transferred her to our automobile from a wheelchair and to a wheelchair from our automobile. Later, appointments required wheelchair capable taxies.

Rita suffered a heart attack on 26 July 2012. After five days of hospital treatment, her condition stabilized with a weakened heart maintaining normal oxygen levels, but with little to no ability to walk. At home her oxygen level slowly dropped, requiring continuous oxygen support. She continued to weaken; and knowing that the end of her journey near, our Pastor, Doctor David Hailey, visited Saturday 4 August. She answered his question, *"How are you Rita?"* with *"Fine thank you."* Her last prayer, that God bless America, began when he asked her to join him in prayer. She began to sing. He joined and together they sang, *"God Bless America."*

Two weeks later Rita died at noon time, Sunday, 19 August 2012. She died peacefully without trauma knowing that she was in her home, in her room and in her own bed. Gail and I sat bedside as I sang *"In the Garden."* Buried 13 September, she rests in the Arlington National Cemetery across the Potomac from Washington, DC.

A good dresser, the true Rita considered that a well-dressed lady wore white gloves and a hat. She made hats and often wore her own brand. In my memory's eye, I still see with pride Rita and Gail dressed for Church wearing hats and gloves. Rita also had a passion for antiques. A shelf around the top of her kitchen wall is still dressed with antique hand painted, hand blown dinner plates. She is buried with one of her plates, with one of her hats, and with a pair of her gloves. That plate's empty space is the missing plate in her missing plate formation.

Rita's grave site is a choice site located within a stone throw of Arlington Visitors' parking lot. In summer and spring, it over-looks a field of headstones row on row, evenly spaced on a ver-dant hill. In Fall, nature's brush paints the scene with reds, browns, and yellows. When trees are bare in winter, the Air Force Memorial, the Washington Monument, and the Lincoln Memorial are visible from her site.

Caring for Rita during her fifteen year journey with Alzheimer gave me a rich and rewarding experience. Throughout those years she remained content knowing that she was at home, loved and cared for. Always grateful for care received, when put to bed; she continued to say *"You are a good husband."* Those statements made each day a good memory. Likewise she contin-ued to occasionally come from out her foggy world and re-live an experience we shared long years ago. These moments contin-ued to make precious memories.

I learned that this world holds much good. For three years, five Certified Nursing Aides took turns caring for Rita. Each, more than competent professionals, gave Rita loving care, and she came to love them. They in turn cared for Rita and were heart-broken by her death. The true Rita, a good conversationalist, could join a group of strangers and depart a group of friends. That trait lingered. When in doctor waiting rooms or other public places she tried to make conversation by repeatedly asking strangers very personal questions; questions that ordinarily gave offense. Strangers, at no time, took offense. Rather, recognizing her handicap, they repeatedly answered the questions and conversed with her.

God has been good to Rita and me. Blessed with education, opportunity, and career, and most importantly, blessed with a good family, all good citizens worthy of their mothers and fathers of earlier generations, our blessings have flowed down like rivers to the sea.

A second blessing; we inherited from our fathers a great nation offering freedoms and opportunity for all. Those freedoms are fragile. Every generation is called to defend them. Rita and I have done so. Let those who follow do likewise, else our children's children will live in tyranny.

Though Rita's headstone stands in Arlington, our family lives the monument that honors her life. Smiling with pride, she stands above with family members on the brickyard of her favorite football stadium.

DURWOOD B. WILLIAMS
CLASS OF 1948
USAF COL. PILOT, P-47
R&S COMMAND - BMEWS
WING COMMANDER OF
A NCSU FAMILY

She stands on a family brick in the brickyard as Co-Wing Commander of a NCSU family.

MEMORY LANE

In memory lane again I walk
a long-long path that I once trod.
Again I see, and touch and talk
To friends of old who smile and nod.
I see
A kitchen warmed by a hot wood stove;
Filled with the smell of a well-cooked dish,
Graced by a Mother's care, and love,
Made safe and secure by a Father's wish.
I see
A school yard filled with laughter and shout,
And friendly games – with bars set tall.
By cheerful playmates – while school is let
out, so long as it lasts – enjoyed by all.
I see
A sister and brother around me they gather,
to beguile me with youthful inventions.
Froth with good will – all times quite clever
always driven by well-meant intentions.
I see
An island so distant in water so blue
A palm tree's small shadow
Gives shades from Sun's hot hue.
In day after day of same-same hot weather
I see
In nearby jungle hang bananas so precious,
yellow and ripe, and ready to treat us.
One dares not to go for the prize so delicious,
The jungle hides snipers ready to shoot us.
I see
Beneath the wings of trusty airplanes,
recently returned from difficult missions.
young men sitting – comrades in pain;
Remembering friends – who now are missing.
I see
A lovely young woman I met one eve,
departing I mentioned some future encounter.
She shakes red hair and blinks brown eyes;
responds with "When?" for a quick rejoinder.

My home is filled with infants still crawling,
watched over by mother–she of red hair.
Soon they are walking – then they are talking.
Fast they grow – to be children so fair.
I See
Years pass quickly and children grow strong.
One by one they leave their home nest.
For schools and careers and lives of their own
With breaking hearts – knowing its best.
I see
My home now graced by Grandmother dear
No longer red – her hair now grey
She comforts a grandchild needing her care,
her joy short-lived, its visit a day.
I see
Grandchildren living lives of their own,
now young adults, caring and giving
to country, to family and home,
Citizens worthy of family tradition.
I see
Squadron companions of wartime days
gone from among us - the Grim Reaper.
A host, once many, is now but a few.
Still soldiering on – to meet their keeper.
I see
The white head now buried in Arlington
With hat, white gloves, and plate
Things that she cherished
When the white head was red.

I now live alone
In a house full of memories
of paths well-traveled
on a long-long journey

It is well
It is well with my soul

263

And now abides faith, hope, love, these three;
but the greatest of these is love.

1 Corinthians 13:13